Group Therapy

Group Therapy: A Group-Analytic Approach is a comprehensive introduction to contemporary group-analytic theory and practice – the prevailing form of group therapy in Europe. Highly accessible yet meticulously referenced, theoretically rich, yet clinically vivid, it is an invaluable resource for all interested in group therapy, providing access to the very heart of working therapeutically with(in) groups.

Nick Barwick is a group analyst who has worked as a psychodynamic practitioner in the educational, NHS and private sectors for over 20 years. He is currently Head of Counselling at The Guildhall School of Music & Drama where he also teaches on the MA in Music Therapy. In private practice, he works individually with writers, overcoming creative blocks and, in group therapy, with vulnerable young adults experiencing difficulties in 'creative living'. In addition to numerous articles published in psychotherapy journals, he has edited *Clinical Counselling in Schools* (Routledge) and co-authored *The Therapeutic Environment* (Open University Press) and *Group Music Therapy* (Routledge). For many years, he was editor of the Routledge journal, *Psychodynamic Practice*. He is also a published writer of fiction and a gigging musician.

Martin Weegmann is a consultant clinical psychologist and group analyst, with many years NHS and private experience. He has specialised in substance misuse, personality disorders and other complex needs. He is a well-known trainer, delivering workshops and lectures throughout the UK. Martin edited *Psychodynamics of Addiction* (Wiley) and *Group Psychotherapy and Addiction* (Wiley) and has published many book chapters and papers in a range of journals. His two most recent books, *The World within the Group: Developing Theory for Group Analysis* (Karnac) and *Permission to Narrate: Explorations in Group Analysis, Psychoanalysis, Culture* (Karnac) have been praised for their originality. Over time, his interests have broadened to include those connected to narration, rhetoric and the 'literary mind'.

'This comprehensive work brings group analysis fully into the twenty-first century. The authors utilize personal experiences, critical eyes, and historical perspectives to provide an integrated view of theory and practice. Rooted firmly in the pioneering work of S.H. Foulkes, the book nevertheless incorporates the rich developments in psychoanalysis, group dynamics, and relational psychology that have evolved since then. This volume will place the reader firmly at the center of contemporary group theory and treatment.'

– **Victor L. Schermer**, *MA, LFAGPA, psychologist, author, Life Fellow of the American Group Psychotherapy Association*

'An outstanding combination of psychological awareness, group-analytic wisdom, artistic ability and literary flair. Together they weave a fascinating, multi-layered and -textured tapestry of the analytic psychotherapy group that is at the same time highly accessible to readers. . . . full of originality, insight, honesty and imagination . . . We are privileged to have [the authors] – and their new book – in our midst.'

– **Morris Nitsun**, *clinical psychologist, Consultant NHS Psychologist in Group Psychotherapy, training group analyst, Institute of Group Analysis, London*

'A joyous, beautiful read, presenting the origins and flourishing of group analysis; the best read for all: students, therapists and teachers. We all can take pleasure and pride in the state of our art so eloquently laid out.'

– **Malcolm Pines**, *MRCPsych, co-founder, Institute of Group Analysis, former president, International Association of Group Psychotherapy*

'A fascinating, beautifully written, accessible, enjoyable book – especially the rich and humane accounts of clinical encounters in groups. I learned a great deal from it and wished such a book had been available when I was training; it would have been like having another wise mentor and supervisor at my elbow. We may be living in anxious times, but we are also living in creative times, when clinicians like Nick Barwick and Martin Weegmann can write so beautifully about their work.'

– **Gwen Adshead**, *consultant forensic psychiatrist, psychotherapist and group analyst, Visiting Gresham Professor of Psychiatry, London*

'*Group Therapy: A Group-Analytic Approach* is what J.R. Rees wrote with regard to Foulkes' first book: A "careful primer" of contemporary group analysis, instructive and indispensable for students and experienced practitioners alike.'

– **Dieter Nitzgen**, *editor of* Group Analysis, *training group analyst, Institute of Group Analysis, Heidelberg, Germany*

Group Therapy

A Group-Analytic Approach

Nick Barwick and
Martin Weegmann

LONDON AND NEW YORK

First published 2018
by Routledge
2 Park Square, Milton Park, Abingdon, Oxon OX14 4RN

and by Routledge
711 Third Avenue, New York, NY 10017

Routledge is an imprint of the Taylor & Francis Group, an informa business

© 2018 Nick Barwick and Martin Weegmann

The right of Nick Barwick and Martin Weegmann to be identified as authors of this work has been asserted by them in accordance with sections 77 and 78 of the Copyright, Designs and Patents Act 1988.

All rights reserved. No part of this book may be reprinted or reproduced or utilised in any form or by any electronic, mechanical, or other means, now known or hereafter invented, including photocopying and recording, or in any information storage or retrieval system, without permission in writing from the publishers.

Trademark notice: Product or corporate names may be trademarks or registered trademarks, and are used only for identification and explanation without intent to infringe.

British Library Cataloguing-in-Publication Data
A catalogue record for this book is available from the British Library

Library of Congress Cataloging-in-Publication Data
Names: Barwick, Nick, 1959– author. | Weegmann, Martin, author.
Title: Group therapy : a group-analytic approach / Nick Barwick and Martin Weegmann.
Description: Abingdon, Oxon ; New York, NY : Routledge, 2018. | Includes bibliographical references and index.
Identifiers: LCCN 2017019706| ISBN 9781138889705 (hardback : alk. paper) | ISBN 9781138889712 (pbk. : alk. paper) | ISBN 9781315676289 (ebk) | ISBN 9781317384717 (Web PDF) | ISBN 9781317384700 (ePub) | ISBN 9781317384694 (Mobipocket/Kindle)
Subjects: | MESH: Psychotherapy, Group | Psychoanalytic Therapy | Psychoanalytic Theory
Classification: LCC RC480.5 | NLM WM 430 | DDC 616.89/14—dc23
LC record available at https://lccn.loc.gov/2017019706

ISBN: 978-1-138-88970-5 (hbk)
ISBN: 978-1-138-88971-2 (pbk)
ISBN: 978-1-315-67628-9 (ebk)

Typeset in Times New Roman and Gill Sans
by Florence Production Ltd, Stoodleigh, Devon, UK

To the spirit of Jo Cox

We are caught in an inescapable network of mutuality, tied in a single garment of destiny. Whatever affects one destiny, affects all indirectly.
(Martin Luther King, Jnr., *Letter from Birmingham City Jail*, 16 April 1963)

Mit unsichtbaren Fäden wird man am festesten gebunden.
Invisible threads are the strongest ties.
(Friedrich Nietzsche, *Nachgelassene Fragmente*, 1822)

Contents

Foreword by Morris Nitsun   xi
Acknowledgements   xv
A note on pronouns by Nick Barwick   xviii
Prologue by Nick Barwick   xix

PART I
Mainly theory   1

1   The development of group analysis: the principle of interconnectedness   3
NICK BARWICK

2   Core concepts: what goes on in groups? (Part one)   18
NICK BARWICK

3   Core concepts: what goes on in groups? (Part two)   31
NICK BARWICK

4   Core concepts: what does the conductor do? (Part one)   51
NICK BARWICK

5   Core concepts: what does the conductor do? (Part two)   70
NICK BARWICK

6   Developments in group analysis: the mother approach   81
NICK BARWICK

7   Developments in group analysis: the 'other' approach   103
NICK BARWICK

PART II
Mainly practice   117

8 Working with(in) groups: a dialogue   119
   MARTIN WEEGMANN AND NICK BARWICK

9 Beginnings: Ted's story   131
   MARTIN WEEGMANN

10 A group in action: making room (Part one)   139
   NICK BARWICK

11 A group in action: making room (Part two)   151
   NICK BARWICK

   Further reflections on 'making room'   161
   MARTIN WEEGMANN

12 Endings   164

   Theoretical reflections   164
   NICK BARWICK

   Clinical discussions   170
   MARTIN WEEGMANN AND NICK BARWICK

   Epilogue   181
   MARTIN WEEGMANN

   References   183
   Author index   206
   Subject index   211

Foreword

Morris Nitsun

Group analysis was, until some years ago, a largely under-published, under-represented field in the broad psychotherapeutic literature, with a predominating focus on S. H. Foulkes' original writings. This has changed significantly in the last decade or two. With the *New International Library of Group Analysis*, published by Karnac, and Routledge's continuing series of books on group analysis, the published literature has grown and diversified in various ways. This includes an increasing number of books aiming to present group-analytic thinking as a whole, as an overall field of clinical inquiry and intervention, clarifying and sifting the strands of theory and practice, as well as historical influences, and putting the discourse in a contemporary context. Examples are the books by Behr and Hearst (2004) and Schlapobersky (2016). What then can the present volume, *Group Therapy: A Group-Analytic Approach*, offer that's different, noteworthy in its own regard, and a valuable contribution to the growing field of literature?

One of the hallmarks of group analysis, and essentially a strength, although sometimes a source of confusion, is its inter-disciplinary origins and orientation. Unlike some schools of psychotherapy that present a unified and bounded theory, group analysis has been formed – and is formed – by divergent input from different fields, offering a complex discipline marked by a high degree of theoretical openness that may be frustrating in some respects but offers the potential for creative development. In keeping with this trend, the joint authors of this book, Nick Barwick and Martin Weegmann, come from fields of considerable interest and relevance to group analysis. Both are colleagues and friends of mine. I know them personally and professionally, with an appreciation of them as people, thinkers, and propagators of group analysis in interconnecting fields. Nick Barwick, presently Head of Counselling at Guildhall School of Music & Drama, where he also teaches on the Music Therapy course, has a strong background in education and active interests in music, not just as appreciator but performer (he learned the saxophone while training to be a group analyst!). He also has a long-standing interest in creative writing, in particular the blocks and defences that stall creativity. He has helped individuals and groups to explore and get to grips with writing difficulties. His eloquent style in this book attests to his own writing skill and his awareness of communicating clearly and meaningfully with his readership. Martin Weegmann is a clinical psychologist with a long career in the NHS and considerable experience working with highly problematic populations, such as borderline disorders and substance misusers. But he also has a rich philosophical background, drawing on sources as diverse as Aristotle and Gadamer, and able to link philosophical perspectives to psychotherapeutic inquiry. Martin is also a photographer and painter, keenly aware of visual harmonies and their parallels in psychotherapeutic work. Further, he shares Nick's strong interest in writing and is presently researching creative writing as a dynamic process, with plans to publish a collection of papers by well-known authors on the topic. Nick and Martin approach their joint book with an outstanding combination of psychological awareness, group-analytic wisdom, artistic ability and literary flair. Together they weave a fascinating, multi-layered and -textured tapestry of the analytic psychotherapy group that is at the same time highly accessible to readers: qualified group analysts, students in the field and interested others who may wish to explore and understand this developing field.

Another valuable aspect of this book is its clear focus on the clinical, on what happens in the consulting room. I highlight this because of my view, often stated in my own writing, that group psychotherapy is the most complex of all the psychological therapies, with a sometimes fragile and inconsistent link between theory and practice (Nitsun, 1996, 2006, 2015). What the group-analytic approach gains in openness, it can lose in specificity and rigour. I have also noted in the literature a seeming tendency to 'escape' from the pressures of the consulting room, and the very immediate problems presented by groups, to a globalizing approach that encourages 'wide-scale' thinking, with concepts such as the social unconscious commanding attention. Important as this approach is, I suggest that it may compromise the clinical endeavour. In my view, it de-centres the individual and risks separating itself from the main thrust of contemporary psychotherapy theory, practice and research and ending up on the margins of recognised clinical practice. Nick and Martin's book is a refreshing antidote to this. The book, while fully cognizant of social influences and, as Nick points out in his prologue, of the wider social and political context, is unambiguously rooted in the clinical, giving a clear account of group-analytic theory but always within the framework of practice, strongly reflecting the vicissitudes and demands of group psychotherapy.

The next quality I admire is the authors' ability to write about groups in a detailed, microscopic way that remains readable and meaningful. In my view, this cannot be overemphasised. Half the problem with the literature on groups is the sheer challenge of writing detailed, readable group case studies. The complexity and intensity of group material, given the number of people, and the rapidity and unpredictability of group process, can be extremely difficult to capture in writing. There are, as far as I know, no particularly well-known group-analytic case studies in the way that exists in the individual psychoanalytic/psychotherapeutic literature (e.g. Melanie Klein's narrative of a child analysis or Kohut's detailed accounts of 'guilty man' and 'tragic man'). The present authors' book comes close, in my view, to reaching a standard of clinical writing that is truly convincing, readable and thought provoking. Not only that, but there is high degree of honesty and openness in the reporting style. I found myself engrossed, touched and moved by the authors' candour and capacity for self-scrutiny. Chapters 10 and 11, in which Nick Barwick writes about the group on which he cut his teeth as a group analyst, are especially good examples and stand a chance of becoming the standard to which other writers aspire.

In these two beautifully written chapters, Nick tackles courageously the at times overwhelming difficulty of working with a group of severely disturbed NHS patients. He gives a vivid account of a fledgling group therapist's shock at meeting head on the full impact of borderline and narcissistic disorders in a group. Confronted by waves of destructive and self-destructive behaviour, he struggles to hold onto his belief in the process and his wavering confidence in his own ability. He cannot find his own authority, nor with the group establish a mode of communication that can assist the therapeutic process. The chapters are aptly sub-titled 'making room', the analogy reflecting the struggle to make room spatially, psychologically and emotionally. His reflections on the nature of borderline anguish and the deep anxiety and despair inherent in it, as well as its traumatic roots – as revealed in the group – are among the finest I have read in this field of writing. Ultimately, through his own struggle, indeed suffering, and the help of supervisors and his own group analysis, Nick not only survives but finds his voice as a group analyst.

Readers may know that I come to group work with a pronounced sense of the anti-group. As a manager of psychotherapy services over several decades, I have consistently noted that the actual conduct of groups, and the task of the conductor, are harder than usually acknowledged and that this may have to do with complex group processes that I have termed 'anti-group' (Nitsun, 1996, 2015). Both Nick and Martin show a marked, unflinching recognition of processes of this kind and the great demands they make on the conductor. The anti-group as a concept is itself covered generously in Chapter 7 of the book that deals with 'alternative' group-analytic approaches. One of the themes I highlight in my writing is the difficulty of reconciling individual and group needs and how this can contribute to the anti-group (a point strongly pursued by Bion), notwithstanding our understanding that ultimately group and individual needs are inseparable. The importance of the individual-group tension, however, is another reason I have difficulty with much of the Foulkesian literature that seeks to obscure or problematise 'the individual', in deference to a sweeping social emphasis. Foulkes's statement that 'the individual is an abstraction' is sometimes taken quite literally and reverentially in the field. But without adequate attention to the individual, I believe, the work of the group is limited. In Nick and Martin's chapters, individual and group are both fully recognised, in the figure-ground configuration that is the hallmark of flexible group analysis. The individual, in their descriptions, is not an 'abstraction' but a living, breathing, deeply conflicted human being who both wants to belong and not belong, and whose dilemma is both a source and consequence of isolation and alienation.

The brilliance of Nick's writing in the chapters I have cited is matched by the searching and sometimes painfully honest dialogue Nick and Martin engage in in Chapter 8. Here, comparing groups that are frustrating and unsatisfying and others that are growthful and deeply satisfying, the two authors traverse important pathways of theory as well as their own subjective reactions to groups that frustrate or those that satisfy. Again, they bring their distinctive backgrounds to bear on the discussion, Martin drawing on his philosophical knowledge and citing thinkers as wide-ranging as Erasmus, Shakespeare and Gadamer. His mention of Erasmus as saying that 'in the beginning was the conversation' rather than 'the word' (a decidedly group-analytic standpoint) is one delightful and illuminating example. Nick, in turn, brings his musical understanding to bear on the discourse. He quotes a statement from jazz that 'there is no such thing as a wrong note', an analogy used to throw light on 'notes' in the communication of the group. Together, the authors weave a compelling account of the life of groups and the conductors who lead them.

Nick Barwick and Martin Weegmann are among the younger generation of group analysts, bringing fresh energy and initiative to the field, but not without the questioning, sometimes uncertain stance that marks the responsible clinician. As younger practitioner/theorists, their work, I suspect, is not yet as well known as it deserves to be. They have yet to gain full recognition. I hope that this book will encourage such recognition. The book is full of originality, insight, honesty and imagination, deeply rooted clinically and strengthened by a rich allusive tendency. We are privileged to have them – and their new book – in our midst.

Acknowledgements

Although this book is co-authored, it has been a project driven mainly by myself. I would therefore like to express my particular gratitude to Martin Weegmann, my friend, colleague and fellow author, first for agreeing to join me on this venture a while after I had already set out on it and, through our developing dialogue, for finding ways to contribute his own distinct and valuable voice while very much supporting mine.

Even when not co-authored, a book is always a group affair, brought into being by a community past as well as present. In particular, in addition to Martin, I would like to thank my group-analytic supervisors, Keith Hyde, Linda Anderson, Morris Nitsun and Malcolm Pines, with whom I have grown at different times in different ways. Malcolm was also particularly supportive of this project in its early days and of course Morris's warm generosity speaks for itself in the Foreword. I would like too to thank Christine Thornton with whom I struck up a valued friendship while training and from whose thoughtful counsel I have continued to benefit in peer supervision. Further, I would like to thank Harold Behr, my own group conductor, from whom, by osmosis as well as emulation, I have imbibed a great deal. And, for generously giving their time to read and comment on the manuscript, my thanks to: Dieter Nitzgen, Gwen Adshead, Malcolm Pines, Robi Friedman, Vic Schermer, Walt Stone.

It is a truism to say that therapists learn most from the people they seek to help but it is worth saying nonetheless. Although I have been pleased to work with all age groups, for much of my professional life, my work has been with young adults who, though often painfully vulnerable, have courageously struggled to forge creative lives. It has been enormously rewarding and a great privilege to play a part in such struggles.

On a personal note, I would like to say 'thank you', once again, to my wife, Carol, who, as always, has been both my very best critic and my deepest support. Upholding, as she does, so many of the 'permanently rickety elaborate/Structures of living' (Fanthorpe, 1995) while I burrow in the labyrinths of writing, I'm acutely aware that, without her, not only would I be far less able to bear so much of the anxiety inherent in the process of writing but much simply would not happen. And I would like to apologise too, both to her and to my beautiful grandchildren,

Charlie, Livvy, Ted and Claudia, the four of whom, being much more interested in playing pirates and stormy seas, have often been more than a little bemused about how the telling of one story could possibly take so long!

Every effort has been made to contact the relevant copyright holders for permission to use some of the extracts used in this book. The publishers would be grateful to hear from any copyright holder who is not here acknowledged and we will undertake to rectify any errors or omissions in future editions of this book.

Excerpt in Acknowledgements from 'Atlas' by U. A. Fanthorpe from *U. A. Fanthorpe, New and Collected Poems*, Enitharmon Press, 2010, reprinted with kind permission of Rosie Bailey.

Epigraph featured at the start Prologue from Jo Cox MP's maiden speech in The Houses of Parliament, June 2015. Reprinted with the kind permission of Brandon Cox.

Chapter 2 first published as Barwick, N. (2015), 'Core Concepts in Group Analysis: What goes on in groups? (part one)' in A. Davies, E. Richards, & N. Barwick, *Group Music Therapy: a group analytic approach*. London: Routledge, pp. 27–35. Reprinted in a revised and expanded version by permission of Taylor & Francis, LLC.

Chapter 3 first published as Barwick, N. (2015) 'Core Concepts in Group Analysis: What goes on in groups? (part two)', in A. Davies, E. Richards, & N. Barwick, *Group Music Therapy: a group analytic approach*, pp. 36–47. London: Routledge. Reprinted in a revised and expanded version by permission of Taylor & Francis, LLC.

Chapter 4 and 5 first published as Barwick, N. (2015) 'Core Concepts in Group Analysis: What does the conductor do?', in A. Davies, E. Richards, & N. Barwick, *Group Music Therapy: a group analytic approach*. London: Routledge, pp. 48–66. Reprinted in a revised and expanded version by permission of Taylor & Francis, LLC.

Chapter 6 first published as Barwick, N. (2015) 'Developments in Group Analysis: the mother approach', in A. Davies, E. Richards, & N. Barwick, *Group Music Therapy: a group analytic approach*. London: Routledge, pp. 67–77. Reprinted in a revised and expanded version by permission of Taylor & Francis, LLC.

Chapter 7 first published as Barwick, N. (2015) 'Developments in Group Analysis: the 'other' approach', in A. Davies, E. Richards, & N. Barwick, *Group Music Therapy: a group analytic approach*. London: Routledge, pp. 78–88. Reprinted in a revised and expanded version by permission of Taylor & Francis, LLC.

Chapter 10 first published as Barwick, N. (2006) 'Making room: Developing reflective capacity through group analytic psychotherapy (Part one)', *Psychodynamic Practice*, 12: 37–51. Reprinted as a revised version by permission of Taylor & Francis, LLC.

Epigraph featured at the start of Chapter 10 from 'Remorse for Intemperate Speech' by W. B. Yeats from *Collected Poems of W. B. Yeats*, 2nd edn, Macmillan, 1950. Reprinted with permission of United Agents LLP on behalf of Caitriona Yeats.

Chapter 11 first published as Barwick, N. (2006) 'Making room: Developing reflective capacity through group analytic psychotherapy (Part two)', *Psychodynamic Practice*, 12: 53–65. Reprinted as revised version by permission of Taylor & Francis, LLC.

Excerpt in Chapter 12 from 'Ghosts' by Elizabeth Jennings from *Elizabeth Jennings, Collected Poems*, Carcanet, 1986. Reprinted with permission of David Higham Associates.

Excerpts from 'East Coker' and 'Little Gidding' from FOUR QUARTETS by T.S. Eliot. Copyright © 1940 by T.S. Eliot. Copyright renewed 1968 by Esme Valerie Eliot. Used by permission of Houghton Mifflin Harcourt Publishing Company. All rights reserved. Also reprinted by permission of Faber & Faber Ltd.

Excerpt from *Howards End* by E. M. Forster published by Penguin. Reprinted with permission of The Provost and Scholars of King's College, Cambridge and The Society of Authors as the E. M. Forster Estate.

Lastly, my thanks to Joanne Forshaw, Samantha Birchall and Charles Bath at Taylor & Francis for their support, understanding and flexibility as life (and death) sometimes intervened in the writing of this book.

A note on pronouns

Whenever I write, I always find myself in a bit of a tangle over the use of gender pronouns. In this respect, to write with both fluency *and* inclusivity, not to mention without flouting too many grammatical mores, is a challenge which I find well nigh impossible to meet. I do hope this particular shortcoming will not prove too distracting for the reader.

Nick Barwick

Prologue

Nick Barwick

> While we celebrate our diversity . . . we are far more united and have far more in common with each other than things that divide us.
> (Jo Cox, MP Maiden Speech in The Houses of Parliament, June 2015)

This prologue describes aspects of 'context' – a concept fundamental to group-analytic thinking – in and out of which this book has been written. Earl Hopper (2003a), unpacking the etymology of the word, notes that 'con' – meaning 'together with', 'in combination' – and 'text' – referring both to 'tissue' (*textus*) and 'weave' (*texture*) – produces connotations that alert us to the intriguing idea that 'a thread and its properties will always be governed by its location within a larger whole, in this instance a fabric or textile' (p. 331).

On an immediate level, the weave out of which the textual thread of this book has been woven finds its source in another text – *Group Music Therapy* (Davies, Richards & Barwick, 2015). *Group Therapy* builds on the theory outlined there, extending, elaborating and updating it to produce the first section of this book entitled, 'Mainly Theory'. As this book took shape, I realised that I and it would benefit from further input, particularly in terms of the second, 'Mainly Practice' section. This is when I invited Martin Weegmann, with whom I had developed an easy and satisfying friendship during our group-analytic training, to join me. Martin, acting as careful, critical reader, has generously contributed his thinking throughout the theoretical section of this book, but it is to the clinical section that he has provided the greatest input and is most responsible for shaping. As someone whose own clinical experience has been dominated by work in the educational and private sectors, it has felt good (and important) to have such an experienced and able clinician, particularly in the context of the NHS, sharing and sometimes steering the clinical aspect of this project.

Group Therapy: A group-analytic approach is intended as a concise introduction to the field of group analysis, organised and referenced in such a way that readers looking for a fulsome one-stop meal will find sufficient fare, while others, wishing to explore further will find ample signposts of where to go. However, beyond the reference to the two sections of the book just mentioned, I am going to forgo the usual outline common to many introductions. I hope the chapter titles speak for themselves and together with careful subtitling offer sufficient guidance as to content. Instead, I would like to give brief further thought to two broader aspects of context, one past and personal, one present and social; though, of course, group analysis construes both past and present, personal and social as interwoven.

A context of which I am particularly aware at the moment is the dramatic resurgence of nationalism during a period in which, until recently, the general trend has been that of inter-nationalism. A core principle of the latter, and one shared with group analysis, is that of interconnectedness. It is, today, a principle nowhere more apparent in political life than the intense and often fraught inter-governmental discussions about global warming. Here, a recognition of joint responsibility and the need, in concert, to act, has been hard won. Yet it is not only the environment that is no respecter of national boundaries. Deprivation, disease, oppression and war all have an impact far beyond their geographical origins, spreading like acrid ripples in a global pond. Expressing a spiritual vision, though using a geographical metaphor peculiarly apt for our times, the seventeenth century English poet, John Donne, poignantly captures the 'inter-nationalist' perspective:

> No man is an island, entire in itself; every man is a piece of a continent, a part of the main . . . any man's death diminishes me, because I am involved in mankind; and therefore never send to know for whom the bell tolls; it tolls for thee.
>
> (Meditation XVII, 1624)

In stark contrast, the cry of 'Britain First' – both the name of a far right UK political party and the words of Thomas Mair, as he murdered Jo Cox, MP in the run up to the EU referendum – and of 'America First' – the election slogan and now the political policy of the Trump administration – proffer a creed very different from the more cooperative internationalist one. Yet such cries are not isolated phenomena. In Western Europe alone, UKIP in the UK, the National Front in France, the Freedom Party in Austria (Norbert Hofer only narrowly losing the 2016 presidential election), Fidesz in Hungary (with Victor Orban, its leader, elected prime minister), Law and Justice in Poland, the Party of Freedom in Holland and Alternative for Germany in Germany, all prosper, expressing a vision of 'new nationalism' that, broadly associated with right-wing populism, is nativist, protectionist, anti-immigration and anti-globalisation. No wonder The Economist (2016) observes that:

> new nationalists are riding high on promises to close borders and restore societies to a past homogeneity.

Though economic insecurities experienced by some 'overlooked' sections of society have been proffered as *the* rationale for this resurgence – the revenge of the 'have-nots' – Inglehart and Norris (2016) argue that of even greater import are psychological factors; factors that have prompted a powerful cultural backlash. Already hastened by technological advances in transport and communication, the spread of 'progressive values', of multi-culturalism and, most recently, of mass migration, have marked the growing dissolution of many traditional boundaries: mental, physical and moral. Fears provoked by this sweep of 'progress' – fears, at heart, of a loss of identity – have led to an intensified nostalgia; a yearning, in the face of a growing sense of impotence, irrelevance and invisibility, for a return to more solid boundaries (borders, barriers, walls indeed), and a longing for one's tribe to be 'great again'. Accompanying this nostalgia has been a revolt against the perceived establishment, those mainstream parties who, appearing at ease with a broadly 'progressive' international agenda have come to be viewed by the disgruntled and disaffected as being led by a morally corrupt elite.

What relevance can this broad ideological context have to the intimate relations and psychological explorations of a group-analytic psychotherapy group? For S. H. Foulkes (the founder of group analysis), the therapy group is a microcosm of society. Thus, just as nations, as a species indeed, in struggling to survive as well as grow, we both guard and reach out beyond our boundaries, finding both succour and limitation in sameness, both fear and hope of enrichment in difference, so the small group and each member within in it, struggles with these very same paradoxes and challenges; challenges that are at once profoundly, inextricably personal, social and political. Failure to meet these challenges and, instead of seeking an ever more articulate form of communication about our experience of them, retreating into the seeming safety of isolationism is, from a group-analytic perspective, a sign of psychological disturbance and distress.

Group analysts view individual psychological disturbance and distress as symptoms of disturbance and distress in the wider social network. This speaks again of an appreciation of the permeability of boundaries. There are no psychological islands. We are all 'part of the main'. However, though a group-analytic perspective is rooted in the principle of interconnectedness and in a belief that our lives can be immeasurably enriched by the accommodation of difference – a 'fusion of horizons' (Gadamer, 1975) – if this is to happen without precipitating, at worst, breakdown, at best defensive regression, then we also need to pay due heed to what the psychoanalyst Ferenczi (1928/1980) called 'timing' and 'tact'; that is, the pace of change must be tolerable and our explorations take us no further from our secure base than psychic stability allows. Further, when some of us find it difficult to manage either the pace and/or intensity of change, from a group-analytic perspective, there is a sense in which all of us do.

Just post the EU referendum, one young woman texted me that she would not be coming to the young persons' group that week. It was her first absence, having travelled nearly 200 miles there and back to attend each week till then. She had little but the group in terms of social contact, leading a chronically isolated and tortured life, wrestling constantly with feelings of worthlessness, contempt for self and others and fraught with suicidal despair. Her text read: 'And yes, I did vote Brexit! And no, I'm not a racist, northerner or pensioner and if everyone in the group is going to attack me as people have done on Facebook, I don't want to talk about it.'

Half of Britain voted to leave the EU. Half the US voted for Trump. Politics is always, of course, an arena of antagonisms, but something about the stark intensity of these divisions, of the difficulty we are having of finding common ground across the deep divide, seems to me to speak of 'malignant mirroring' (Zinkin, 1983) – of splitting and of projective mechanisms at work. To heal the split does not mean that those who believe in the principle of interconnectedness need ditch their values. But we do need to facilitate a process of communication in which real fears can be aired, in which feelings of shame, invisibility and impotence can be safely explored; fears and feelings which, at some level, according to group-analytic principles, are likely to be common to all.

Neuroscientific research demonstrates that we are hard-wired to connect deeply with others and that these connections, in turn, mould the way we are 'wired'. Simply speaking, we are made, through literal and metaphorical intercourse, to create. Although our long and chequered history as a species shows all too well how capable we are, as unthinking groups, of committing the most horrendous attrocities, we are capable too, together, of great compassion, immense generosity and laudable, civilised advance. It is, in the end, our 'groupishness' that, though capable of threatening both us and other life forms with extinction, on balance, enables us to develop, prosper, thrive. That the group, with all its psycho-social intricacies, can be both so dangerous and so life-enhancing, is a clear indication that to ignore its complexities, and to ignore how we both contribute to and are made from them, is to ignore the principle of interconnectedness at our peril.

I would like to finish with an apocryphal story, told to me when I was 10. I am grateful to John Schlapobersky (2016) for reminding me of it, be it in a slightly different form.

> One night, a wise man dreamt that a messenger of God visited him and offered to show him both heaven and hell. Accepting this offer, the messenger took him first to visit the damned. How surprised he was to be shown a beautiful banqueting hall in which, at its centre, a huge table stood, laden with the most delicious food. On the table were many pairs of chopsticks, each six foot long. The damned, who were seated around the table, were allowed, said the messenger, to eat as much as they wanted whenever they wanted, but they could only do so if they used the long chopsticks. It was at this point that the wise man noticed how all those who sat at the table, unable to feed themselves with the use of such unwieldy utensils, were groaning in the most terrible agony, their figures emaciated, starving. And so it would be, always, for eternity.
>
> Overwhelmed with this horror, the wise man pleaded to be taken from this terrible place and instead to be shown heaven. In an instant, he found himself transported, to another equally beautiful banqueting hall in which, as with hell, a huge table stood at its centre, equally laden with delicious food. Again,

on the table were many pairs of six foot long chopsticks and the wise men was told that here, as in hell, the same rules of feeding applied. Yet when he looked at the people gathered there, he realised that far from seeing the living corpses he had seen in hell, here they were all well nourished, cheerful, content.

'How can this be?' the wise man asked. 'The same hall, the same table, the same food, the same chopsticks and the same rules! And yet here in heaven all thrive! What then makes the difference between heaven and hell?'

'Ah!' replied the messenger. 'In heaven, people feed each other.'

Group-analytic therapy is a therapy whose primary aim is to enable the individuals who engage in it to lead less pain-wrought, more creative, more productive lives. However, therapy in a group-analytic group aspires to do more than this; or rather, it believes that it must do more than this if it is to help the individual fully thrive. It aspires to engage its members in a complex psycho-social-educational experience. The process of such engagement is inextricably both personal *and* social, both psychological *and* political, since the future it seeks to enable for each person – one that is more hopeful than despairing, more creative than destructive – is a future which, as Donne well understood, involves all mankind.

Part I
Mainly theory

Chapter 1

The development of group analysis

The principle of interconnectedness

Nick Barwick

Although Group Analysis (also known as Group-Analytic Psychotherapy) was conceived out of creative, interdisciplinary intercourse – in particular, between psychoanalysis, gestalt psychology, neurology and sociology – it was destruction, chaos and despair that were midwives to its birth. Flooded by the traumatised casualties of The Second World War, hard-pressed military psychiatrists turned to a group model as the pragmatic, if not quite last, resort. What emerged were 'The Northfield Experiments' – experiments in group psychotherapy held at the Northfield Military Hospital, Birmingham. The first of these (led by John Rickman and Wilfred Bion) failed to establish a workable model;[1] the second (led by Harold Bridger, Tom Main and S. H. Foulkes), learning in part from the previous cohort's mistakes, fared better (Harrison, 2000).

Many of these pioneering psychoanalytically-trained psychiatrists, whether successful or not in those early group ventures, went on to make significant contributions to the development of group-work in civilian contexts. Bion, for example, returning to the Tavistock Clinic, developed his 'basic assumption theory', prompted a therapeutic approach to groups that became known as the 'Tavistock model' and, in helping to establish The Tavistock Institute of Human Relations, began a tradition of psychoanalytically-oriented organisational consultancy that continued to develop long after his own relatively brief interest in groups waned. Bridger, another founder member of The Tavistock Institute and, later, The Institute of Human Relations at Lucerne, also became highly influential in developing a psychoanalytic approach to working with organisations, while Main, following his appointment as Medical Director at the Cassel Hospital, began to conceptualise the therapeutic community – an approach that has been immensely significant in the field of inpatient and later, day-centre therapeutic care, providing a key method of working with patients with moderate to severe personality disorders. Foulkes meanwhile, perhaps rather quietly in comparison, returned to private practice before taking up posts first at St Bartholomew's and then, as Consultant in Psychotherapy, at The Maudsley, London. There he continued his group experiments, meeting regularly with a circle of interested colleagues to discuss their findings, and all the while developing and disseminating his own particular, distinctive model of group psychotherapy: Group Analysis.

Psychoanalysis and group analysis

Foulkes trained as a psychoanalyst in Vienna in 1923. Unequivocal about psychoanalysis's centrality in his thinking, Foulkes (1948) makes his allegiance clear:

> The contributions which Psycho-Analysis has made have inaugurated an epoch in the understanding of the human mind. It will take another half century until the momentum of its impact has reached its climax.
>
> (p. 7)

As a consequence, what Foulkes refers to as three fundamental psychoanalytic 'tools' – 'a method of investigation called free association', 'the knowledge of the unconscious' and 'the analysis of the transference situation' (pp. 7–9) – he claims as being of equal import in group as dyadic work.

Even so, Foulkes, in conceptualising group analysis, challenged psychoanalytic orthodoxy on two major counts. First, in contrast to Freud (1921/1991), he believed it was possible to 'do therapy' in groups; that, under the right therapeutic conditions, a group had a natural capacity to nurture its members and to encourage reflective capacity and the development of thought. Second, he believed that a group was a natural medium in which to facilitate such development because it was within a group – the family embedded as it is within the wider group of community and culture – that 'individuals' are formed. This socio-historical perspective went counter to the dominant psychoanalytic model of the time which, based on a biological perspective, construed the psyche as being formed not by social context, but by innate sexual and aggressive drives, albeit modified by their encounter with the realities of the external world.

Though challenging psychoanalytic attitudes of the time, as Weegmann (2016) notes, Foulkes did so diplomatically, managing to be both the radical and 'the gradualist who charmed and retained his audience' (Pines, 2013: xxii) – his orthodox, psychoanalytic audience. Thus Foulkes (1948) dutifully notes how:

> . . . the mental topography evolved by Psycho-Analysis, assigning certain functions of mind to an 'Id', 'Ego' and 'Super Ego' has done justice, theoretically, to the fact that the 'outer' world becomes internalised, that man's inner dynamic world is a microcosmic reflection of the whole world, at least his whole world. It has, in fact, allowed man's social nature to be represented in man's innermost structure.
>
> (p. 10)

Referring to Freud, father of psychoanalysis, is a common rhetorical device in psychoanalytic writing. In this way, debts are paid and added gravitas accrued. Drawing on Freud (1930), Vella (1999) suggests another, unconscious motive: an attempt to allay 'ambivalence and guilt over the murder of the primal father' – a murder Vella associates 'with the injuries our contemporary theories inflict upon ideas which Freud held precious . . . Guilty theorists therefore seek to atone for their heresy with a rich crop of deferential references to the master' (p. 8).[2]

Being both loyalist and dissenter,[3] Foulkes fits well this guilt-ridden, murderer's profile. Indeed, in the very next sentence comes the first soft hammer-blow:

> . . . Psycho-Analysis has not yet allotted to this social side of man the same basic importance as it has to his instinctual aspect.
> (Foulkes, 1948: 10)

Politely indicating limitations in orthodox psychoanalytic thinking – where primacy is given to drive theory – Foulkes offers for inclusion, a second, though not secondary, perspective: a social construction of human psychology.

Such a construction, today, would put Foulkes in good company. Contemporary psychoanalytic thinking has moved away from the predominantly nativist perspective, embracing instead a more interactional model of psychological development. At the time, however, Foulkes's proposal, in its foregrounding of an emergent social paradigm, challenged Freudian thinking, as did the very notion of conducting credible therapy in groups.

Freud on groups

Summarising the characteristics of group mentality, Freud identifies:

> . . . weakness of intellectual ability . . . lack of emotional restraint . . . incapacity for moderation and delay . . . inclination to exceed every limit in the expression of emotion and to work it off completely in the form of action . . . an unmistakable picture of a regression of mental activity to an earlier stage such as we are not surprised to find among savages and children.
> (1921/1991: 148)

This characterisation draws heavily upon the work of Le Bon (1895), whom he quotes at length:

> . . . by the mere fact that he forms part of an organised group, a man descends several rungs in the ladder of civilisation. Isolated, he may be a cultivated individual; in a crowd, he is a barbarian – that is a creature acting by instinct.
> (Le Bon cited in Freud 1921/1991: 103–104)

In so doing, he affirms a very Nietzschian maxim:

> Madness is something rare in individuals – but in groups, parties, peoples, ages, it is the rule.
> (1886/1973: no 156 p. 85)

Le Bon, a social psychologist steeped in reactionary politics, had been deeply disturbed by the mayhem surrounding the Paris Commune of 1871. Although, to contemporary sensibilities, it is the violent curtailment, by government forces, of this experiment in social democratic republicanism that is most shocking,[4] for Le Bon, it was the experiment itself that served to confirm his scepticism about democratic politics and his suspicion that the more power gained by the 'common man', the more marked would be society's regressive descent into barbarism. Consequently, conflating terms such as 'group', 'mass', 'crowd' and 'mob', Le Bon dismisses the group's capacity to act as 'a medium for civilised discourse' (Behr & Hearst, 2005: 18).[5]

Although further ironies (in terms of Freud's allegiance to Le Bon) lie in the fact that both Hitler and Mussolini drew upon his work – Mussolini apparently keeping a copy of Le Bon's *La Psychologie des Foules* by his bed – Le Bon's depiction of the masses under the influence of uncontrollable, primitive forces fits well Freud's own theorising:

> when individuals come together in a group all their individual inhibitions fall away and all the cruel, brutal and destructive instincts, which lie dormant in individuals as relics of a primitive epoch, are stirred up to find free gratification.
>
> (1921: 106)

This is a bleak view of groups; one 'shaped by [Freud's] ... preoccupation with the leader as the central figure at the apex of a power hierarchy and the ever-present danger of a breakdown into mob-ridden destructive behaviour' (Behr, 2004: 336).[6] Outside the happy coincidence of finding itself under the hypnotic influence of an enlightened leader, Freud construes groups as lacking capacity for thought or altruism. They may construct systems that appear civilised, but these are not the product of thinking but of psychological defence. For example, hostile sibling rivalry may be transformed, by means of identification and reaction-formation: the hated object becoming the loved. Group cohesion may be further enhanced 'by directing hostilities towards others; hence, 'the Englishman casts aspersion upon the Scot, the Spaniard despises the Portuguese' (Freud, 1921/1991: 131) – what Freud refers to as 'the narcissism of minor differences' (1930/1991: 305). As for social justice, this is simply how we manage envy and jealousy: 'we deny ourselves many things so that others may have to do without them as well' (1921/1991: 152). For Freud, most damning of all:

> ... groups have never thirsted for truth. They demand illusions and cannot do without them
>
> (p. 80)

All this proffers reason enough for apprehension in any psychoanalyst with a mind to develop a group approach. And if this alone were not enough, there is always the salutary case of Trigant Burrow.

The salutary case of Trigant Burrow

Trigant Burrow (1975–1950), psychiatrist, psychoanalyst, co-founder of The American Psychoanalytic Association and, in the United States, founder of 'phyloanalysis' (originally called 'group analysis'), is a figure, until recently, widely unacknowledged if not actively ignored.

In 1921, an analysand of Burrow's, Clarence Shields, claimed that if they were to swop roles, Burrow would surely reveal himself as riddled with neuroses as Shields himself. Burrow, taking up this challenge, discovered the truth in it. Indeed, concluding that some of these neuroses were rooted in the inequities of power in the therapeutic relationship, he argued that the individualistic application of psycho-analysis was inseparable from authoritarianism. Consequently, he sought to extend (some say replace) the asymmetrical model of analytic work with a project of mutual analysis, first within the dyad, and then, over time, as he experimented with gradually increasing numbers of participants, within a group context. This psycho-social experiment led him to construct a 'highly original conception of the social nature of human beings' (Hinshelwood, 2004: 327).

Burrow argued that Western culture had taken a 'wrong turn'. In progressing towards greater individualism, a hyper-individualised consciousness had evolved which had 'sever[ed] the natural bond between elements of the societal body' (1927a: 45), causing people to become alienated, forgetting the essential nature of their relatedness. For Burrow, psychoanalysis needed to restore the balance between self-consciousness and social-relational or group-consciousness; a balance he termed 'cotention'. Such a view, and the experiments with the group situation – 'a medium for addressing the societal forces that create our separative, alienated sense of 'I' (Gilden, 2013: xxviii) – won Burrow few favours among the psychoanalytic establishment, most notably, Freud. For example, in response to Burrow's enthusiastic, approval-seeking reports on his group-analytic project, Freud writes:

> ... my expectations are not at all favourable to you ... The mass[7] situation will either result immediately in a leader and those led by him, that is, it will become similar to the family situation but entailing great difficulties in the function of expression and unnecessary complications of jealousy and competition, or it will bring into effect the 'brother horde' where everybody has the same right and where, I believe, analytical influence is impossible.
> (Freud, 1926, cited in Campos, 1992: 6)

Chiding Burrow for his 'speculative analogies', Freud completes the intellectual castration:

> I do not believe that we should be grateful to you for the fact that you want to extend our therapeutic task to improving the world
> (ibid.)

Explicit references in the psychoanalytic literature to Burrow's work are relatively rare; this, despite the fact that, as Pertegato (1999) suggests, he has clearly been 'widely read'. Given the contempt Freud expressed for both the man and what have been referred to as his 'extravagant claims' (Scheidlinger, 1992), such omission is, perhaps, hardly surprising. Given Burrow's ignominious professional fate – this eminent, respected co-founder and one-time president of the American Psychoanalytic Association had, by 1932, been expelled from its ranks – any hesitancy a group-sympathetic psychoanalyst might have had in fully acknowledging him, might surprise even less.

Other influences on Foulkes's development of group analysis

Considering the fate of Burrow, considering the psychoanalytic orthodoxy's attitude to group therapy, considering Foulkes's own nature – according to Pines, a 'modest and approachable man' – what is perhaps striking is that Foulkes should feel able and willing to challenge psychoanalytic orthodoxy at all. For this he certainly did, with increasing clarity and confidence, noting that, for psychoanalysis to 'extend its dimension' to include group analysis, 'the whole of psychoanalytic theory and practice would have to be changed, and far removed from the mind and intention of its originator':

> In the meantime, we firmly reject the idea that experiences in group psychotherapy should be limited by present-day psycho-analytical concepts. Group-analysis is free to develop within the larger framework of psychotherapy. Its effects inside this have been described as a revolution.
> (1965/1984)

Aptly, Foulkes's pioneering strength is born not out of strident individualism but the complex group context in which his professional life developed. In his first public account of group analysis (1946/1990), he clearly indicates two influential areas of discourse, of analytic heritage, in addition to psychoanalysis:

> ... the qualifying word 'analysis' does not refer to psychoanalysis alone, but reflects at least three different influences, all of which operate actively.
> (p. 129)

These two other influences he refers to as 'psychological analysis' – particularly the work of Goldstein – and 'sociological analysis, or socio-analysis' – particularly the work of Elias. Of Burrow, he makes no mention.[8]

'Psychological analysis'

As a young man, Foulkes aspired to be a 'different psychiatrist' (Foulkes, 1967; cf. Campos, 2009: 6); one that was 'a psychoanalyst as we understand nowadays'.

Significant then, that with such ambitions, rather than going to Berlin ('then the capital of the world in medicine'), or Vienna (the home and hub of psychoanalysis) he decided instead to remain in Frankfurt. Although affairs of the heart may have contributed to this decision, professionally what kept him, suggests Campos, was Frankfurt's radical intellectual atmosphere and, in particular, his desire to continue his studies with the distinguished neurologist and Professor of Psychiatry, Kurt Goldstein.

Goldstein and his colleague, Adhemar Gelb,[9] had been studying brain-damaged casualties of the Great War. Increasingly, they became aware that 'reductive' biological approaches – where causal links were made between symptom and 'localised' brain lesion – were insufficient to explain the complexity of patient behaviour. For example, when instructed, a brain-damaged patient had difficulty in pointing to his nose. However, when involved in a network of familiar needs, such as blowing his nose, he experienced no such difficulty. Such phenomenon led Goldstein to champion a holistic approach to his research, deeply informed by Gestalt psychology. As Foulkes (1936/1990) put it, in his review of Goldstein's work:

> No finding to be considered without reference to the whole organism and to the total situation.
>
> (p. 43)

In the opening pages of his seminal introductory text to group-analytic psychotherapy, Foulkes (1948) paraphrases Goldstein's holistic, gestalt-informed, neuro-biological perspective:

> Life is a complex whole. It can only artificially be separated into parts, analysed.... This is of immediate importance in dealing with disturbances, for instance, in the field of Medicine ... The healthy organism functions as a whole and can be described as a system in dynamic equilibrium ... [having] constantly to adjust actively to the ever changing circumstances, milieu, conditions in which it lives.
>
> (p. 1)

When the organism is not healthy, when there is dysfunction, though the cause may be identified as a malfunctioning aspect of the organism, a deeper understanding reveals that:

> Disturbed function is due to the disturbance of the equilibrium of the total situation.
>
> (p. 2)

Foulkes adopts a neurological metaphor to describe how, in a therapy group, each individual is 'a little nodal point' in a 'communicational network' (of people rather than neurons). Each contribution an individual makes not only gains fuller meaning when read against the context of the dynamic network of relationships in which it is made – 'the total situation' – but may also be understood as an expression of the communications and/or lack of communications at work within the dynamic system-as-a-whole. This understanding, informed as it is by the gestalt psychological concept of figure-ground relations[10] allowed Foulkes to re-frame individual psychological disturbance as an expression of disturbed interpersonal processes of, initially, the 'group of origin' (the family), embedded as it is within wider social groups/communities. Thus, though 'disturbance' may be

> embodied in a particular patient, [it] is in fact the expression of a disturbed balance in a total field of interaction which involves a number of different people.
> (Foulkes & Anthony, 1965/1984: 54)

Further, in becoming the focal point for disturbed interpersonal processes – the 'multipersonal network of conflict' (p. 117) – the 'disturbed' individual may become increasingly isolated from the wider network. This is so because the network begins to experience the individual concerned as potentially contaminating, while both network and individual/nodal point experience each other as incompatible.

Foulkes's indebtedness to Goldstein, to Holism and to Gestalt psychology then, is clear. Indeed, the very tenor of Foulkesian optimism in the natural capacity of groups to develop and mature can be seen as emanating, in significant measure, from this same source. As Goldstein (1940/1951) notes:

> Under adequate conditions, the tendency of normal life is toward activity and progress.
> (cited in Nitzgen, 2008: 328)

Indeed, 'there is only one motive by which human activity is set going, the tendency to actualise oneself'. This sentiment, one of 'creative intentionality', is in striking contrast to Freud's, one which gives greater weight, especially in groups, to darker, more destructive forces. Interestingly, in this respect, despite Foulkes's Freudian allegiance, his belief in a 'self-actualizing tendency' as 'the basic drive' links him to key figures in the field of humanistic psychology who have also been strongly influenced by Goldstein, among them, Carl Rogers and Abraham Maslow.[11]

The Frankfurt school

Following studies with Goldstein, Foulkes pursued psychoanalytic training in Vienna. In 1930, returning to Frankfurt as director of the Institute of Psychoanalysis, he became involved in a crucible of radical inter-disciplinary thinking, spear-headed by the Institute of Social Studies.[12] This crucible, known as 'The Frankfurt School', gave birth to 'critical theory': a Marxist critique of bourgeois individualism elaborated to include not only economic but also cultural and psychological perspectives.

Although there is no consensus on the full impact that contact with the Frankfurt School had upon Foulkes and his development of group analysis, certainly it might be argued that it inculcated, perhaps more implicitly than explicitly, a respect for the importance of an *inter-disciplinary* understanding of psychic and social life. Cooper (1999) suggests that many themes arising out of the School's critical scrutiny of social phenomena had clinical implications which Foulkes later took up and developed. Most crucial among these is the issue of 'authority' and of the 'family' as the 'vehicle which transmits the individual's susceptibility to the structures of authority' (p. 41). Indeed, Foulkes takes the term 'conductor' (group therapist) from cultural theorist and musicologist, Adorno, a member of the Frankfurt School, who studied the subtle fluctuations in the location of authority within the orchestra-conductor relationship (see Chapter 4).

The Frankfurt School grew in the context of and, to some extent in response to, Fascism. Committed to the realisation of a better society, its challenging explorations soon drew the attention of the Nazis (itself a subject of the Institute of Social Studies' critical scrutiny), and, in turn, led to a 'dismemberment of the network' and 'dispersal of its members' (Behr & Hearst, 2005: 3). In 1933, The Institute, together with most of its members moved temporarily to Geneva and then, in 1935, to the States, to the universities of Columbia and New York. Others, such as Adorno (initially), Foulkes and, via Paris, Norbert Elias, left for England.

'Socio-analysis'

Elias, a sociologist, was another key influence on Foulkes, providing him with the backbone for his third strand of 'analysis' – 'socio-analysis'.

Elias's sociological perspective further challenges the 'false dichotomy' between 'individual' and group/'society'. Individuals, can only be understood, he argues, indeed can only exist, in the context of their 'interdependencies' with each other, as part of networks of social relations, or 'figurations'. Although much modern thinking emphasises the notion 'Homo Clausus' or 'Closed Man' – a view of individuals as autonomous and independent – the true picture, according to Elias, is of 'Homines Apertis' or 'open people' (the singular/plural contrast – man versus people – being deliberate). 'Homines Apertis' is characterised by interdependence rather than autonomy and bound to the figurations in which they develop.

In *The Civilizing Process*, Elias (1939/2000) describes how, over time, culture defines the very nature of individual psychic structure; i.e. we are social to the very core. His example is of how 'manners' – standards regarding violence, sexual behaviour, bodily function, forms of speech – change as the threshold of shame and repugnance increases over time. This threshold (intra-psychically what psychoanalysis might refer to as the superego) is, says Elias, the result of 'restraints' imposed by an increasingly differentiated and complex network of social relations (figurations). These restraints then become internalised; meaning they require less enforcement by external social institutions. They become 'habitus' or 'second nature'.

'Nature' is thus reframed as 'nurture', though not necessarily of a nurturing kind. This is so because the concept of figuration is about not only interdependence but also function and coercion, and therefore about power. Both individuals and groups are interdependent because each fulfills a need for the other. They have some function. What function they serve depends on the resources available and who has control of them. In effect, their interdependence leaves each party 'capable of exercising some form of reciprocal constraint' (Quintaneiro, 2004). Such constraint is not simply top down. Even absolute monarchs are not autonomous and depend upon other members of the figuration to achieve and maintain their power. Nevertheless, differences of power among groups and individuals do exist and lie in the type and proportion of resources which different parts of the figuration control.

The falsity of the individual-group dichotomy described by this model fits well Foulkes's own developing perspective. Drawing on Elias he states:

> ... each individual – itself an artificial, though plausible abstraction – is basically and centrally determined, inevitably, by the world in which he lives, by the community, the group, of which he forms a part. ... the old juxtaposition of an inside and outside world, constitution and environment, individual and society, phantasy and reality, body and mind and so on, are untenable. They can at no stage be separated from each other, except by artificial isolation.
>
> (1948: 10)

Burrow 'reloaded'

The fate of Burrow as salutary warning for psychoanalysts considering promoting the therapeutic efficacy of groups has already been discussed. Possibly as a consequence, despite being 'stimulated' by Burrow's writing (cf. Foulkes, 1990) and despite acknowledging gaining a 'number of profound insights' from studying him, Foulkes (1948) confesses 'mixed feelings ... of interest and prejudice' on reading him, concluding that Burrow's method was 'probably different from the outset to the one here described and has ... developed in quite different directions'. (p. 37). Recent scholarly research (Pertegato, 2013; 2014), however, suggests otherwise.

Pertegato (2014) offers numerous examples of both group-analytic theory and method rooted in Burrow. Theoretically, for example, Burrow focuses on the importance of 'overcoming ... the dichotomy between individual and group' since:

at the basis of his thinking there is the unitary conception of the human being and the primary continuity of the individual with the group, be it one's social group or the species as a whole.

(Gatti Pertegato, 1994 cited in Pertegato, 2014: 319)

Burrow sees the individual as an integral part of the environment and cannot be artificially separated from it (Syz, 1927: 607 cited in Pertegato, 2014); indeed to do so, is to attempt to study 'a fish out of water' – a metaphor common, interestingly, to both Burrow (1928a) and Foulkes (1948). Such understanding leads Burrow to state:

man is not an individual, its mentation is not individualistic. He is part of a societal continuum.

(1926a/2013: 148)

Criticising the 'fallacy of the individualistic approach' in psychoanalysis, with its limited study of the 'individual unconscious' and its neglect of the 'mass or social unconscious of which the individual is a part' (1926b/2013: 157), he states:

It is futile to attempt to remedy mental disease occurring within the individual mind as long as psychiatry remains blind to the existence of mental disease within the social mind.

(ibid.)

This includes:

... the actual presence of demonstrable disordered mental states within the social organizations that form our present day civilization.

(ibid.)

As Pines (2013) puts it, Burrow's accusation, not dissimilar to Foulkes's more diplomatic challenge, was that the psychoanalytic community shared in a 'social cover-up':

the fact that we all disguise is that neurosis is social and that a social neurosis can only be met through a social analysis.

(p. xxi)

As for group method, several key areas of a group-analytic approach Pertegato (2014) also identifies as originating in Burrow's work, for example:

- the concept of the group-as-a-whole – one in which 'no reaction of anyone [is] regarded as isolated or separate' – and, following this, that the group itself may also be seen as being representative of society at large (Burrow, 1928b/2013: 183);

- due emphasis on the here-and-now free communication of the group (1927b/2013: 177; 1928b/2013: 186);
- the importance of the patient experiencing himself as an observer of 'common human problems, personal and social' (Burrow, 1927b/2103: 173)
- an appreciation of certain group specific therapeutic factors such as:
  - mirroring: 'the opportunity for each student to see disinterestedly the elements composing his own neurosis as they are directly reflected to him in the neurosis of another' (ibid.: 174);
  - universality: becoming 'part of a societal plexus . . . along with people pursuing an interest common with his own' (ibid.: 173);
- an appreciation of a more mutual, democratic form of therapy encapsulated by Burrow's comment that 'group analysis is not my analysis of the group, but is the group's analysis of me or of any other individual of the group' (1927c/2013: 138).

All this brings an undeniable weight of counter-evidence against Foulkes's close collaborator James Anthony's assertion that Burrow, though having 'a background of psychoanalytic knowledge and working in groups . . . did not strongly affect the field of current group psychotherapy' (1971: 10).

Did Foulkes then, together with a number of other group-oriented psychoanalysts, collude in a 'copious ransacking' of Burrow's ideas while, ironically, remaining complicit in 'the iron censorship of the psychoanalytic orthodoxy'? The Pertegatos (2013: lxxxviii) suggest as much. Whatever the truth, for Foulkes, his indebtedness to this group pioneer is a complex, conflicted, nuanced matter and one that Power (2013) nicely alerts us to. For, while in the first edition of *Group Psychotherapy* (Foulkes & Anthony, 1957), Foulkes refers to Burrow as 'one of the most important pioneers of group-analysis' and 'one of the first to recognise the group's role in the individual's neurosis . . . [providing] us with many deep insights into the understanding of groups' (p. 41), in the second, 1965 edition, of Trigant Burrow there is no mention.[13]

Conclusion

Throughout his writing, Foulkes continues to elaborate the notion of individual and group as 'two sides of the same coin' (Foulkes & Anthony, 1965/1984: 26). Fusing Goldstein's notion of a 'network of neurons' with Elias's notion of 'social network'/'figuration', Foulkes suggests the group is 'the essential frame of reference in psychology' and that:

> the individual is inevitably a fragment shaped dynamically by the group in which he first grew up. . . . a piece of a jig-saw puzzle . . . When you take this individual fragment out of its context, it is shaped and formed, or deformed, according to the place it had and the experiences it received in this group. The first group is normally the family. This family, willy-nilly,

reflects the culture to which it belongs and in turn transmits the cultural norms and values.

(Foulkes, 1974: 275)

What is so powerful here, at an ethical, philosophical and political level, is the notion of shared responsibility for mental disturbance and mental health:

Ultimately it would mean that the whole community must take a far greater responsibility for outbreaks of disturbing psychopathology generally. There is therefore a very specific defensive interest at play in denying the fact of the interdependence which is here claimed; the cry 'but each is an individual' and 'surely the mind is a matter for the individual' means, in this sense, 'each for himself, I am not to blame for what happens to the other person, whether he is obviously near to me, or whether I am involved in concealed ways, or even quite unconsciously.

(1973: 225)

In contrast, Foulkes (1964) states that:

Neurosis is not a disease, but arises from problems which concern everybody.
(p. 296)

In this light, a group-analytic group, representing a microcosm of society, may be seen not only as a pragmatic method of delivering therapy (much as it was at its inception) but also as a preferred method too, for:

... if people live from birth on as inter-relational open entities[14] ... if individuals are thoroughly socialised and individualized at the same time, and if, during this process, they are liable to produce psychopathological conditions ... we *not only may, but must*, assemble them in a therapeutic group ... to treat them.

(Lavie, 2005: 520)

Such a claim echoes that which Cody Marsh, psychiatrist, minister and pioneer of psychiatric group work, made nearly 80 years earlier when he announced that the motto on his psychiatric shield would read:

By the crowd they have been broken, by the crowd they shall be healed.
(Marsh, 1933)

Notes

1 The failure was not a clinical one but a failure to consider the wider organisation in the planning and maintenance of the therapeutic approach. As a consequence,

the disapproving military authorities forced the closure and reassignment of the experiments within 6 weeks (cf. Harrison, 2000).

2 Similar oedipal dynamics evident in the writing process are noted by Britton (1998) and Barwick (2003).

3 According to Foulkes (cited in Cooper, 1999), Ernest Jones, president of the British Psycho-Analytic Society (1920–1924 & 1932–1949), as well as other senior psychoanalysts, considered Foulkes's preoccupation with groups as a 'breach of faith'.

4 In the slaughter of commune sympathisers by government forces, 30,000 were killed, perhaps as many as 50,000 later executed or imprisoned (Cobban, 1965).

5 Recent research has traced Le Bon's contributions within a wider, emergent field of 'crowd psychology', coincident with the growth of sociology, based predominantly on negative images of group life and reflective of certain bourgeois concerns and anxieties of the era (Borch, 2012).

6 In 'Group Psychology and the Analysis of the Ego', Freud (1921/1991) refers to the process of 'mass binding' in which the ego submerges itself by means of narcissistic identification with the now idealised leader and, losing individuality, merges with the mass (of members) prostrating itself in 'humble subjection, compliance and absence of criticism' (p. 112).

7 Here we can hear Le Bon's conflation of terms: small group, large group, mass. They are all the same.

8 It is sometimes suggested that 'field theory' and the work of Kurt Lewin had a major influence on the development of group analysis. Tubert-Oklander (2014) notes, however, Foulkes himself denied such influence, commenting that though 'our own group-analytic views married well with concepts used in "field theory", and that the latter helped us in our orientation' (Foulkes & Anthony, 1957: 20), the commonality between the two approaches derived from their 'common background as regards Gestalt psychology' which, for Foulkes, came from Goldstein.

9 Adhemar Gelb had, together with Max Wertheimer (one of the founder members of the Gestalt Psychology movement) set up a centre for research in Gestalt Psychology at Frankfurt.

10 What we perceive at any one time – the figure – is only perceivable by dint of the background (ground) out of which it emerges (is made meaningful). The text is not discernible without the page. Meaning is incomplete without context. Rubin's vase drawing (in which either two faces facing each other or a vase can be discerned) is perhaps the best known example of this principle.

11 Goldstein, another German Jewish exile and émigré, left Germany in 1935 to settle in the United States. There, as a university teacher, he became a founding figure of holism, influencing, as Harrington (1996) notes, a whole generation of American psychologists.

12 Ilse Seglow, a colleague of Foulkes, recalls the rich exchange of ideas between the disciplines of economics, politics, psychoanalysis, medicine, history, philosophy, cultural theory, anthropology and sociology (Campos, 2009). The roll call of leading participants is impressive and includes Max Horkheimer (the influential second director of the Institute), Theodor Adorno, Walter Benjamin, Norbert Elias, Erich Fromm, Leo Lowenthal, Herbert Marcuse, Friedrich Pollock, Paul Tillich, Max Wertheimer and, on occasions, Kurt Lewin. Kurt Goldstein was also a contributor though he left for Berlin before Foulkes returned.

13 Pichon-Riviere, whose work on groups began 4 years prior to Foulkes's own, has also been proposed as an alternative 'true pioneer of group analysis' (Tubert-Oklander, 2014: 15).

14 This is a reference to Elias's (1969) notion, already mentioned above, of Homo Clausus – 'closed man' – versus 'Homines Aperti' – 'open people'; the latter being

'open entities with open valences of bonding to other individuals'. Elias was interested in what historical and ideological conditions gave rise to the conception of the former, isolated, singular description of the human state as proposed by many modern psychologies, especially psychoanalysis, as opposed to what he viewed to be the more realistic and scientific conception of individuals (in the plural), in all their rich inter-relational complexity.

Chapter 2

Core concepts
What goes on in groups? (Part one)

Nick Barwick

Building upon the principle of interconnectedness, Foulkes elaborates several core concepts to describe group-analytic theory. Grappling with processes of immense complexity, these descriptions are sometimes more 'metaphoric' than precise. For group analysts, this has been a source both of frustration and inspiration,[1] prompting many to draw upon diverse fields, from within and outside psychoanalysis, in search of greater clarity.

What is a group-analytic psychotherapy group?

Slow open and time-limited groups

The classic group-analytic group is a *slow open group*. 'Open' refers to changing composition; members join, members leave. 'Slow' refers to the pace at which these 'beginnings' and 'endings', 'births' and 'deaths' occur. In this 'slow open' way, the group builds a complex family, social and cultural history which is different from, but resonant with, each members' own family, social and cultural history.

Often, for reasons of pragmatism as well as service delivery, time-limited group-analytic groups are also run. Here, usually, everyone starts and finishes together. The more limited the time, the more limited/focused will be the group's aims, and, most likely, the more homogenous the group, particularly in terms of problems presented.

Combined, conjoint and group-analytic psychotherapy groups

Foulkes first developed group practice as a 'combined' model – that is, seeing patients both for individual and group therapy. However, group analysis as a stand-alone model soon superseded this approach. Although combined therapy thrives in some parts of the world, in Europe it is rarely practiced, certainly in a sustained, organised way. Group Analysis in the context of conjoint therapy (a programme of parallel individual and group sessions with different therapists) is also relatively rare.[2]

Established contemporary group-analytic wisdom then suggests all group members commit, exclusively, to group therapy. Even so, best practice is not always quite so clear cut. For example, new members may seek to join groups while still in individual therapy and, though it is usually helpful to recommend terminating such therapy before commencing a group, in certain circumstances, it may be important to negotiate a weaning process: a period of transition during which the patient engages in both modalities, even though aiming to relinquish individual therapy over time. Similarly, it is not unknown, though not common, for members to have periods where they might supplement, say, a once-weekly group therapy with a period of individual therapy – for example, with a period of cognitive behavioural therapy (CBT) intended to address an immediate and distressing symptom. However, it is important that any such variant on the standard approach – that is, group analysis as a standalone therapy – is carefully discussed in the group (why has it arisen? how do other group members feel about it? what might be the benefits and/or concerns for both the individual concerned and the group?) and carefully monitored, since the relative informality of such arrangements can easily lead to unhelpful splitting and a potential leaking out of part of the group's life-blood.

Size

Foulkes recommends a group of seven or eight, plus 'the conductor'. (The conductor is the group-analytic term for therapist. See Chapter 4 for a discussion of this term.) A larger group tends to prompt greater, often annihilatory, anxieties. Intimacy is also often more inhibited and the opportunity for self-presentation reduced. Too small a group, however, pressures the conductor into being more active; less able to allow group dynamics to unfold and the group to do the work. Indeed, certain dynamics, for example those around conflict and difference, may feel riskier, harder to explore. Further, absences threaten group identity when numbers are few.

The stranger group

The classic group-analytic group, unstructured in its approach (i.e. without pre-determined agenda or rules of engagement), meeting once or twice-weekly for 90 minutes, is a *stranger group*. This means members do not know or meet each other outside the group. Any such encounter is regarded as a *boundary incident*, and is discussed, provided that it has been reported.

Boundary incidents are not necessarily anti-therapeutic. Once discussed in the group, they can provide important opportunities for learning. Unchecked, however, they lead to psychic leakage, depleting the group's life-blood. Secret, they promote sub-groupings that undermine trust in confidentiality and the group's capacity to contain.

On rare occasions, therapists meet members one-to-one. Such meetings demand careful thought regarding what they mean to individual and to group. Opportunities for exploring feelings arising out of such events need to be made.

Composition, cohesion, coherence

Foulkes recommends *heterogeneous* groups – ' "a mixed bag" of diagnoses and disturbances' (1965/1984: 66). Nevertheless, he also recommends no one should be socially or psychologically isolated – for example, one young person in a group of older people, one black person in an all-white group, one heterosexual in a group otherwise all gay, one person with more manic traits among a group otherwise constituted of people presenting as introverted and/or depressed. This is sometimes referred to as selection according to 'the Noah's Ark principle' – at least two of each type (Lorentzen, 2014: 4).[3] The reasons for applying such a principle are many, including providing the best opportunities for *mirroring* (see Chapter 3) as well as helping to guard against potential *scapegoating* of the individual (see Chapters 5 and 6). However, more fundamental is an appreciation that both commonality *and* difference are vital to psychological development, for while the foundations (and maintenance) of self depend upon the experience of safety gained through an encounter with sameness, the development of self, of identity, grows out of an encounter with difference.

Sometimes, the principle of sameness/safety takes precedence over the principle of difference/exploration. For example, group analysts run groups for women, the elderly, those with eating disorders, those who have experienced torture, those who have suffered abuse, and for many other relatively homogenous groups. Such homogeneity (be it in terms of social grouping, diagnosis, personality structure and/or life-history/experience) can promote *cohesion* – a sticking together, or 'bonding' vital to a basic sense of safety without which no exploratory work can be done. The experience of sharing similar experience helps break down feelings of isolation, strengthens self-identity and a sense of 'we-ness' – 'belonging groups' (Rouchy, 1995) – and reduces feelings of abnormality and shame. Unsurprising, then, that several studies (cf. Marziali *et al.*, 1997; Lorentzen *et al.*, 2004; Johnson *et al.*, 2005; Bakali *et al.*, 2010, 2013) have demonstrated a clear relationship between outcome and cohesion (in many respects the group equivalent of the therapeutic alliance).[4]

Some time-limited groups, in efforts to promote sharing, make establishing safety their main aim. Nonetheless, for any group, it is important to remember that sameness is an illusion, even if, at first, a vital one. To reach its therapeutic potential in terms of interpersonal learning, a group must relinquish sameness and, though valuing similarity, work with difference. Otherwise, cohesion becomes a defensive posture with impermeable boundaries within which difference is expunged.[5] Pertinent here is Thygesen's (1992) notion of difference itself (the 'diversity' within a group) as a 'group-specific therapeutic factor' – a third object that helps dissolve the over-cohesive matrix symbolising the mother-infant dyad.[6] The development of a group can thus be described as a move from cohesion, in which security is based on identification, to *coherence* (Pines, 1985a/1998; 1994a) – 'a mindful . . . unity: an aesthetic achievement reached through the reflective and resonant interaction of different parts'. (Barwick, 2004: 132). However, though coherence describes a higher level of group functioning and a capacity to sustain more diverse and complex relationships (between individuals and between individual and group identity), it is not a permanent state but one which, depending on levels of real and/or perceived threat, oscillates with the more primitive and undifferentiated group formations characteristic of cohesion (Ezquerro, 2010).

Development

In closed and/or time-limited groups especially, linear developmental patterns are observable. For example, a new group concerned with boundaries and searching for structure, goals and dependence on a leader could be described as being in an 'orientation' phase (Bennis & Shepard, 1956). This may be followed by a 'conflict' phase where norms are argued over and struggles regarding authority and control engaged in. Only gradually may a more mature state of 'coherence' be achieved in which the focus on structure, authority and power relations gives way to a focus on issues of intimacy and interdependence. This description matches Tuckman's (1965) group-stage summary – *forming, storming, norming, performing* and *adjourning*;[7] a summary that is widely drawn upon in group psychotherapy (e.g. Yalom, 1970/1985; MacKenzie, 1997), including group analysis (e.g. Dick, 1975; Lorentzen, 2014).[8]

For the clinician, the framework provided by a staged or phased group developmental perspective is an attractive one. It promises some means of orientation among the dizzying complexity of group life. However, in the context of slow-open group-analytic groups, unmodified it is a perspective that inevitably oversimplifies. Slow open groups, characterised as they are by a changing membership (and by the sometimes hopeful but also often anxiety-ridden challenges that accompany this) are likely to be particularly susceptible to regressive forces at different times in their life, even if such forces, within a sufficiently robust and containing group-analytic culture, may be in the end, creatively harnessed in the service of progression. For this reason, group development in group analysis tends to be understood as oscillating and/or cyclical rather than linear, despite a hoped-for growing capacity for coherence and containment over time.

Another criticism of many stage/phase descriptions of group development is that they cannot easily capture the complexity of, and variation in, each individual group members' development and developmental needs at any given time. Von Fraunhofer (2008) addresses this problem with a three-phase model focusing on the individual's development within a group rather than the development of the group itself. Drawing on Fairbairn (1952/2003), she describes the progression from immature dependence ('fusion') through a transitional phase of partial independence ('joining') to a phase of more mature interdependence ('belonging'). Each phase, she suggests, is characterised by an 'attitude towards exchange' (reciprocity): fusion being characterised by an attitude of non-reciprocality, joining by an attitude of experimentation, and belonging by an attitude of reciprocity – a capacity for mutual exchange. Similarly, drawing on Schlapobersky (1994), she describes how each attitude is characterised by a quality of communication, namely monologue, emergent dialogue and discourse (see Chapter 3 for further discussion of these terms).

Drawing on von Fraunhofer (2008), together with other group schemata, Schlapobersky (2016) offers an integrated perspective, one which gives due weight to both group and individual development, first elaborated with Pines (Schlapobersky & Pines, 2009). Utilising Tuckman's group development model, he identifies a set of five developmental tasks:

- *Engagement*. The individual/group struggles with anxiety about being involved in a new situation. Boundary issues, confidentiality and issues of safety predominate.
- *Authority*. Tension about group norms, disclosures and who is confident or not are focused upon.
- *Intimacy*. Questions of trust, attachment and affiliations become core.
- *Change*. Group trust grows; so does self-disclosure. Greater self-exploration allows greater recognition of difference and greater individuation.
- *Termination*. Reflection on changes inside/outside the group are characteristic. What has been 'generalised'? What has not?

These tasks both group-as-a-whole and individual members repeatedly return to 'in a spiral of increasingly *coherent* exploration' (Schlapobersky, 2016: 96). Such deepening exploration is consistent with 'working through' (Freud, 1914). Thus this task-focused perspective proffers a useful orienting map (a sense of logical progression) but avoids the pitfalls associated with a linear, phasic description of a group's developmental journey.

A further useful 'developmental' frame that Schlapobersky describes, though not group-specific, is the 'three dimensions of therapy' – relational, reflective and reparative; the therapeutic course through which the analyst must act as facilitating guide. Again this course is cyclical rather than linear, though a more mature, well-established group is likely to work with greater frequency and depth in the second and third dimensions while a 'young' group is likely to spend more time in the first. In the first, relational dimension, 'relational moments' are generated through attachment and friction. These offer fertile ground for 'reflective moments' where new meaning can be made. Such reflective moments of self-consciousness may give rise to remorse and concern which in turn may fuel a potential re-configuration of relational patterns. Such new patterns, characterised by generosity and gratitude, are core to the 'reparative moment', a concept that incorporates Yalom's (1970/1985) group specific therapeutic factor 'corrective recapitulation', itself an elaboration of the corrective emotional experience (Alexander & French, 1946).

Core psychoanalytic processes at work in groups

Foulkes suggests three core aspects of psychoanalysis – the unconscious, free association, transference – are equally valid in group analysis. However, even these take on modified forms.

The unconscious

In the Freudian tradition, the unconscious refers to mental processes and phenomena outside an individual's conscious awareness. Because its contents – desires, fears, memories – carry painful and/or unacceptable emotional associations, it is made and/or kept unconscious by dint of 'defences' such as repression and splitting, which are themselves unconsciously deployed. In this way, as individuals, we manage to adapt to and survive the experience of internal conflicts and the difficult demands and often traumatising impact of the external world. However, in managing in this way, we also begin to become depleted of basic resources which otherwise might be available to us (for example, the 'psychic energy' consumed in maintaining or refusing aspects of the unconscious and the potential learning from experience which is lost to conscious awareness when the impact of 'experience' itself proves too difficult to consciously digest). Further, though gaining a level of mental safety by these unconscious manoeuvres, we become not only psychically depleted but also remain prey to the influence of what is consigned to the unconscious. This influence, revealing itself in unhelpful, irrational behaviours as well as a variety of potentially distressing mental and physical symptoms, proves counterproductive to what Winnicott (1970) calls 'creative living'. For this reason, a central aim of Freudian psychoanalysis is to render the unconscious conscious or, according to Freud's later structural theory of mind: 'Where id was there shall ego be' (1932: 112).[9]

For Foulkes, as for Freud, making the unconscious conscious is core to therapy. However, while for Freud the unconscious is embodied and biological in origin, growing out of the individual's id, Foulkes broadens this perspective:

> the group-analytic situation, while dealing intensively with the unconscious in the Freudian sense, brings into operation and perspective a totally different area of which the individual is equally unaware ... the individual is as much compelled and modelled by these colossal forces as by his own id and defends himself as strongly against their recognition without being aware of it ... One might speak of a social or interpersonal unconscious.
>
> (1964: 52)

Initially, these two collocations – 'social unconscious' and 'interpersonal unconscious' – Foulkes uses interchangeably. He soon drops, however, the latter. Why this is so becomes clearer as he introduces another descriptor – 'transpersonal' – to describe the unconscious dynamics at play in a group setting. For Foulkes, the descriptor 'interpersonal' becomes inadequate, it seems, in his efforts to capture the state of 'endo-psychic common union' (1966 [1990]: 154) he is trying to portray. This 'union' arises out of web of formative communications that pass not only 'between' but also 'through' people and that therefore proffer, at the profoundest level, a determining contribution to each person's psychological identity.

For Foulkes then, mind, including unconscious aspects of mind, are seen as being co-constructed and thus inherently social.[10] As a process, this co-construction can be seen to be at work in any group. It arises not only out of the complex network of interpenetrating communications (past and present) that constitute the therapy group's life, but also out of the communicational networks that constitute the life and history of the wider groups, communities and societies out of which the therapy group has emerged; that is to say, its context. This is what Foulkes (1964) alludes to when he says 'the individual is . . . compelled and modelled by these colossal forces' (p. 54), that he is 'social through and through' (1948). Thus, when Foulkes notes that, in a group-analytic group, the conductor 'is put in the position of the primordial leader' (p. 59), he is suggesting not only the presence of unconscious, interpersonal, familial transferences co-constructed by the group but also something far more 'colossal' and transpersonal in nature.[11]

Although Foulkes argued with increasing confidence for the significance of the social unconscious in determining identity and for the need, if therapy was to be effective, for opportunities to access and work with it, his concept of the social unconscious remained essentially intuitive and his explanatory elaborations, scant. Among group analysts who have sought to provide more detailed elaborations, Hopper (Hopper, 2001; 2003b & d; Hopper & Weinberg, 2011; 2015) has been key. For Hopper, the social unconscious refers to the *constraints* of social objects – socio-cultural communicational arrangements (i.e. institutions, organisations, political, economic and other systems) – that have been internalised and of which people are 'unaware'. This is to recognise the impact of 'social facts and forces' on both the individual and the group, a necessary prerequisite if the group analyst is to be 'sensitive to the unconscious re-creation of them within the therapeutic situation' and 'provide a space for patients to imagine how their identities have been formed at particular historical and political junctures, and how this continues to affect them throughout their lives' (Hopper, 2001: 9–10).

As developing individuals (Hopper prefers the word 'person', to avoid colluding with a view of a psychological entity that can be understood out of its social context) we not only internalise such constraints as we develop but also emerge from them. This is to emphasise that 'in the beginning there is no such thing as an infant but only an infant/mother couple in a social context: two bodies, one mind'. (p. 24). To be mindful of this, suggests Hopper, is not only to recognise that such constraints can be facilitative as well as restrictive, but also to appreciate that psychic life begins not with projection (of the anxiety inherent in the putative 'death instinct') but with processes of internalisation.

The way that the constraints of the social unconscious affect us, for better or worse, can be seen in the way language influences thinking. For example, if we have a word for something we are more likely to see it – certainly to see it more quickly. Further, the connotations the word has colours the way we see it. Since language is a socio-cultural construct, it carries certain assumptions and prejudices specific to the culture of construction. Hence, to enter into language is to have language (and culture) enter into us: to have our perception shaped by socio-political forces of which we are largely unaware.

For example, Dalal (2002a) notes how 'black' in modern Britain has many more negative than positive connotations. This seems 'natural' – black being the colour of the dangerous dark. Yet such connotations are neither a-social nor a-historical. Indeed, in early seventeenth century England, positive connotations of black were much more common, 'black' suggesting the exotic – 'black and comely' – more than the illicit or bestial. By the turn of the eighteenth century, however, a marked rise in negative connotations occurs; a change coinciding with colonial expansion. Could it be that the 'de-*nigration*' of 'black' – that is, the 'blackening' of 'black' – became a way of dehumanising non-Christian cultures, so managing/avoiding, in the wake of our exploitations, European guilt? Such conscious and unconscious linguistic manipulation quickly becomes embedded, expressing a social unconscious that constrains thought in generations to come.[12]

Understandably, we experience resistance to becoming aware of such constraints, partly because we are so caught up in them, partly because the concept compromises the notion of 'free will' (a narcissistic blow), partly because of the guilt awareness exposes us to and, partly, because society achieves a certain functional stability by being constrained in this way, even when that stability is particularly disadvantageous to the development of some individuals and sub-groups within it.

An appreciation of the social unconscious makes available for analytic scrutiny not only unconscious processes within people but also between people and through people. The latter takes the form of 'assumptions' (what is taken for granted and natural in society), 'disavowals' (disowning knowledge or social responsibility for things), 'social defences' (what is defended against by projective mechanisms) and 'structural oppression' (the control of power and information by competing social interests so that awareness is restricted) (Brown, 2001).

Dalal (2001), however, takes issue with the dual model of unconscious – one individual/biological and one social – proposed by Brown (2001) and others. This model, Dalal (1998) argues, follows 'orthodox Foulkes' (one constrained by Freud) rather than 'radical Foulkes' (one informed by Elias) who proffers a different perspective:

> [the] group, the community, is the ultimate primary unit of consideration, and the so-called inner processes in the individual are internalizations of the forces operating in the group to which he belongs.
>
> (Foulkes, 1971a/1990: 212)

In effect, 'the things that look like the instincts – the so-called natural ways of behaving – are internalizations of group forces . . . the id itself is acculturated'. (Dalal, 2001: 543).

In what Dalal (2011) refers to as an 'Eliasian/radical Foulkesian schema', the social precedes the individual and the social is the domain of the political –

the conflicted field of power relations. Foulkes's 'social unconscious' is one name, suggests Dalal, for this *social a priori*. It follows that the social unconscious is fundamentally political. Further, the mind that emerges from such a social context is thus inevitably constrained by the ideologies (the unconscious assumptions as to why things are the way they are or the way they should be) and discourses that are an expression of the power relations that constitute political life. Neither patients nor analysts are free from such constraints.

Although there is no single view of what constitutes the social unconscious or how its 'colossal forces' are transmitted – see, for example, the diverse views expressed in Hopper and Weinberg's (2011, 2016) edited collections – what unifies these views is an interest in deepening our awareness and understanding of the principle of interconnectedness and the importance of social context. For example, Scanlon (2015) argues how, ironically, improving access to psychological therapies (IAPT) can, in failing to engage 'deeper questions about the (dis)organised nature of our *communal* 'depression' and the associated socio-economic and political oppression and suppression that gives rise to it' (p. 40), leave those receiving treatment scapegoated, burdened with sole responsibility for their predicament and persecuted by the system ostensibly designed to help them. Even so, for some group analysts, an over-emphasis on the social 'neglects crucial aspects of psychotherapeutic insight, research and experience' (Nitsun, 2015: 70). Furthermore, Nitsun notes how many of his 'particularly socially orientated colleagues' struggle:

> to argue the utility of the social perspective in clinical work only to resort to psychodynamic, psychoanalytic, humanistic or other clinically based theories as ways of understanding complex group problems.
> (Nitsun, 2015: 70)

Free association

Free Association is a fundamental method, in individual psychoanalysis, of accessing the unconscious. The assumption is: all lines of thought lead to what is significant – 'the logic of association' being a form of 'unconscious thinking' (Bollas, 2008: 21) – except where there is 'resistance'. In group analysis, free association becomes 'group association' or 'free-floating discussion' and refers to thoughts communicated *between* members. As Foulkes comments, 'We now treat association as based on the common ground of unconscious *instinctive understanding* of each other'. (1964: 4).

What Foulkes does is link Freud's fundamental psychoanalytic method with Goldstein's fundamental concept of the 'total situation'. (Nitzgen, 2013a). This was a decisive theoretical step and led him to 'accept that ideas and comments expressed by different members (of the group) have the value of *unconscious interpretations*' (Foulkes & Anthony, 1965/1984 cited in Nitzgen, 2013a: 150). Not only are 'all communications, from whatever individual they may come' now seen 'as meaningful associations in the context of the group' (Foulkes, 1968/1990: 181) but 'the conversation of *any* group could be considered in its unconscious aspects as the equivalent of free association' (1964: 117), though such association is most prevalent in groups, like the group-analytic group, which are unstructured and have no 'occupation' (no explicit focus/task). Indeed, in the analytic group, reduced censorship elicited by its unstructured nature and the *free floating discussion* or *group association* – Foulkes's names for the group equivalent of free association in individual therapy – that flourishes in this environment, 'enables us to approach what might be called the social unconscious' (Foulkes, 1965/1984: 56).

The ongoing process of mutual interpretation, both at a conscious and unconscious level, that group association describes becomes, for Foulkes, the very process of 'analysing' (1975/1986) – the core work of a group-analytic group. Hence, in establishing the concept of group association, Foulkes takes not only a decisive theoretical step but a decisive methodological one as well. This is so because the conductor can no longer be deemed the sole holder of interpretative authority, but rather one whose primary task is to facilitate the natural interpretative capacity of the group; what Foulkes refers to as 'analysis'. This is not to suggest conductors should not interpret but that they should be careful that doing so does not interrupt the group associations that in themselves can fulfill this function with far greater therapeutic effect – hence Foulkes's dictum: '*interpretation comes in where analysis fails*' (1975/1986: 117) (See Chapter 4 for a fuller discussion of the conductor's interpretative function). For these reasons and more, many group analysts would agree with de Maré's (1991) assessment that:

> the first and deepest insight, the initial unique and major contribution that Foulkes (Foulkes & Anthony, 1957/1965) ever made, was that of the simple but quintessential significance of free-floating group discussion.
>
> (p. 51)

Transference

A contemporary understanding of transference combines both 'whole' and 'part object' perspectives. Whole object transference refers to figures from the past – for example, mother, father, siblings – and a person's experience of them, that are unconsciously transferred to the present, thus strongly colouring that person's experience of 'new' relationships. Part object transference refers to the fact that our experience of present relationships is not only unconsciously informed by our experience of past relationships but also that those past relationships in themselves are coloured by our projections – split off and denied, because unacceptable, aspects of ourselves we assign to others and parts of others – for example, our own aggression. In effect, often what we see in others is what we find difficult to see in ourselves.

Transference and its interpretation is core to the work of individual psychoanalytic psychotherapy. Foulkes notes how the group analyst is always a Transference figure (capital 'T' denoting transference to the conductor) and that the Transference is likely to be strongly coloured by past authority relations. Such Transference – to a more or less omnipotent figure, be it the primal father or early mother, though at first inevitable and needing to be borne, also needs to be 'counteracted'. Without such counteraction, it threatens to produce the kind of unthinking mass against which Freud (1921) so clearly warned. In such groups, characterised by compliance, conformity and self-subjugation to the idealised leader, free group discussion, upon which the whole group-analytic process depends, is critically undermined. Hence, for Foulkes, though allowing Transference 'to the full', he recommends '*not* to use it, but . . . to free the group from the automatic force of this tendency to compliance and conformity' (1971a/1990: 211). Foulkes's method of counteracting – in effect, developing 'an ever expanding network of communication' (p. 212) – is discussed further in Chapters 3 and 5. However, even beyond the dangers outlined here, Transference use or, more accurately, its over-use is, at the very least, to cultivate a dyadic relationship – therapist-patient, therapist-group – which fails to utilise the group's broader life, including multiple transferences (small 't' denoting transferences to other group members) characteristic of the group-analytic approach.

T/transferences tend to be seen more vividly in a group and negative Transferences, because of safety in numbers, more freely voiced. Oedipal T/transferences are just such a case in point. Members constantly encounter triadic relationships in which possession of and exclusion from 'the gaze' of another is key. Indeed, individuals can experience, in the here-and-now of the group, whole past patterns of functioning rooted in their family network, just as they can more recent communicational networks such as playgroups, classes, workgroups. Further, a common transference is to the group-as-a-whole as an early, pre-oedipal mother (Grotjahn, 1983; see also Chapter 6).

In addition to multiple individual T/transferences, multiple group T/transferences are also evident. The group T/transferences are collective and often usefully contextualised by the notion of group-as-a-whole development. For example, when a group reaches a certain 'developmental stage', it flexes its muscles, asserting its own authority. Sometimes referred to as the 'barometric event' (Bennis & Shepard, 1956), the group Transference can be seen as being to the tribal father whose authority is challenged and must be overcome if it is to be incorporated and the group to 'come of age'.

When there is group transference to individuals, a group member may be seen by the group as personifying certain characteristics – the result of collective projections. For example, in a group fearful of loss of control, one member may be identified as personifying uncontrolled aspects of the group. Similarly, in a group assailed by persecutory guilt arising, for example, from surfacing aggression, one person may become identified as aggressor, around whom the whole group carefully treads. Individuals are both coerced into playing these 'parts' as well as often unconsciously drawn to them – what Bion (1961) refers to as 'valency'.

Group members may also unconsciously co-create situations belonging to present and/or past wider social, cultural and political contexts (Hopper, 2007). Thus feelings of helplessness and loss – perhaps residues from socio-cultural conflicts and traumas transmitted across generations – can forcefully re-emerge within a group (Volkan, 2001; Hopper, 2003b, 2003c). These types of group transferences are likely to be more prevalent in certain homogenous groups – such as a group of people who have experienced torture and/or persecution – but may be co-created by group members when relevant to a particular member or members within it.

It is not any single Transference then but the web of T/transferences in its entirety that is core to group analysis since it is the 'evolving context of the group' that gives its members an opportunity to 'transcend and transform these powerfully laid down early patterns' (Pines, 1985a/1998: 63). Foulkes (1964) calls this 'ego training in action'– a training based on 'an ongoing corrective interaction with others' (Pines, 1985a/1998: 63). Such training, going beyond the classical psychoanalytic aim of making the unconscious conscious, can also be construed as a training for democratic citizenship (de Maré et al., 1991; Nitzgen, 2001).

Notes

1 Skynner 1983/1987 was among the first group analysts to comment on the 'deficiency' of Foulkesian theory, noting that Foulkes 'prided himself on his ability for conceptualisation which was not one of his strong points' (p. 235). Several prominent group analysts (e.g. Nitsun, 1996) have since elaborated on this concern, though others (e.g. Weegman, 2011) have argued that group analysis's theoretical incompleteness has protected it from reductive manualisation.
2 Combined and conjoint therapy is common practice in the States. Could this aspect of clinical culture have its source in the more individualistic culture characteristic of the US?
3 It may also even be helpful at times, when bringing a new member on board, to consider bringing two, not least because the new member will represent the 'stranger in the group' (Bacha, 1997). This 'role', before being properly worked through in a group, can often be a difficult one and so is sometimes beneficially shared. This possible benefit for the new person(s) joining needs of course to be weighed against the likely impact on the group of having double the change-cum-load to manage.
4 MacDonald (2004) and Begovac and Begovac (2013) also note the relationship between cohesion and loss/trauma, the former being drawn on, at least temporarily, in managing the experience of the latter.
5 Nitsun (1996) refers to 'all-consuming affiliation' as a characteristic of anti-group culture, twinned with its polar opposite, 'isolation'. Anti-group forces are discussed in Chapter 7.
6 Thygesen (1992) also raises an interesting issue, though one not fully explored in her paper, of whether female conductors tend to prolong group cohesion at the expense of more mature coherent states, while men tend to do the opposite, prematurely pressing toward coherence and underestimating the need for cohesion.
7 This last stage was a later addition (see Tuckman & Jensen, 1977).
8 Dick (1975) suggests 7 phases: magical beginning, anger and rebellion, depression and hopelessness, overt sibling rivalry, individuation, reflections about time, mourning and hope. Lorentzen (2014) simplifying MacKenzie (1997) suggests 4:

opening engagement (characterised by building a feeling of community), differentiation (characertised by assertion of the individual and finding strategies for handling tension and conflict), interpersonal work (characterised by confrontation and introspection: 'work with own and others' dysfunctional interpersonal patterns') (Lorentzen, 2014: 50) and termination, (where loss and separation elicit an exploration of whether one has received enough in therapy in life and the concept of self-responsibility).

9 Although the id is clearly associated with the unconscious, they are not synonymous; that is to say, though all that is id is unconscious, not all that is unconscious is id since both ego and superego have unconscious aspects. Indeed, group analysis gives special attention to the unconscious aspects of the superego in its efforts to modify each member's relationship to authority and liberate their capacity, in collaboration with the group, to re-make themselves, freer of the more restrictive aspects of authority's 'civilizing' influence.

10 Moreno developed the notion of the 'co-unconscious'. Interested readers are referred to Fluery & Knobel (2011). For a broader consideration of Moreno's influence on group analysis see Hamer (1990); also Hinshelwood (2004).

11 Associations with the 'collective unconscious' are evident here and Nitzgen (2011) notes that, initially, Foulkes appears to conflate this Jungian term with his own. Several group analysts (e.g. Zinkin (1979) have drawn on the concept of the collective unconscious to emphasise the co-construction of anxieties and defences and the internalisation of aspects of culture. The impact of this internalisation of values and beliefs transmitted through the generations has been called the 'cultural complex' (Singer & Kimbles, 2004) and is further explored in the context of group analysis by Noack (2011) and Fariss (2011).

12 As Dalal points out, racist language can be implicit as well as explicit. For example, the word 'lie' appears to have no colour bias until juxtaposed with the collocation 'white lie'.

Chapter 3

Core concepts
What goes on in groups? (Part two)

Nick Barwick

In addition to the three core aspects of psychoanalysis described in the previous chapter – the unconscious, free association and transference – Foulkes describes several 'group-specific factors' and phenomena central to group analysis. These he derives not from psychoanalysis but 'from the field of observation of the small group' (Pines, 1982/1998: 18).

Core phenomena

The matrix

The concept of the 'matrix' epitomises the principle of interconnectedness. Foulkes describes it as 'the hypothetical web of communication and relationship' (1964: 292). He also refers to it as 'the network of all individual mental processes, the psychological medium in which they meet, communicate and interact' (1965/1984: 26). Further, matrix's Latin root, *mater*, means 'mother', while the OED defines it as: 'the uterus or womb', 'a place or medium in which something is bred, produced, or developed'. What then is born out of the matrix? What is caught in its web? What develops amidst its connections? It is the individual 'conceived of as a nodal point' and an 'open' rather than 'closed system' (Foulkes, 1964: 70). The individual, however, is not passive, for thought-processes in the matrix pass 'right through all individuals' like 'X-rays', 'each elaborates them and contributes to them and modifies them in his own way' (1971b/1990: 229).

Foulkes refers to the individual as a 'fragment' of a group, 'a piece of a jigsaw' (Foulkes, 1974/1990: 275). The first jigsaw of which he is a part is his family (itself, of course, a part of the larger multi-dimensional jigsaws of community, culture and history). Thus the patient brings to the group his *personal group matrix*: an 'individual' mind forged in relation to his group of origin and therefore, in a profound way, an expression of it. Yet, as the group develops, a new matrix, formed from the interweaving personal matrices, develops too. This *dynamic matrix* becomes the background against which each individual communication can be understood. Each personal story, each interaction, comes to have a group meaning as well as personal one. It expresses something on behalf of the group as well as something on behalf of the individual.

To these two matrices, Foulkes adds a preceding third: the *foundation matrix*, 'based on the biological properties of the species, but also on the culturally firmly embedded values and reactions' (1975a/1986: 131). Since, 'even a group of total strangers ... share a fundamental mental matrix' (1971b/1990: 228), it follows that, 'What we traditionally look upon as our innermost self, the intrapsychic against the external world, is thus not only shareable, but is in fact already shared' (Foulkes, 1975b: 62).

Nitzgen (2015) describes Foulkes's development of the concept of the matrix; a matrix that is not only personal and interpersonal but also transpersonal. The latter calls for a model of socio-cultural transmission – the foundation matrix and the social unconscious – that appreciates how 'groups not only ... communicate about the psychic facts of their members, but also ... social facts and their social contexts' (p. 132). Conductors need to be alert to these layers of communication (personal, interpersonal and social) if they are to facilitate the linking of psychic facts with social-historical facts, thereby identifying the 'personification' of social facts in individuals, in what may be, in effect, 'social psychopathology' (Foulkes, 1984 cited in Nitzgen, 2015: 134).

Elaborations of the foundation matrix include the 'social matrix' (Bhurruth, 2008) – which recognises that group therapy boundaries are permeable to past and present societal, political and cultural events (Ettin, 1993; Stone, 2001) and that out of different socio-political environments different psyches are formed – and the more 'mystical', Jungian-influenced perspectives articulated by, for example, Powell (1994) and Zinkin (1998):

> As the group progresses, the members have a growing experience of being connected in their ultimate unity; not just their own unity as a group but a sense of this unity reflecting some ultimate reality which goes far beyond their small circle.
>
> (p. 193)

Powell, noting how an ideology of individualism easily overlooks even our literal interconnections (such as our immersion, when we sit together in a group, in each others' electromagnetic fields) weaves together analytical psychology and modern physics to argue a metaphysical *and* a physical basis to human interconnectedness:

> Even within the ambit of our universe, events are not related in a linear fashion but form a matrix in space and time in which everything is intimately connected to everything else (the "holoverse").
>
> (1991: 312)

Whether or not such speculations are of clinical use, at the very least, the concept of the matrix continues to convey a powerful understanding of 'individuals as well as of society as *units consistently under construction by communication*'

(Scholz, 2003: 551). Indeed, it is essentially an intersubjective concept conceived by Foulkes a generation before the 'intersubjective turn' in psychoanalysis coalesced into being.[1] Further, by identifying different matrices, Foulkes alerts us to the '*different time rhythms*' of different types of 'crowd'. The rhythm of change in the foundation matrix (a matter of biological and cultural evolution) is 'slow' while the personal matrix, though naturally conservative – preferring to maintain even a difficult psychic status quo – is, potentially, relatively rapid. Most rapid and least conservative is the dynamic matrix and it is within the more fluid, translatable communications of this matrix that the pre-set jigsaw fragment of the individual is most effectively challenged to change. Further, as individuals do change, so does the dynamic matrix to which they belong. This helps develop greater group coherence and an enhanced capacity to contain. Thus the 'web' becomes 'womb', in which the individual alternately submerges and struggles to emerge, 'strengthened', 're-defined' and 'revitalised' (Roberts, 1983).

Location and the 'group mind'

Describing the group matrix, Foulkes (1964) comments:

> Looked at in this way it becomes easier to understand our claim that the group associates, responds and reacts as a whole. The group as it were avails itself now of one speaker, now of another, but it is always the transpersonal network which is sensitized and gives utterance or responds. In this sense we can postulate the existence of a group mind in the same ways as we postulate the existence of an individual mind.
>
> (p. 118)

The notion of 'group mind' is not welcomed by all. Can a group really have a mind when it does not have a brain? (Hopper, 2001). As Weinberg (2007) notes, however, the term does not suggest groups have brains but rather shared hidden motives, myths and defences that guide behaviour. The concept of 'group mind' thus challenges the notion of mind as private individual possession, reframing it as 'interacting processes between a number of closely linked persons, commonly called a group' (Foulkes, 1973/1994: 224).[2]

Location is an aspect of 'group mind'. It refers to a group phenomenon where 'interacting processes' of the group emerge as a communication from an individual or set of individuals in the form of some 'event':

> Every event, even though apparently confined to one or two participants, in fact involves the group as a whole. Such events are part of a *gestalt* configuration, of which they constitute the 'figures' (foreground), whereas the ground (background) is manifested in the rest of the group. We have described as *location* the process which brings to life this concealed configuration.
>
> (Foulkes, 1964: 110)[3]

This is true even of what is often considered to be the epitome of intrapsychic material, the dream; thus Foulkes's maxim: 'Every dream told in the group is the property of that group' (p. 127).

Recognising the phenomenon of location makes what is located in the individual (or sub-group) available as a resource (even if, initially at times, a disturbing one) for the whole group. This promotes psychic development in both individual(s) and group. If the process of location is not acknowledged, however, the individual(s) in whom an aspect of 'group mind' is located may begin to lose psychic flexibility, adopting instead (by dint of past and present group pressures) particular 'roles' – the carer, the victim, the patient, the aggressor.[4] This group enforced role adoption has sometimes been referred to as 'role suction' (Redl, 1942).[5] When qualities experienced by the 'group mind' as particularly unacceptable become not only located but also more permanently lodged in an individual or sub-group, *scapegoating* occurs. This means the individual/sub-group concerned becomes, in the mind of the group, synonymous with a symptom which the group then finds difficult to tolerate. Without an appropriate intervention from the conductor, the individual is likely to be sacrificed as a way of cleansing the group of the disturbance. This 'final solution' is likely, however, to be deadly not only for the individual sacrificed but also for the group that is left behind; temporarily relieved perhaps but frequently creatively impoverished.

Weegmann (2014, 2016) develops a broader socio-historical understanding of the exclusionary process described above through the notion of the 'exclusionary matrix'.[6] This describes configurations whereby certain social groups or beings are dominant and 'see', while others are subordinate and 'seen'; seen as behaving outside a norm of acceptability or respectability. Although scapegoating accompanies exclusion, the exclusionary matrix involves multiple, overlapping subjects which change over time, though with 'a metonymic sliding of associations between them' (2014: 104). Weegmann suggests that a 'complex process of refraction' or 'negative mirroring' (see below) leads to some groups occupying a position of 'healthiness' and 'fullness' (e.g. decent citizens, the ruling class, hard-working families), while others are assigned to an 'unwholesome', 'degenerate', potentially 'contaminating' or 'polluting' position (over time, e.g. Jews, 'dangerous classes', addicts, homosexuals, scroungers, immigrants). The latter are then experienced by the former as posing a threat to the social body.[7]

The processes that produce the exclusionary matrix inevitably permeate the small group and need, suggests Weegmann, to be understood not only in terms of 'projection' but also of 'construction' – the 'discourse, rules and narratives that constitute the very objects that they derogate or malign' (p. 104).

Communication and translation

Nitzgen (2008; 2013a) notes 'Foulkes's persistent efforts to integrate Freudian drive theory into an overall theory of communication' (2013a: 318). Only the link between the two:

would explain satisfactorily that neurotic disturbance, symptoms, in themselves autistic [i.e. without a voice] and unsuitable for sharing, exert for this very reason an increasing pressure on the individual for expressing them. As long as he cannot express them in a better communicable way he finds no real relief. He must therefore set to work again and again so long until he has transformed them into socially acceptable articulate language . . . *this working towards an ever more articulate form of communication* is . . . *identical with the therapeutic process itself* [italics in the original].

(Foulkes, 1948/1983: 169–170)

The 'autistic symptom' that 'mumbles to itself secretly, hoping to be overheard' (Foulkes & Anthony, 1965/1984: 259) is 'autistic' because, though lodged in the individual, it is a symptom arising out a breakdown in the communicational network of origin (the family) from which the individual has become communicationally isolated. The therapy group thus offers a re-contextualising network in which the symptom finds a way of being both shared and articulated. The communicational process of moving from isolated symptom (closed communication with predictable outcome) to shared problem (open communication in the dynamic matrix of the group with unpredictable outcome) to shareable meaning and shared understanding, Foulkes refers to as *translation*; 'the equivalent of the making conscious of the repressed unconscious in psychoanalysis' (Foulkes, 1964: 111).

In facilitating the emergence of 'ever more articulate . . . communication' – that is, communication that, in having meaning to both self and other is both understandable and understood – Foulkes (1964) identifies four levels of communication that need to be addressed:

- *the current level* (sometimes referred to as 'reality': e.g. John is late; Ellen is hurt by the group's response to her)
- *the T/transference level* (whole object transference – e.g. Ellen treats the conductor as if he were her father; Alan responds to Jane as if she were his youngest sibling)
- *the projective level* (i.e. part objects: members split off and project parts of themselves onto and into others: e.g. Jane recoils at Mark's anger though it is Jane who is (also) angry, though she is not conscious of it)
- *the primordial level* (Here Foulkes draws on Jung's notion of 'collective unconscious'. The group finds itself 'gripped by an archetype' (Zinkin, 1994: 115) often evident in profound resonance to a dream or group metaphors that gather depth of meaning.

Part of the group's task is to develop its communicative awareness and range and an understanding of how different levels of communication constantly influence each other.[8] In this, the composition of the group can help. For example, a group that includes over-rationalising members may be complimented by those with freer access to 'lower' (more deeply unconscious) levels of communication (Foulkes, 1965/1984: 260–263). The capacity for individualised divergent communicational sensibilities to be woven together to form a stronger, healthier whole has been continually confirmed in clinical practice.

Brown (1986) describes group analysis as a way of developing 'dialogue for change'. Schlapobersky (1994) elaborates this notion by distinguishing three forms of dialogue: *monologue* (speaking alone with or without an audience), *dialogue* (a conversation between two people – his use of the word being more specific than Brown's) and *discourse* (the speech pattern of three or more people). In this 'dramatic' model, all speech forms have a place, the movement from one to the next being vital to the therapeutic process. Thus monologue is understood as a form of individual self-expression and self-reflection (as in a soliloquy), dialogue a search for intimacy or for 'a resolution of opposites' and discourse, 'the work of the chorus' (Schlapobersky & Pines, 2009: 1360), 'true discourse' being the 'defining attribute of group communication' (Schlapobersky, 1994: 212).

Habitual monologuing, however, is likely to be defensive rather than developmental. It may be a form of hallucinatory gratification, obliterating feared absence, loss and the need for other. It may be a way of protecting the self against feared intrusion, abuse. Or it may be evidence of a lack of attuned, rhythmical exchanges in the early mother-infant dyad. Here, the act of giving can become muddled with the act of possession, monologuing becoming a socially deviant effort to make contact by colonising the world (see Chapter 10). The group's capacity to help shift monologue to dialogue to discourse reflects a shift from isolation to belonging and marks a growing willingness 'to take the non-problem seriously':

> ... there is a period in which an individual's presenting problem is accepted by the group. However, after a while, mysteriously the presenting problem is dropped ... in favour of something which is not the problem, not what the individual patient believed he joined the group to involve himself with – it is dropped in favour of the passionate discussion of and involvement with the shifting roles, relationships and behavioural communications which make up the system of the group itself.
>
> (Garland, 1982: 6)

Mediated by free-floating, reflective *dialogue*, this shift becomes 'an evolution from *despair* and *impotence* to active *desire* and *hope*' as the experience 'of being part of an ensemble in which candid and daring communication brings about transcendence of what seemed to be an inescapable hopelessness, helps the group members to develop a new stance towards life' (Tubert-Oklander, 2010: 137). Such a stance is defined by a deep valuing of 'true intersubjective relationships' and a deeper empathy and understanding not only of self, but also of others, the two being inextricably bound.

Elaborating the intersubjective perspective and drawing on the philosophy of Gadamer (1975) to do so, Weegmann (2014) develops further the notion of dialogue. Conceiving the group as a progressive unfolding of the experiential worlds of its participants, through dialogue, group members' 'horizons' are differentiated, expanded, explored.

Weegmann links the concept of 'horizons' to Stolorow's (2002) 'organising principles'- unconscious, though not primarily defensive, principles that 'govern how we see ourselves and our expectancies of being with others' (p. 3). In effect, we look at life from particular viewpoints and with an inevitable degree of bias born out of the socio-historical context which has helped shape us and in which we find ourselves embedded.

> When we are better aware of the historicity of our background beliefs and prejudices, alternative organisations of meaning become possible and with this can arise a greater understanding of the context within which the other's meaning exists.
>
> (Weegmann, 2014: 21)

This shift, Gadamer (1975) calls 'fusion of horizons'. Such fusion is not an end point but part of endless 'incomplete acts of understanding'; understanding that 'involves a relation between horizons that is continually subject to revision' (Weegman, 2014: 21). Such understanding 'emerges in the play of dialogue . . . neither predictable nor possessed by either party' (ibid.). By developing a group culture of openness to other possibilities, others' horizons (all of which, productive or not, have their own biases), we join with others in an intersubjective space in which we become not only more able to understand others but also more aware of the 'contours of our own prejudice (background beliefs)' (ibid.).

In cultivating the type of open, communicative culture best suited to an ever-developing 'fusion of horizons', Weegmann (2016) suggests the conductor might usefully turn to a contemporary approach to rhetoric. Such an approach, he says, provides greater complexity and depth to the more descriptive Foulkesian notion of 'communication'. Further, a rhetoric-informed perspective enables us, he argues, better to delineate the intricate interactional order of group life – with its different 'voices', the 'positions' from which people talk and the 'speech acts' in which they (including the conductor) are engaged; acts which aim to persuade, show, protest, co-operate, justify and so on. There is a veritable grammar of motives here, to use Burke's (1969) phrase, all of which help to give group life its great presence and power. Indeed, says Weegmann (2016), through engaging in this way in 'discourses':

> we participate in micro-seconds, led by language and reactions beyond ourselves. Language grounds us through a honing of meaning, while leading us beyond what we expect, as it forms, unfolds, and reforms itself.

Language allows us to identify with others, to be consubstantial ... to differ, to mark ourselves off, in loops of communication that do not cease; communication and communion actively combine.

(p. 12)

Group-specific factors (process dynamics)[9]

Resonance

For Foulkes, the concept of resonance 'threw new light on the question: how is it possible that the group context produces a shared life from a modality usually conceded only to the "inner" mental life' (1977/1990: 299). Foulkes and Anthony (1965/1984) originally describe resonance as individuals 'reverberating' to some 'common stimulus' – a comment, an absence, a conflict, a dream – 'in a manner specific to the stage [of development] to which they belong' or 'key' to which they are 'attuned':

> These individual vibrations ... create a sort of contrapuntal effect. The overtones add a peculiar richness to a group life occasioning cross-currents of argument, surprise, incredulity, opposition, and interest. It is as if a player, habituated to the narrow range of a single instrument, was suddenly and unexpectedly confronted with a symphonic extension of his little theme.
>
> (p. 166)[10]

Resonance to the 'common stimulus' might be expressed verbally, but equally in any number of ways: behaviour, somatic events, accidents and so on. Always, instinctively, it 'takes into account the unconscious meaning and "wavelength" of the stimulating event' (1977/1990: 299). This helps explain how 'that which is neither realised or realizable for the individual is nevertheless activated by the shared processes in the group' (Thygesen, 2008). Further, what may start out as isolated communications, through resonance, begin to connect harmonically with yet unconscious group preoccupations, like variations on a still emerging theme.[11] As this occurs, 'there is a feeling of well-being', suggests Pines (2003a):

> which arises when responses of the other resonate with what is sensed as being the most personal of one's experience. This is the essence of progress in group analysis, the presence of other-resonating persons whose inner processes are made both visible and audible through mirroring and resonance.
>
> (pp. 512–513)

Such organically developing, expansive, socially bonding and affirming orchestrations can be understood to be possible because of humanity's 'innate musicality', suggests Wotton (2012): our 'capacity to develop a sense of intersubjective time within which to construct joint meaning', to be 'in time and in tune' with each other. Drawing here on the notion of 'communicative musicality' (Malloch & Trevarthen, 2009), Wotton (2012; 2015) describes how this 'innate musicality', though biologically inherited, is also culturally specific (in that it has identifiable culturally influenced characteristics and nuances) and creative (in that it is co-constructed between people – e.g. mother and infant – through a process of improvisation). An appreciation of this kind of communicative musicality can, she argues, enrich 'our understanding of the social processes of belonging, identity and change' (2015: 448).

It is important to bear in mind, nevertheless, that resonance is a dynamic process that is not necessarily therapeutic, even though group-analytic psychotherapy (and indeed all relational therapies) attempts to utilise it to therapeutic effect. Recent studies in 'limbic resonance' (Lewis *et al.*, 2001), in which our brain chemistry and nervous systems are understood, through synchronising manoeuvres (limbic regulation), as being deeply affected by significant others, not only proffers a biological understanding of the potentially positive effects of therapy (limbic revision) but also an insight into how problems with empathic resonance may form the basis of many psychopathologies (Farrow & Woodruff, 2007) and how deficits in 'normative' 'limbic regulation' can lead to 'flooding' and 'emotional contagion'. In short, resonance can traumatise and/or re-traumatise as well as heal.

Foulkes describes resonance as occurring at the 'primordial level of communication'. This level he associates with the 'collective unconscious' (Jung, 1968) – an inherited aspect of the psyche, common to all. Although he does not elaborate on this association, others have. Thygesen (2008), drawing on both contemporary analytical psychology (Spiegelman & Mansfield, 1996, Stein, 1995) and psychoanalysis (Gerson, 2004, Ogden, 2004, Stern, 2004), concludes:

> *Resonance* correlates with the constellation of a common connecting mental field ... a changed, often widened state of mind. A 'tuning in' or 'attunement' to what is unconscious to our 'normal ego-consciousness', namely to the group-matrix, takes place ... In the process, ... a dissolution of boundaries, of resistance and defences happens, so that fantasies, thoughts, imagination, feelings, themes lying latent or hidden in the group's matrix, are brought into conscious reflection
>
> (Thygesen, 2008: 80)

Schlapobersky (2016), defining resonance as *'the elementary conveyor of emotions'* (p. 252) argues that it only fully makes sense when partnered with the concept of 'interpersonal valency' – valency being essential to the process of transmission. Bion (1961) defines valency as 'the individual's readiness to enter into combination with the group' in the context of basic assumptions (p. 116). Divorcing this concept from its basic assumption context, Schlapobersky (2016) draws it within the group-analytic frame by marrying it with resonance. He concludes:

Valency to others' affect and the resonating consequences of this valency
... can be understood as a basic set of human attributes.

(2016: 254)

Condensation and Amplification

Condensation refers to a deep and intense build-up of resonance in the group resulting in a type of compression which, under pressure, is suddenly released as a condenser phenomenon. Foulkes and Anthony (1965/1984) describe it thus:

> The sudden discharge of deep and primitive material following the pooling of associated ideas ... an accumulative activation at the deepest levels ... as if the "collective unconscious" acted as a condenser covertly storing up emotional charges generated by the group, and discharging them under the stimulus of some shared group event.
>
> (p. 151)

In the release of such energies – for example through the telling of a 'group dream' (one told by an individual but clearly having group relevance), a fantasy, story or through a charged interaction – there is always an element of surprise, as resonating aspects of the group suddenly coalesce into shared and shareable meaning.

The term amplification, drawn from analytical psychology, is often twinned with condenser phenomena. Like condensation it describes an intensification of resonance. However, rather than being characterised by compression and sudden release, its intensification arises out of a broadening of resonance among group members. Schlapobersky (2016) defines the two terms, condensation and amplification, thus:

> Condenser governs the intensity of emotional association and amplification describes the range of spread.
>
> (p. 256)

Mirroring

Foulkes likens the small group to a 'hall of mirrors' in which 'an individual is confronted with various aspects of his social, psychological, or body image' (Foulkes & Anthony, 1965/1984: 150):

> A person sees himself, or part of himself – often a repressed part of himself – reflected in the interactions of other group members. He sees them reacting in the way he does himself, or in contrast to his own behaviour. He also gets to know himself ... by the effect he has upon others and the picture they form of him.
>
> (Foulkes, 1964: 110)

Although the pictures formed by others may, as Foulkes concedes, carry distortions rooted in others' own individual neuroses, Foulkes asserts that such distortions 'cancel out'; that is, taken across the group, they compensate for each other so the 'composite reflection approximates to the image obtainable in a normal group' (Foulkes & Anthony, 1965/1984: 151). Although this assertion arguably oversimplifies, the recognition of mirrored parts of self proffers important opportunities for identity integration and psychological growth since, 'looking and being looked at is a fundamental process in personality development, in finding out who one is and who one is not'. (Pines, 1982/1998: 34). Indeed Schlapobersky (2016), defining mirroring as 'a complex form of resonance through which affect, understanding or intuition, seen in or associated with others, can reveal truths about the self that may be welcomed, opposed, taken flight from or attacked' suggests that it is the creative 'harvesting of these reactions', with the aim of promoting self-development, that is core to group-analytic work (pp. 254–255).

The mirror phenomenon's therapeutic import has been richly elaborated by Wooster (1983), Zinkin (1983) and, most notably, Pines (1982/1998; 1985b/1998; 2003a). Drawing on the work of Mahler, Winnicott, Lacan, Kohut, Stern and others, Pines explores the mirror metaphor in terms of early developmental self-other interactions. Where deficits have occurred (interactions that have undermined or failed to facilitate identity development) they are ripe for corrective re-encounter. For example, contemporary infant research (Stern, 1985) identifies the manner in which a sense of self ('the early psychic matrix') begins to form on the basis of reciprocity of gaze, sound and touch. The child's gestures are given meaning by the mother. The mother insists on being recognised and that the baby recognises itself as the source of intentionality, of self. So too, with the group:

> The more the group members can see and feel their very experience to be meaningful to the group as a whole, so their basic matrix of self is remobilised and worked through in the new group field.
>
> (Pines, 1983: 12)

Mirroring can also be seen as a conceptual development of projective identification – where aspects of self-experience are unconsciously pushed into another so the other experiences those projected feelings as if their own (see Chapter 6). Such projections are rife within a group – an integral part of the communicational process (see levels of communication above). If such projections can find a containing voice, reflection rather than reaction may ensue. This is often a fraught process in which inter-psychic 'use' of each other can easily, without the help of the conductor and of the group, become 'ab-use'. Ideally, the matrix takes up the role of container rather than any individual within it.

The discovery of mirror neurons has offered further support for the group-analytic view of the importance of mirroring and of the validity of a social mind. Mirror neurons are brain cells that fire up in response to the activity of others. They register 'perceived behaviour, emotions and intentions of others "as if" one were enacting or experiencing them oneself' (Schermer, 2010a: 221; 2010b). They thus allow us to 'recognise' human experience in each other, to 'leap into' the mirror of the other and to respond internally as if the other were the self. In other words, 'individuals attune to one another and represent themselves in and through each other, challenging the premise that minds function in relative isolation'. (Schermer, 2010a: 222). Instead, the embodied mind/brain is revealed as an open, rather than closed energy system (Damasio, 1999), inherently biosocial and inextricably linked to its group context (Cozolino, 2006). This new knowledge recasts individuals not as social 'atoms' but as 'reflecting mirrors' of the interpersonal world that surrounds them' (Schermer, 2010a: 222). Hence, in a group, in a vital and vitalising sense, 'We do not only reflect each other, we *are* each other, until we begin to sort out our own individual nature and tendencies within the group, what Bollas (1989: 109–113) calls our unique "idiom"' (Schermer, 2010a: 224). This is to say that, paradoxically, the individuation process depends upon 'the mirroring self-reflection and self-consciousness that can only occur within a social context'. (2010: 225)

Negative mirroring

Foulkes focuses on the nurturing, empathic aspects of mirroring. Nitsun (1996), however, contrasts such benevolent, developmental, 'communicational' mirroring with 'archaic' mirroring. Based on resonances that never achieve higher levels of articulation, archaic mirroring can quickly lead to 'mimetic engulfment' – a loss of separate identity as a result of an unconscious, *en masse* process of imitation – prompting defensive and/or destructive reactions rather than creative reflections.

Weinberg and Toder (2004) identify a number of negative mirrors:

- *the shrinking mirror*: selective mirroring where difference is eschewed; only one aspect of a member, sub-group or group-as-a-whole is seen e.g. we are all all-nurturing; you/I are/am completely hopeless.
- *the magnifying mirror*: no selectivity here; early in its maturation, before developing into a sound-enough container, the group encourages everyone 'to let it all hang out'. It then finds itself 'flooded' with affect without the means to deal with the flood.
- *the all-knowing mirror:* no room for complexity or doubt. No tolerance of divergent thinking.
- *lack of a mirror*: everything is seen in terms of the self. Every utterance collapses into the narcissistic pool – 'I feel like that' – followed, often, by empty, unconnected silence; until the next isolated, stone-prompted ripple. This points to 'early developmental deprivation ... a lack of primary mirroring' (p. 502) – mirroring in the primary care giver's eyes that helps establish an experience of belonging and worth.

All these mirrorings can be seen as malignant. However, 'malignant mirroring' (Zinkin, 1983), usually refers to a specific form of negative mirroring: an aversive reaction between two people, as if each sees in the other some aspect of themselves that is too horrifying and/or shameful to acknowledge. Intensified denial and projection follow. Locked in a terrorised and terrorising gaze based on mutual projective identifications, each participant is both repelled and fascinated by the mirror in which they look. Zinkin identifies malignant mirroring as an interpersonal interaction – between pairs of individuals or sets of individuals. However, the pair thus engaged often also enacts transpersonal dynamics at work more broadly within the group.

Triadic mirroring and the 'model of three'

'Observation and self-observation in a social setting' is a crucial therapeutic activity (Foulkes, 1948/1983). Foulkes refers to the contribution of the 'observer', in his 'model of three':

> ... if A and B are two persons between whom this interaction takes place, it would appear to me that the presence of a third person C is required if this interrelationship is to be seen in perspective.... This model, which one might call the *model of three*, is to my mind the simplest elementary model for the understanding of interpersonal relationships. C represents that new third dimension group observation introduces.
>
> (1964: 49)

Foulkes does not elaborate greatly upon this model. However, elsewhere, linking this to a contemporary object relations view of the oedipal situation, I suggest that the development of observational capacity or 'witness training in action' is a vital aspect of group-analytic work (Barwick, 2004). The capacity to 'bear witness' is founded upon the capacity to bear exclusion; that is to remain empathically connected to that which one is not entirely a part. This is an important developmental achievement having many psychological ramifications, not least the development of:

> a capacity for seeing ourselves in interaction with others and for entertaining another point of view whilst retaining our own, for reflecting on ourselves whilst being ourselves ...
>
> (Britton, 1989: 87)

The capacity to witness in this way, Britton refers to as maintaining 'a third position', creating a 'triangular space' essential for reflection (Britton, 2004).

Pines (1982) draws on the story of Perseus to illustrate the need for a perspectival third position in the slaying of personal gorgons. Perseus's journey is into the inner depths of the Psyche, of which the gorgon, Medusa, is symbolic of one 'shadow-oriented' aspect (Diel, 1980, cited in Pines, 1982/1998). The stony paralysis and consequent demise of those who have previously made the venture can be understood as resulting from an inability to contemplate the objective truth about oneself. Yet the success of the venture is vital to psychic development. Only by facing one's inner demon is the individuation process furthered, the shadow-self integrated, and the creative potential both liberated and controlled. Thus the blood from Medusa's neck gives life to Pegasus, the horse of the Muses, which enables Perseus to continue his psychic quest.

The point is that the gorgon can only be faced with the help of a third, in this instance, Athena's armour which, polished, becomes a mirror (a reflecting object) in which Perseus can witness Medusa and, in the witnessing, deal with her. Relating this to the group in which individual members may see mirrored, in other members' interactions with each other, hated and disavowed aspects of their own selves, Pines suggests that what otherwise might lead to 'entranced' or 'entangled' forms of projection – such as malignant mirroring – 'receives a triadic form of mirroring, one at a higher developmental level'. Through this triadic mirroring, 'a benign cycle of projection and introjection is initiated which can often lead to the freeing up of the closed psychic system and thereby to renewed psychic growth' (p. 27).

Wooster (1983) suggests malignant mirroring – where there is an absence of a third position – may find its source in deficits in early triangulation experiences. Drawing upon Abelin (1971, 1980) to identify the developmental stage at which the child is forced, by the intrusion of the father, to become aware of exclusion from an imitative, narcissistically mirroring relationship with his mother, Wooster notes that the child must take up a position as an observer and, in recognising his separateness, enter a shared symbolic realm. This is a realm in which 'reflection begins to replace reaction' (Pines, 1982/1998: 30). Indeed, in part, the child learns the capacity to observe and reflect *from* his father. The father, after all, will have experienced exclusion from the 'nursing couple' and will, ideally, not only have tolerated it but, in the early stages, also by protecting the mother-child dyad, have actively encouraged it as well. Thus, in addition to being a rival, it is *with* the father that the child must identify. In effect, a 'favourable outcome' to the child's witness training programme may depend 'on the positive and emulatory aspect of the three-person jealousy inherent in the situation'. This, in turn, is very much informed by the 'father's own capacity to work through his initial jealousy about this intrusive newcomer breaking up the original husband/wife duo' (Wooster, 1983: 38). It is the absence of such a 'favourable outcome' that may lead to malignant mirroring.

The intervention in the negative dyadic relationship, then, of the mirror as 'third element', creates the psychological space for dialogue, for the holding of different points of view about the same experience, and for exploration. Where there is no triangulation of space, there is 'no capacity for reflection and for meeting on shared ground'. This means that there can be 'no acceptance of an aspect of self that is reflected in the other and also of the other in the self' (Pines, 1982/1998: 34). In the therapy group, if neither party can manage the reflective activity of witnessing their own interactions, other witnesses – the therapist and other group members – must be called (Barwick, 2004).

Exchange

Exchange is the process of interactive sharing in a group. Friedman (2014) refers to it, together with resonance and mirroring, as 'aspects of intersubjective dialogue' (p. 4). It is usefully paired with mirroring: the latter implying similarity or sameness; the former difference. And, as Zinkin (1994) states, 'People are helped both by identifying with others and by recognising their differences' (p. 103).

Essentially, what is exchanged is 'information' (Foulkes, 1964: 34): 'information' as 'news of difference'; 'differences that make a difference' (Bateson, 1979). Constant exposure to reported and enacted different ways of seeing, being and doing, can be deeply and productively challenging, producing a liveliness and directness of exchange, particularly in terms of feedback, that is more difficult to envisage in the asymmetrical relationship of the therapy dyad.

Dalal (1998) also emphasises the potentially transformational nature of ex-changing 'information':

> Information is another name for what Elias has called knowledge, and ... this is the same as language and thought. Elias's insight was that the state of knowledge is inextricably entwined with the state of the psyche. When this is joined up with Foulkes' notion of communication, we can see how and why speech is potentially a transformational and therapeutic act.
>
> (Dalal, 1998: 223)

Dalal's metaphor is penetrative, dramatic:

> To speak is one thing, to listen is another. To listen is potentially a very frightening process, because to hear the words of another is literally to let their words and meanings into the self – it is to let a stranger into the home. And once they have entered, who knows where they may go, what havoc they may wreak, or what changes they may precipitate?
>
> (ibid.)

Drawing on the analogy of exchange in the early mother-infant relationship, Thornton's (2004) is less dramatic, though far-reaching in its impact nonetheless:

> Exchange in that first relationship is of far more than milk and bodily contacts; there is acknowledgement of feelings and of mutuality in feeling, and there is reciprocal observation.
>
> (Padel, 1985: 275 cited in Thornton, 2004: 312)

In groups then, the vitality of exchange is pre-verbal as well as verbal, having transformative value independent of content. This is not to underestimate the impact of linguistic exchange, only to compliment it, for language, as a carrier of 'content', has always had a significant role to play in shaping our experience of ourselves in the presence of others. This is so since 'with language, infants, for the first time, can share their personal experience . . . including 'being with' others in intimacy, isolation, loneliness, awe, fear and love' (Stern, 1985: 182).

In the group, as feeling states are put into words and exchanged, as difference is encountered, recognised and identified with, as isolating experience is converted into 'exchangeable currency' (Behr & Hearst, 2005: 86), the 'shareable universe', inner and outer, expands, giving truth to Merleau-Ponty's (1964) poignant observation:

> I borrow myself from others; man is a mirror for man.
> (cited in Pines, 1985a/1998: 68)

The socialising process

Early in his development of group analysis, Foulkes (1948) establishes the 'Basic Law of Group Dynamics':

> The deepest reason why patients . . . can enforce each other's normal reactions and wear down and correct each other's neurotic reaction, is that *collectively they constitute the very norm, from which, individually, they deviate.*
> (Foulkes, 1948: 29)

Drawing on this 'law', Brown (1998a) equates socialisation with normalisation whereby the individual is brought into line with group norms. Brown emphasises the notion of 'norm' here, not as an ordained constant, but something that develops within the context of the group's dynamic matrix; a matrix continually both imbibing and developing its group-analytic culture. Hence, a Foulkesian take on normalisation/socialisation needs to be understood, Brown suggests, not in terms of the imposition of uniformity but the elaboration of humanity.

Nitsun (2006) considers Brown's interpretation as overly benign. His own reading of Foulkes's Law is of something more coercive than creative; a law that is repressive, prey to the ideology of its time and demanding of social conformity, including, a restraining of the exploration of all things sexual. Instead, Nitsun opts for a less recognised notion – 'the Group as Forum' (Foulkes, 1948: 167) – in which the group helps the individual to revise the boundaries of the ego and the 'restrictions imposed by the community' (p. 168) represented in the superego. Instead of presenting a picture of a group 'slavishly struggling to fulfil the norms and standards of society', suggests Nitsun (2006: 115), this vision is of 'a group that aims to interrogate orthodox norms and helps to redraw individual boundaries in the social context' (p. 141).[12]

Nitzgen (2016) also refers to the creative potential of the group as forum. Noting that community cultural values and norms are never directly transmitted but are necessarily coloured by parental interpretation, the process of any individuals' socialisation can be understood as being based not on '*generally* accepted norms and values' but 'particularised, "familio-centric" *versions* of them' (p. 26) internalised as the superego. It is only by working through 'the (repressed) authority of the parental superego can we become free(d) enough to confront and to modify unconscious socio-cultural constraints, which are often based on political oppression, and vice versa' (p. 27). This 'liberation' becomes possible because:

> the group sets up its own boundaries under its own weighty authority, which is a good match for the ancient Superego.
> (Foulkes, 1948/1983: 164)

Though differing on the niceties of group-analytic theory, Brown, Nitsun and Nitzgen all see group analysis offering a radical, liberalising form of socialisation; one which offers 'the possibilities of providing a fairer, kinder morality' (Nitsun, 2006: 151). Indeed, suggests Brown (1998a), the socialising process means that even patients with profound psychopathology, (including criminals and anti-social characters encountered in forensic settings) who might, in individual therapy, prove too frustrating or threatening for the therapist can, in the context of a group, through mutual confrontation and empathy, be transformed/reformed (cf. Weldon, 1997).

Such transformations result from the filling out of what at first may be tenuous connections between members within a context that is fundamentally egalitarian:

> The patient is brought out of his isolation into a social situation in which he can feel adequate ... he can feel understood as well as show understanding of others. He is a fellow being on equal terms.
> (Foulkes, 1964: 33)

In short, socialisation promotes an experience of feeling part of the human world; a belongingness achieved by gaining insight *and* outsight (an understanding not only of the other but also of the self through one's understanding of the other (de Maré, 1972: 159; Pines, 1982/1998: 31; Schlapobersky, 2016).

The notion of a 'social instinct' – the psychological effects of our genes – expounded by Ormay (2012) places the process of socialisation within a modified (and socialised) version of Freudian drive theory and of Freud's structural theory of mind. Though drawing on socio-biological (e.g. Hamilton, 1963) and psycho-biological research (see Ormay, 2012: 81–99), the seed of this concept is Darwinian.

Darwin (1879/2004) describes 'social instincts' as an innate (i.e. genetic) propensity in man 'to take pleasure in the society of its fellows, to feel a certain amount of *sympathy* with them, and to perform various services for them' [my italics] (p. 121). Indeed, it is from an understanding of the evolution of sympathy (in contemporary parlance, empathy) – rooted initially in direct kinship relationships (e.g. mother and infant) and reinforced and elaborated through the evident survival advantages of groups that achieve a level of solidarity/cohesion – that

Darwin develops his theory of altruism and morality (see De Waal, 2006; Joyce, 2006).

Based upon this understanding of social instinct, Ormay (2012) posits a 'social function that makes us perform social acts, not out of masochism and fear of punishment, but from a relevant drive of belonging, in the interest of the whole race' (p. xx). He calls this social function 'nos' – we – the 'psychic function of "relatedness"' (p. 189) which allows us to 'relate to the various wholes of groups' (p. 47) and which he uses to modify Freud's structural theory of mind, 're-formed' and re-stated as id, ego and nos.

Just as the development of ego draws upon the principle of difference, helping to identify our uniqueness in the world, the development of nos draws upon the principle of similarity. Without ego we would dissolve into the whole. Without nos we would fail to recognise our belonging, our common humanity.

Ormay's view of the social instinct appears congruent with Foulkes's view of the natural propensities for nurture active in groups. Noting how social instinct among animals generally 'seems to dictate that we do not harm each other', he concludes:

> If we let our social instinct drive us and become human in the social function of nos, our love for each other will make us feel when we might harm, or when we can help one another.
>
> (2013: 363)

Again, in accord with Foulkes, Ormay identifies the superego – 'an artificial product of civilization' (p. 354) – as being problematic, not the nos. Hence the development of nos, suggests Ormay, oscillating with further developments of the ego, characterise the maturing of both individual and group, proffering relief from aspects of the social unconscious (enshrined in the superego) that restrict rather than enhance our lives. As Power (2012) summarises:

> Where id and superego are, there ego and nos shall be.

Conclusion

Each new development in group-analytic theory often produces as many differences in opinion as it does a furthering of a unified approach and Ormay's exposition is no exception.[13] Nevertheless, what is diverse also remains unified in that group analysis remains committed to promoting an ever-evolving understanding of how we have become and are constantly becoming who we are; how identity is formed and re-formed within and by the matrices *to* which we contribute and *of* which we are a part. That it is an active as well as a passive process – that is, not only is the individual impacted upon by the group but also the group and each of its members are impacted upon by the individual – encourages both a developing clarification of individual needs as well as a greater sense of individual responsibility for others. This is to recognise that change and growth arise not only out of 'regressive behaviour' – what others can do for oneself – but also 'progressive behaviour' – what one can do for others. Thus, by releasing the individual from isolation – that is, promoting in him the capacity for empathy as well as the experience of being empathised with – the socialising process is a therapeutic enactment of the principle of interconnectedness and lies at the heart of the experientially based, biologically informed, psycho-social venture that is group analysis.

Notes

1 'Intersubjectivity' is a paradigm within psychoanalysis associated with several relational strands of thinking: self-psychology and its elaboration in the work of Stolorow (e.g. Stolorow *et al.*, 1987; Stolorow & Atwood, 1992), psychoanalytically oriented developmental psychology/infant research (e.g. Stern, 1985) and relational psychoanalysis/relational perspectivism (e.g. Mitchell, 1988; Aron, 1996; Orange *et al.*, 1997). As Weegmann (2001) notes:

> A common emphasis within this paradigm is that of conceiving complex relational fields and organising principles, within which psychological processes come together and through which experience is continually shaped and re-shaped (p. 516).

This leads to an understanding of both development and pathology as 'irreducibly relational, embedded in many intersubjective contexts' (ibid.). Interestingly, Mitchell (1988) uses the term 'relational matrix' to capture the way that personality emerges out of early formative relationships, though without any reference to Foulkes.

2 With the notable exception of de Maré (de Maré & Schollberger, 2004, 2006, 2008) and Hopper (2003 c, d; Hopper & Weinberg, 2011), Tubert-Oklander (2014) notes there has been little written concerning the metapsychology of group analysis. Advocating a need for a general theory of mind, one that articulates individual and collective processes, he offers a contribution to its development with his 'syncretic paradigm'. This suggests there is a part of mental functioning that does not differentiate – between subject-object, material-mental etc – and that 'This undifferentiated (syncretic) dimension . . . allows individuals to engage in relations and participate in groups, institutions, communities, and society' (p. 61).

3 Elsewhere, Foulkes (1948/1983) notes:

> If one looks at a psychological disturbance principally as located, taking place, in between persons, it follows that it can never be wholly confined to a person in isolation . . . The total configuration then puts a different emphasis on the disturbance as manifested in any individual concerned' (p. 127).

This recognition of pathology as 'inter-personal', of reframing the notion of the 'sick mind' as a 'relational pathology' (Friedman, 2013), places Foulkes as 'a pioneer of intersubjective thinking' (Friedman, 2014).

4 Friedman (2014) notes how an intersubjective understanding of pathology is connected to the concept of location. As Foulkes (1948) himself states, the location of pathology is not in the individual alone but in his relationships, or as Friedman (2015) puts it, 'in the space in between related people' (p. 246).

5 The concept of 'role suction' is deemed inadequate by some (e.g. Hopper, 2003c) who notes its failure to acknowledge sufficiently the personality of the person taking on the role.

6 This term, initially coined by Mills (2005), signifies the production of 'a dangerous, abject reign that circumscribes the identities of ideas, institution and selves' (p. 7).
7 The 'excluded' are seen as embodying 'core dangers' – a term Weegmann (2014) borrows from social anthropology. What lies close to, yet beyond, acceptable boundaries is met with horror and disquiet.
8 Schlapobersky (2016) replaces the term 'level' with 'domain', suggesting the hierarchy implied by the former fails to convey their interdependent, more fluid nature. However, despite a useful hologram analogy – where the domain we see changes as we change our viewing point – he still refers to each domain as being 'beneath' the other.
9 Schlapobersky (2016) recasts 'group-specific factors' as 'process dynamics'.
10 The musical analogy, often elaborated in group-analytic literature, is itself embedded in 'analogical terms derived from the physical sciences' (Foulkes & Anthony, 1965: 152). This links it to oscillations within and between (sympathetic resonance) a range of 'bodies' from the sub-atomic to the inter-planetary, providing us with a sense of the principle of interconnectedness at every level of existence.
11 As Potthoff (2014) notes: 'Resonance explains the spread of free association in groups . . . Without resonance there can be no intersubjectivity' (p. 274).
12 For a full account of how repressive orthodox norms can be seen as having marginalised sexuality and desire and its exploration in the group psychotherapy literature, see *The Group as an Object of Desire* (Nitsun, 2006).
13 See, for example, Blackwell (2013), Nitzgen (2013b) Wotton (2013), Sordano (2013).

Chapter 4

Core concepts
What does the conductor do? (Part one)

Nick Barwick

Group analysis is 'a form of psychotherapy *by* the group, *of* the group, including the conductor' (Foulkes, 1975a/1986: 3). The group is thus the agent of change; the conductor simply part of the group. And yet, the conductor is also different. The very name makes him so; someone who 'sets a pattern of desirable behaviour ... puts emphasis on the 'here and now' ... promotes tolerance and appreciation of individual differences.... represents and promotes reality, reason, tolerance, understanding, insight, catharsis, independence, frankness and an open mind for new experiences' (1964: 57)! As conductor then, he contributes powerfully to the development of a 'group-analytic culture'; a culture in which radical reconfiguration of identity can occur.

The conductor and authority

The term 'conductor' Foulkes takes from Theodor Adorno. Adorno's research into the fluctuating authority in the orchestra-conductor relationship offered Foulkes a blueprint for understanding the therapist's authority in relation to the psychotherapy group; broadly speaking, one which assumes a more active role early in the group's life – modulating tempo, attending to individual instruments, linking instruments and sections of instruments together, interpreting the score – and works towards a 'decrescendo' of such activity over time.[1]

Unsurprisingly, as both Nitzgen (2001) and Nitsun (2009) note, Foulkes was wary of a group's tendency to conform to the conscious and unconscious beliefs of a leader and felt that the term (in German, 'Führer') had been deeply compromised by fascism. Indeed, since Foulkes saw the 'correction' of authority relations (internalised in the superego) as a key therapeutic task, the manner in which the conductor 'leads' the group becomes a significant factor in facilitating this 'correction'.

Foulkes identifies two roles for the conductor, each requiring the adoption of a 'position'. As 'administrator' (the person responsible for establishing and maintaining the structure of therapy) the position is of 'executive authority'. As 'therapist' (the person facilitating process and interpreting content), it is of 'expert authority', shaping the therapeutic culture of the group (Hutchinson, 2009). In the executive position, wielding a non-transferable 'power over others', the conductor must manage a number of challenges to his authority. By responding with genuine curiosity as well as non-punitive firmness, he contributes significantly to the internalisation of a modifying experience of authority relations; that is, to a maturing of the superego.

In contrast, expert authority *is* transferrable; its transfer being one of the conductor's aims. The process is analogous to 'weaning'. Initially, recognising the inevitability of the 'immature' group's 'craving for a leader in the image of an omnipotent, godlike father-figure' (Foulkes, 1964/1984: 60), the conductor accepts the group's projections – the power, 'the One-who knows or the one-who-cures' (Foulkes & Anthony, 1965/1984: 127).[2] Yet he does so only to relinquish it; to change 'from a leader of the group to a leader in the group' (Foulkes, 1964/1984: 60), thereby replacing 'the leader's authority by that of the group' (p. 61). In short, group analysis seeks 'to free the group from the automatic force of this tendency to compliance and conformity' (1971a/1990: 211) and 'to replace submission by co-operation on equal terms between equals' (1964/184: 65).

Since a leader's power is based largely upon projections of parts of the superego of those 'following', the process of shifting the locus of power is inevitably accompanied by a re-introjection of a modified superego. Further, since, as Nitzgen (2001) suggests, the 'transference love, "especially in the infantile and trust sense of the term" (Foulkes, 1971a/1990: 216) can be said to be the biggest obstacle to "cooperation between equals"' (Nitzgen, 2001: 337), this shift is achieved through '*transference analysis in action*' (Foulkes, 1975a/1986: 112). Describing the conductor's active contribution to the decrescendo in the therapist's expert authority and the accompanying crescendo in the group's, Foulkes also draws on a less clinical analogy: 'The conductor', he says, 'digs his own grave' (1964: 62).[3]

Conductor as group member

Foulkes also highlighted the importance of the conductor's role as 'group member'. This is core to the group-analytic spirit since the conductor is inevitably embedded in the matrix in which and with which he works – a participant in what he observes. As such, in intervening he will make frequent use of 'we' when exploring what is being experienced and observed and, from the outset, is responsible for modelling important group-analytic attitudes such attentiveness, tolerance, frankness and curiosity which all group members must develop.

Ofer (2013), describing the 'growth-enhancing leadership' qualities of the choir conductor, Daniel, in the film *As It Is In Heaven*, not only reiterates the importance of declining the regressive pull of the group to play God, advocating instead, in an attuned and timely fashion, the spirit of a cooperative endeavour among equals, but also identifies the conductor's personal flexibility, his ability to make personal change, as key. However, though it is important that the conductor is as open to the transformative power of the group as any member and though he or she can undoubtedly gain much that is therapeutic from the groups they conduct, such gains can never, of course, become a dominant motivator of their work. In other words, the conductor's role as group member is used in the service of the group not, primarily, in the service of their own psychological development, even though their own psychological development may, one would hope, inevitably grow out of working within the group.

Another way of understanding the idea of the conductor consciously utilising their membership of a group in the service of conducting it, is to recognise the importance of the countertransference. Since countertransference is a vital part of any contemporary analytic therapist's tools, for the purposes of brevity and simplicity, in this chapter, I have subsumed the conductor's role of group member within that of therapist.

A note on group structure, process and content

The conductor attends to three aspects of group life: *structure, process and content* (Foulkes & Anthony, 1957, de Maré, 1972).[4] Structure describes the 'architecture' in which the group's interpersonal life is housed: the analytic setting, the organisational setting and, in terms of composition, the membership itself. Process refers to fluctuations of emotion and experience within the group: the 'business of relating and communicating' (Schlapobersky & Pines, 2009: 1355). Content refers to verbal and non-verbal events: emergent narratives, themes and their development. As dynamic administrator[5] (Pines *et al.*, 1982), structure is the main focus of attention. Process and content are mainly the therapist's domain. Nevertheless, as we shall see, such categorisation of the dimensions of group life and their associated conductor roles is not absolute and both dimensions and roles, in certain instances, inevitably bleed into each other.

Conductor as dynamic administrator

Managing the analytic and organisational settings

The analytic setting includes the room and its contents (chairs, table, etc.) and the boundaries (time, frequency) in which the physical setting is placed. The room and its contents – ideally, identical seats arranged in a circle with a small table[6] at its centre – can be understood as an extension of the conductor's body and of his 'holding' capacity. Thus the room's constancy, apt quietness and freedom from external impingements help cultivate a sense of dependability and safety. Further, by keeping the setting relatively constant, the significance of any changes that do occur becomes available for analytic scrutiny.

Attending to the relationship between the wider organisation and the analytic setting is also vital. This is perhaps particularly so in public health settings, where the group has a location as part of the services on offer. As part of this reality, the group conductor needs to have good working relations with colleagues, both clinical and non-clinical. Apart from anything else, the conductor is usually dependent on others for referral. All this is to acknowledge that the group meets in the context of a network of social interdependencies, the neglect of which risks, at best, de-stabilising impingements on the *boundaries* of the analytic setting, at worst, the dissolution of the group itself.[7]

Selection

> Group composition is the therapist's first and most enduring contribution to the group for its membership will determine the outcome of therapy.
> (Schlapobersky & Pines, 2009: 362)

In assessing membership, the conductor keeps three things in mind: suitability for group therapy, for this particular group, for this particular group at this particular time. These last two aspects concern patient 'fit': matching individual with group resources and needs. At a basic level this may mean maintaining 'the Noah's Ark principle' as discussed in Chapter 2. At a more complex level it may mean assessing the level of disturbance the group is likely to be able to manage and indeed make good use of for the benefit of all. For example, if the prospective group is mature (i.e. not overly dependent, reasonably capable of containing disturbance without feeling overwhelmed and reasonably reflective) introducing a member with borderline personality disorder may be mutually beneficial. Having quicker access to unconscious forces, such members can help fuel group momentum. In return, the group can help regulate the intensity of their affective swings. However, if the group is insufficiently mature, interpersonal disturbances provoked are unlikely to benefit either individual or group and could threaten fundamental cohesion (Pines, 1984/1998).

In terms of general suitability, Foulkes suggests anyone suited for individual psychotherapy is suited for group. Brown (1991) tempers this view but agrees with Foulkes that, vital, is the ability to communicate in a group. This calls for assessment based on interpersonal skills. Related contra-indicators might be people who are too narcissistic to be capable of identification with other members, too needy to contemplate sharing attention (something often linked with very early traumatic loss/deprivation), too undifferentiated to withstand the group's emotional currents/storms, have very poor impulse control or hold such rigid belief systems they appear impervious to other perspectives (Behr & Hearst, 2005). On the other hand, for some whose attachment patterns can make them wary of the intimacy of a one-to-one relationship or conversely, have 'a tendency to get overly enmeshed in sticky, clingy and perhaps parasitic transferences in dyads' (Hopper, 2006: 555) group therapy may be especially helpful.

Friedman (2013) suggests the following questions should guide assessment:

> *What* is the disorder that needs to be treated? *What* is the *optimal* therapeutic *space*, and *when* should a specific *optimal* space be recommended?
> (p. 165)

Building on Foulkes's 'fundamental turn of mind' (1964: 18) – that individual neurosis arises out of dysfunction at a 'multipersonal' level – Friedman (2013) suggests adding relational disorders to the classic definition of individual pathology used in assessment. Drawing on Agazarian (1994), he focuses on co-created, interpersonal dysfunctional patterns which he categorises as:

- *deficiency relational disorder* – where the participant difficulty in containing the duality of strength and weakness leads to relating in split ways (e.g. patient and caretaker).
- *rejection relational disorder* – where participant difficulty in containing aggression leads to a dysfunctional relational dynamic between rejecter and rejected.
- *relation disorders of the self* – where 'social over-identification' results in an 'under-development of an autonomic, mature Self. Selfless 'heroes' ... and their 'selfish' counterparts collude ... to serve the 'cause' while harming them-selves and others'. (Friedman, 2013: 167)
- *exclusion relation disorder* – not as aggressive as 'rejection' (above), but where the relationship solidifies between those who experience being socially central and those who are (and at some level accept being) marginalised.

Such disorders, being co-created, require therapeutic interventions that challenge the reciprocal relations contributing to them. However, though Friedman concludes that '*Relation disorders characterized by dysfunctional patterns, need to be treated where they were created*' (p. 168) – that is in a group, be it small (for the first two disorders) or median (for the last two) – he acknowledges that most patients prefer to start with individual therapy and so suggests a pragmatic two step model – a dyadic experience followed by a group.

Schlapobersky and Pines (2009: 1362) offer a useful summary of inclusion and exclusion criteria:

Inclusion

1 motivation to address personal issues/problems
2 willingness to participate
3 some experience of successful relationships
4 some interest in exploring/understanding self
5 some capacity to talk, listen and relate
6 some interest in others
7 some sense that being among others might be helpful
8 some ability to sympathise/empathise with others
9 some indication of future reliability in attendance

Exclusion

1. acute crisis
2. history of broken attendance in therapy
3. major problems of self-disclosure
4. major problems with reality testing
5. pathological narcissism
6. difficulties with intimacy generalised into personal distrust
7. defences that rely excessively on denial and disassociation
8. emotional unavailability
9. verbally subdued or withdrawn
10. hostile and aggressive, verbally or otherwise

Suitability for a group would require prospective members to meet at least four inclusion and no more than four exclusion criteria.

Preparation and principles of conduct

Preparing members for the group is likely to enhance group functioning and reduce drop-out (Slavendy, 1993). As part of this preparation, the conductor introduces each member, prior to joining, to certain 'principles of conduct' (Foulkes, 1975a/1986). These help regulate the boundaries of the setting:

- discretion (what is presented in the group remains in the group);
- regularity and punctuality;
- notification of absences;
- payment of fees (if the work is private);
- no contact outside the group;
- abstinence (to refrain from behaving in ways that reduce tension or distract attention from emotional content).

It is important that all such 'principles' as well as the principle of 'openness' or 'active disclosure' are discussed not in any authoritarian way but in a way that is in keeping with the group-analytic culture the conductor tries to promote. Indeed, that these are principles rather than 'rules' acknowledges that any transgression (boundary incident) requires analytic interest more than enforcement since, well-handled, such incidents usually offer opportunities for development.

Motivational work may also be an important part of participant preparation, particularly where high levels of anxiety are mobilised by the prospect of joining a group. Not only can patient goals be usefully discussed but also the preparatory one-to-one sessions offer an opportunity to explore 'nightmare scenarios' – fears of what might prove overwhelming. Lorentzen (2014) notes how it is particularly important to explore all negative ideas and expectations since shared awareness of and preliminary reflection on them makes them less likely to lead to destructive acting out.

Selection and preparation usually occur over several sessions. Concerned about patient-therapist attachment complicating member-group attachment – the shift from sole to shared 'ownership' of 'conductor-parent' being potentially problematic – some conductors keep one-to-one contact to a minimum. Others, however, see such secure one-to-one attachment as providing an important anchor for the patient negotiating entry into the group – the therapeutic alliance being a stepping stone to the broader alliance(s) with and within the group (i.e. the experience of cohesion) – and any patient concerns that might get provoked by the prospect of moving from dyadic to triadic relationships, as an opportunity for further preparatory work/reflection.

Of course, just as each new member needs preparation for entry into the group, the established group needs preparation for the entry of a new member. Essentially, this means finding a way of talking about members' hopes and concerns regarding the impact of the imminent arrival and, indeed, about the fact that the conductor has initiated such an impingement upon the boundary of the existing group. Mature groups may make such preparations themselves. However, when there is reluctance to do so, the conductor must encourage such expression and reflection, simultaneously noting, with interest, any reluctance shown. In doing so, the roles of conductor as dynamic administrator and therapist begin to blur.

Boundaries and other fundamental safety conditions

The careful establishment and maintenance of boundaries of time, space, roles and principles of conduct, including stable participation, are fundamentals in creating a safe enough environment for group members to work, to explore. Not infrequently, the conductor will need to attend to 'boundary incidents'; incidents where some aspects of these boundaries are challenged. Absences, and lateness are common examples of such incidents and they need to be addressed, ideally by group members, but if not, by the conductor directly in a manner which shows interest (and, where necessary, firmness) rather than punitiveness and rigidity. Other examples, seemingly less transgressive, might include, for example, a member offering to help ready furniture prior to the group. In such circumstances, the conductor must remember he is a 'Transference figure' and that any such offer has meanings that should not be lost to the emerging matrix of the group. Similarly, after a group, should a member approach the conductor about some 'private' matter, the conductor must encourage them to bring the matter to the group. Indeed, all communications (conversations, emails, texts, telephone messages) that take place between members (including the conductor) outside the group belong to the same network as those that take place inside the group. It follows, if the group's matrix is not to be depleted, all need to be made available *to* the group.

Challenges to the physical setting – members re-arranging chairs, shifting the table – can also occur. Whether to confront these immediately and concretely – for example, by returning a moved table – or whether, noting them, to wait until session material offers an opportunity for a more reflective intervention, is a matter of clinical judgement. Whichever the approach, both holding the boundary and making such communications available for analytic scrutiny are essential for group safety and development. Again, this is another good example of how dynamic administration inevitably bleeds into therapeutic activity.

Weinberg (2016) offers an important rider to the minimal conditions usually deemed necessary for the development of a safe and successful therapy group. Recognising that some groups appear to thrive despite intrusions, frequent arrivals and/or departures, changes of room and timing, lack of punctuality and spates of absences (for practical reasons rather than expressions of internal conflict and ambivalence), he notes that among the essential conditions for successful group therapy are the capabilities of the conductor. Fundamental among these is the capacity to create a 'reflective space'.[8] This requires a 'secure presence' (Neeman-Kantor, 2013): a subjective presence which involves 'his/her immersion, passion, attention, emotional involvement, reverie' (Weinberg, 2016: 15), a readiness to be drawn into 'enactments'[9] and, beyond this, the ability to 'hold the group-as-a-whole in our mind as reflective space and stay hopeful despite the difficult conditions' (Weinberg, 2016: 15). It is this presence that can help compensate for 'fuzzy conditions, loose boundaries and leaking containers' (ibid.) by contributing to a co-created fantasy (of a safe enough space capable of reflective activity) in the mind of the group including the conductor.[10]

Conductor as therapist

Long-term and short-term groups: a difference of emphasis

Although the focus in this chapter is upon conducting classic slow open, long-term group-analytic psychotherapy groups, much of the approach described is also applicable to conducting short-term, time-limited groups. Nevertheless, there are differences. Summarising these differences, Lorentzen (2014) identifies that, in the context of short-term groups, there will need to be increased therapist activity, more structure, more active focusing on problem areas, greater focus on working in the here-an-now and more attention to the process of termination. These are essentially differences of emphasis.

Therapist activity: passive and active interventions

A conductor's therapeutic activity is synonymous with their *interventions*. Interventions generally describe verbal utterances: questions, clarifications, challenges, observations, interpretations. However, they also describe behaviours – gestures, entry in and out of the group, the taking of a particular chair. Indeed, even a conductor's seemingly passive presence is an 'intervention', since their capacity to observe and attune to emotional currents in the group can itself provide significant holding and containing functions. Conversely, a conductor's persistent silence and reserve (one might say 'absent' presence) may be experienced as uncaring, neglectful, threatening. This is to recognise the impact of the 'observer effect': the effect of the observer on what is being observed that is co-created by both observed and observing parties.

Interventions can be understood then as being either more 'passive' (such as observing and reflecting – as in reflecting on what is going on) or more 'active' (as in commenting on what has been observed, or articulating some of what is being reflected upon). In terms of a conductor's observations, these must be essentially 'free-floating', as prescribed by Freud: 'a mental poise that matches patient free association' (Barwick, 2000: 16). This observational attitude is complicated by a need for 'bi-focal' orientation – towards both the individual and the group. Each event in the group, even if apparently involving only one or two members, must be observed in itself but also as part of a Gestalt configuration (pattern) that involves the group-as-whole. In other words, the meaning of the individualised event ('figure') is understood as only becoming fully meaningful in the context of the background ('ground') that is the rest of the group.

For the conductor, meaning begins to arise out of reflection. Observations gathered by free-floating attention are subjected to the reflective processes of the conductor's own mind. Roberts (1993) suggests a conductor's reflections should follow the following sequence:

- what is the situation in the group? (assessed on the pace of activity levels, emotional quality, content being discussed)
- what processes contribute to the situation in the group?
- what is not being spoken about?
- is the situation constructive, destructive or neutral?
- is it desirable to change the situation?
- what interventions could affect the situation and the processes which are contributing to it?
- do I have the necessary intervention in my repertoire?
- is the time ripe for an intervention?

A conductor's active interventions can in themselves be understood to belong to a spectrum, some being more active than others. Traditionally they have been described as having 'masculine' (more active) and 'feminine' (less active) elements; reserve, robustness and penetration associated with the first; empathy, support and receptivity with the second. A Foulkesian perspective – epitomised by the motto, 'Trust the group' – considers a well constituted group to be naturally creative, nurturing. This has led to an emphasis upon the conductor's complimentary 'feminine' function. Consequently, even a conductor's more active interventions are often characterised by 'lightness of touch' or 'a nudge in the right direction'. Such an approach was Foulkes's own, modelling[11] group analysis's democratic 'culture of inquiry':

> He believed that the group always knew more, could find out more, than any individual if its creative power could be harnessed. And he assumed the best

way ... to facilitate this creative potential was to throw any question open ... and throw his ideas into the ring like the rest.
(Skynner, 1982: 14–16 cited in Schlapobersky, 2016: 18)

And yet, despite such optimism, the practice of group analysis is littered with casualties – drop-outs, scapegoats, those who have become more disturbed – suggesting group forces at work far less benign than the motto 'trust the group' allows. In the face of such clinical realities, concepts such as 'the anti-group' (Nitsun, 1991; 1996) have helped group analysts more clearly describe and attend to these more destructive aspects (see Chapter 7); ones which perhaps demand, at times, more 'masculine', active interventions.

How do conductors actively intervene?

Maintenance interventions[12]

Maintenance interventions aim to clarify and/or re-affirm relevant boundaries. Ideally, such interventions arise out of the interpersonal communicational processes of the group. For example, one member expresses anger at another for never being on time; another great concern about a member's absence with no message. However, if the group does not 'intervene', the conductor must. This is particularly so if such boundary incidents are pervasive, suggesting anti-group forces at work. Maintenance interventions are a good example of the conductor focusing on both structure and process while acting as both administrator and therapist.

Open facilitation

Open facilitation aims to promote group 'process' without seeking to influence its direction. It is a 'lubricating activity' (Kennard et al., 1993: 109). It may take the form of an observation, a clarification or a reflecting back. Whichever the form, there is no conscious hypothesis regarding underlying dynamics or issues but rather a signal of interest in the process of communication itself and in the worth of thinking about what is going on. The conductor may gain the group's assistance in the task of thinking simply by saying, 'I wonder what everyone thinks is happening in the group at this moment'.

Guided facilitation

Guided facilitation is more directional but typically 'light-handed' nonetheless. The conductor, having some hypothesis about what is going on – latent aspects ripe for translation – finds a way of directing the group's attention to it. In effect, he provides a 'stepping-stone' for an individual and/or for the group towards meaning-making.

Interpretation

Foulkes notes that the individual contributions members make to the process of free-floating discussion can be understood are 'unconscious interpretations' of prior contributions in the group (1968/1990: 181). Organically, this helps develop the meaning-making, group-analytic culture Pines describes:

> At a deeply unconscious level, as when a person speaks of a symptom, of a difficulty in life, of mental pain or conflict, the response of the other group members can often illuminate the presenting person's unconscious processes. This illumination comes from the authentic knowledge that one person has of another, based upon deep personal involvement in the therapeutic situation.
> (Pines, 1993: 100)

As such 'interpretative' processes unfold – as surface is exchanged for depth, symptoms for meaning, isolation for communication – the conductor's role is essentially one of 'watchful gentleness' (Trevarthen, 1977: 337), of 'fundamental unintrusiveness' (Bollas, 1987), rather than direct interpretative intervention.

Nevertheless, conductor interpretations – those offering psychoanalytically informed meaning to patients' contributions and interactions where previously either there was no apparent meaning or where the meaning conveyed is different from that suggested – are necessary at times and Foulkes offers some 'guiding lines' as to when and how they should be made:

> Interpretation is called for when there is a blockage in communication. It will be particularly concerned with resistances, including transference. Its form and content should be determined by the ongoing interaction and communication as experienced by the group. For its location and timing the emotion of the patients should be followed.
> (1975a/1986: 125)

Related to this is his warning against 'plunging interpretations': those that go from surface to primitive depths, stirring such profound anxieties that the patient either responds in an intellectualised manner or ignores the interpretation altogether.[13]

Conductors tend to be sparing in their use of interpretation and, when interpreting, tend to address the group-as-a-whole more than the individual. Such reticence finds its roots in Foulkes's aphorism: *'interpretation comes in where analysis fails'* – analysis being 'the totality of the work directed at making the unconscious conscious': 'the establishment of more and more specific meaning by patient exploration' (p. 117). After all, 'in giving an interpretation we do the work which the patient ought to do' (p. 116) – that is, the work of translation.

Comparing the development of the group's capacity to translate with a child learning to speak, Foulkes adds, 'If the child is too readily understood by its parents on an infantile level it will make no effort to increase its mastery of language'

(Foulkes & Anthony, 1965/1984: 263). Further, conductor-proffered interpretations tend to promote him or her as primary source of analytic wisdom, intensifying projections of authority while simultaneously demoting the authority and creative potential of the group. This does not deny the occasional usefulness of offering a direct interpretation to an individual, particularly if something, despite being near the surface, is not being addressed by the group. If proffered, however, an incomplete interpretation is often preferable. This can prompt group reflections that often have the capacity to take the individual (and the group) far further than the conductor is able to alone.

Always, though Foulkes constantly promotes the conductor's attention to the making of meaning – to interpretation – he does so in the context of the conductor's primary task: facilitating the group's capacity for communicating with ever greater articulateness. This will include the group's capacity to interpret, to make meaning out of its own content – including its symbolic communications – as well as its processes.[14] Hence:

> The conductor should be ahead of his patients . . . in hearing (what Grotjahn calls) 'the voice of the symbol' . . . patiently waiting for them to catch up, cautiously helping . . . but most concerned with what is in the way, blocking the group's own understanding.
>
> (1975a/1986: 132)

Indeed interpretation without due timing and tact is both fruitless and frequently counter-productive whoever its instigator; all the more so when the image itself, not its translation, might be best placed to 'safely hold experience which was too painful, too brittle, or too broken to be firm enough to tolerate analysis' (Bachelard (1969) cited in Cox & Theilgaard 1987/1997: xiii).

A note on 'the interpretation of dreams'

In psychoanalytic therapy, dreams have long been prized as *the royal road to the unconscious* (Freud, 1900). In group analysis, dreams are also highly valued but an understanding is complicated not least by an appreciation of the implications of a 'social or interpersonal unconscious' (Foulkes, 1964: 52). Although any dream told is clearly personal to the dreamer then, from a group-analytic perspective, it cannot be seen as solely so. This is not only because the act of telling is a social act having both conscious and unconscious intent and conscious and unconscious impact, but it is also a 'property' of unconscious dynamics that belong to all levels of the matrix – personal, dynamic and foundational.

A number of creative approaches to dreaming have emerged out of this interpersonal and transpersonal understanding of dreaming (see Neri *et al.*, 2002). Of particular interest, within a large group context, is this 'social dreaming matrix' (see Lawrence, 1998; Lawrence & Biran, 2002). However, with our focus upon the small group and the work of the conductor, Friedman (2002, 2004, 2012,

2015b) is one of the more deliberate exponents of a group-analytic approach to dreams, describing as he does the transpersonal/intersubjective nature of dreams in groups, as well as some of the possible clinical implications of working with them with this perspective in mind.

Friedman (2015b) identifies three approaches: informative, transformative and formative. In the first, the conductor focuses on interpreting the dream's 'latent content' – its hidden meanings. Essentially a classic psychoanalytic approach, Friedman gives it a group-analytic emphasis by viewing the dream as being located in the dynamic and foundation matrices rather than solely the personal matrix. Hence, any interpretation sought would need to address not only the person but also the unconscious dynamics at play at an inter- and trans-personal level in the group. Such interpretative work tends to be quite explicit, whether it is carried out by conductor, group members or both. However, if the interpretative process is monopolised by the 'expert' – the conductor – important aspects of group-analytic culture may be undermined since it is likely to prompt a crescendo rather decrescendo in the group's dependence on authority.

In the second, transformative approach, the conductor encourages the group to make space in which the dream can, through processes of association rather than direct interpretation, resonate. Sharing 'spontaneous individual affective responses (the personal resonance reflecting (unconscious) identifications with latent contents' (p. 50), suggests Friedman, can indeed deepen the informative function. In contrast, precipitous interpretations can 'dissociate the interpreters from the dreamer' and the group, as a consequence, loses opportunities for experiencing quintessentially therapeutic 'moments of meeting' (Stern et al., 1998).

The third 'formative' approach recognises that dream interpretation can 'frighten some dreamers, or may cause them and the relations in the group more damage than good' (Friedman, 2015b: 54). The conductor, taking cues from the dream – is its narrative relatively coherent? does it include humans? does it have a sense of movement? – assesses the level of psychic robustness of both dreamer and group. If robustness is deemed lacking, formative work – 'listening, accompanying the dreamer and the group through fears threatening affective moments as if grabbing an infant's hand through a dark ally' can, Friedman argues, itself engender 'the most powerful "moments of meeting"' (p. 55).

Transference interpretation

Transference provides immediate, live access to a patient's relational history and/or ways of relating. It is thus one of the most significant dynamics active within the therapeutic situation. So valuable is the information it proffers, individual therapists, with neurotic patients at least, tend to encourage its 'maturation'. In part, such 'transference neurosis' is enabled by the nature of the analytic attitude – generally characterised by a high degree of restraint, reserve and neutrality, be it with an affirmative tone. In its most classical form, this amounts to providing a 'blank screen' on which the patient's projections may be 'thrown' (Freud,

1913/2002). Indeed, Kleinians refer to actively 'gathering the transference' (Meltzer, 1968) and to transference in therapy as the 'total situation' (Joseph, 1985). It is unsurprising then that, in individual therapy, research suggests that the transference interpretation (in particular one which links, through the 'transference triangle' (Malan, 1979), the patient's relationship with current others outside the therapy, with the therapist and with figures from the past) is seen by most psychoanalytic practitioners as the single most significant mutative intervention a therapist can make (Hobson & Kapur, 2005).

Foulkes notes the inevitable significance of the conductor as a Transference figure, particularly with reference to his authority in the early stages of a group. However, rather than 'gathering' such f/phantasies, Foulkes (1975a/1986) advises he 'must avoid becoming too important and must keep to the background', for if he manages to 'minimise his significance', not only will he be in a better position to analyse a patient's projections but 'he will make the group into a more confident and active agent'. Hence, 'The group will learn to rely more on itself and be correspondingly more convinced of the truth of its findings' (p. 111).

The fact that, in a group, the Transference is one among many transferences (see Chapter 2), is another reason the conductor declines to 'gather' it. To do so would be to inhibit fuller development of the matrix (including complex multiple transferences) by giving prominence to the dyad: conductor-patient, conductor-group. Further, though the conductor may, at times, offer interpretations regarding these multiple transferences, much of the time such dynamics are challenged by 'real' responses from group members as part of the process of communication. This encourages a 'corrective family group experience' (Grotjhan, 1977):

> There is a built-in correction of the transference phenomena through the peer relationship in groups. The analyst is trained to let the transference neurosis grow to full bloom. Members of a group are neither trained nor willing to accept such projections ... and will correct them.
>
> (p. 14)

For the conductor, a natural outcome of gradually declining aspects of the Transference role is his greater freedom to be himself. Although abstaining from personal disclosure in terms of history or current reality, he has licence to be more spontaneous, more liberal in affective communication and more willing to engage playfully, sometimes humorously, within the matrix of the group.

Though less reserved, the conductor hopes, nonetheless, to monitor rather than enact his own transferences. Even so, such relational purity is unlikely. Although the group will not have access to the conductor's relational context outside the group, they will have access to past and present relations inside. This is enough to prompt observations and hypotheses about the way he relates in the group. Such scrutiny is valid analytic work and, though the conductor must be mindful of whether anti-group or developmental forces motivate, he must also be open to discourse that helps modify authority relations and promotes the growing maturity of the group. In effect, the conductor should be willing to accept and even invite the group's help with his blind spots (Hopper, 2006).

The use and misuse of countertransference

To speak of a therapist's 'blind spots' is to highlight the issue of countertransference. Countertransference has a long, complex history. Seen classically as a form of therapeutic contamination (either the analyst's own transference to the patient, or their emotional response (counter) to the patient's transference), the remedy is further analysis for the analyst. Taking a more contemporary 'totalistic' view (Kernberg, 1965), though still recognising the importance of being alert to potentially contaminating 'blind spots' (both personal and professional[15]), Prodgers (1991) recasts it as an invasion of the analyst's unconscious by the patient's which, as long as the analyst is not captured, becomes a rich source for understanding the patient's internal world.

In some ways, Foulkes took quite a 'classical' view of countertransference. Invasive, destabilising, he refers to it as a 'Trojan horse' (Foulkes, 1958/1990). However, through the concept of resonance, in which the conductor participates as much as any member, Foulkes's view of countertransference is much more totalistic. Indeed, Foulkes goes much further than most analytic models by suggesting the conductor should not only work with such 'communications', helping to translate them into more articulate forms, but should also, at times, offer a form of countertransference disclosure.

The 'best hint' as to whether such disclosure is 'useful or even necessary' is, Foulkes suggests, whether the conductor 'becomes aware that some resistance against communication is located in himself, is involving him if not caused by him' (1975a/1986: 114). This is to take seriously the fact that the conductor is both observer *of* and participant *in* the group. As participant, he is exposed to, penetrated by and, with the other members of the group, co-creator of, the interacting processes that constitute the matrix of the group. This view of countertransference has much in keeping with an inter-subjectivist perspective.

As an intersubjectivist, Orange (1995) suggests the term countertransference should be used only when referring to the analyst's 'reactive emotional memories that interfere with empathic understanding and optimal responsiveness' (p. 74). For her, better suited to identifying countertransference in the 'inclusive sense' – that is the 'concurrent and mutual organising activity of analyst and patient' – is the term 'co-transference'. This is to affirm what Leowald (1986) suggested when arguing that:

> It is ill-advised, indeed impossible to treat transference and countertransference as separate issues. They are two faces of the same dynamic, rooted in the inextricable intertwinings with others in which individual life originates.
>
> (p. 276)

In the context of a group, the implications are that countertransference can no longer be understood simply as the conductor's emotional response to the individual or to the group-as-a-whole since it is construed as a phenomenon that is 'actively co-constitutive of the group process' (Schulte, 2000: 543).[16]

More specifically, this essentially intersubjectivist reading of countertransference has led to a reconsideration, in certain circumstances, of the therapeutic validity of intentional countertransference disclosure (see e.g., Aron, 1996, 2006; Maroda, 1991; Mitchell, 1988). Some disclosures are more forceful (Renik, 1993) – 'an almost blatant disclosure of one's personal feelings and reactions' (Potthoff, 2014: 273) – others much more cautious, selective. A mainly US-led re-evaluation, though in many ways pre-empted by Foulkes, such developments in countertransference disclosure in the psychoanalytic field have not yet clearly translated into a model of good practice within group analysis. This is a fact perhaps not unrelated to Foulkes's own ambiguity in this regard, as well as group analysis's position in relation to the dominant psychoanalytic (anti-countertransference disclosure) mores of group analysis's country of origin, the UK. Nevertheless, Aran (2016), an Israeli group analyst, draws on the correlation of group-analytic and intersubjective approaches to argue for judicious, intentional countertransference disclosure, especially of the negative countertransference and particularly at times of therapeutic impasse.[17] In line with both Yalom and Leszcz (2005) as well as Cohen and Schermer (2001), Aran (2016) suggests that any countertransference self-disclosure needs to be well-timed and appropriate to the group's maturity (e.g. not too early in a group's life when there remains a need to idealise the conductor). Given these provisos, she offers a clinical example of her use of negative countertransference disclosure with a group whose relations, dominated as they were by insult and anger, had become rigid and polarised, so that free floating discussion had ceased and at least one member had threatened to quit the group. In this context, where neither transference interpretations nor invitations to the group to explore the nature of the here-and-now relationships succeeded in offering a way out of the impasse, self-disclosure appeared to facilitate the group's ability 'to own and process emotions, especially when coping with projective identification' (p. 4).

Some group analysts prefer to align themselves more closely with a more conservative object relations approach when working with countertransference. This perspective, though recognising projective identification – the process by which denied, split off aspects of the self are projected into others so that what is projected is experienced by the other as if it were their own (see Chapter 6) – as, potentially, a mutual process, nevertheless emphasises the conductor's role as symbolic parent/therapist/container rather than symbolic sibling/group-member/unconscious co-seeker of containment. The conductor's countertransference is thus thought about in terms of being an emotional response to (resonance with) these projections at work in the group and in need of processing (containing/understanding) rather than reacting to and communicating 'in the raw'. It is the process of containment – making meaning out of what has been projected and re-presenting it in more digestible, knowable form – that brings the patient psychic growth (through re-introjection of the projected aspects) and relief rather than what might be seen as a communication about a failure to do so.

Drawing on Argelander (1970), Beck (2006) introduces the notion of 'scenic understanding' to the idea of working with the countertransference – 'scenic' referring to dramatic enactments (or re-enactments) on a stage. In a group, a particular member's traumatising relationships from the past begin to be re-enacted in the here-and-now relationships of the group. Resonance then takes over, helping to find 'a common denominator, a trauma or conflict shared more or less by the whole group' (p. 103). The conductor's first job is one of 'scenic observation': a careful watching, from an analytically informed perspective, of the creation of the enactment. 'Scenic experience' quickly accompanies such observation: the conductor's own resonance, his experience of being invaded by the resonances at work in the group as a consequence of the enactment and of being pulled towards a particular way of relating. This needs to be followed by 'scenic intervention': the conductor's description, offered to the group, of 'the roles and attitudes evolving within him/her during this process, and the ideas he/she has in the state of functional regression' (p. 104). Although some group analysts might be wary of too interpretative an intervention, such descriptions may also be offered by way of invitation – part of hermeneutic research in which the whole group may join. Whichever the approach, Beck's summary remarks are unlikely to be contested:

> It is not enough to become nothing but a part of the situation. Also, it is not enough to observe the situation from outside and just think about its meaning. In a therapeutic ego-split, we have to oscillate between being affected by and involved in the situation, and to reflect about what is being enacted.
> (pp. 104–105)

In a group context, although the conductor has the role of therapist, all members work in a therapeutic capacity. Further, since transference and associated projective processes are ubiquitous, each member, as well as the group-as-a-whole, is likely to experience countertransference responses to interactions within and of the group. Indeed:

> Communication through projective identification is a vital part of group life and often provides an effective pathway for psychological growth.
> (Rogers, 1987: 99)

The conductor's job is to encourage a maturing of such primitive communicational methods into more sophisticated forms, such as 'putting it into words'. Since this tends not to happen easily, those finding themselves used as a container for split off and projected aspects of others will themselves need help (and support) in recognising that this dynamic may be at play. In effect, part of the 'witness training in action' already described (see Chapter 3), in its development of a capacity for self-observation and the observation of interactions in which one is involved, can also be seen as a form of 'countertransference training in action'.

Notes

1 Pisani (2014) and Koukis (2016) offer a fuller comparison of the work of the conductor in orchestras/choirs and in the group-analytic group. Koukis also explores the 'musicality' of group-analytic groups as does Powell (1983), Strich (1983), Thygeson (2008) and Wotton (2012, 2013, 2015).
2 This mantel of authority which the leader is inevitably given early in group formation is in keeping with Freud's theory of mass formation where the individual egos of group members become narcissistically identified with an idealised leader (see Ch 1). As Nitzgen (2001) notes, many contemporary psychoanalytic writers have identified a shift in which the early mother rather than the primal father has become the centre of mass psychological dynamics. This still follows, however, 'Freud's structural analysis of the willing submission of the self under the idealised other in mass formation, hypnosis and transference'. It is still, structurally, 'a re-enactment of a past relation between an omnipotent other and a passive-masochistic self' (p. 336).
3 Foulkes's pithy exhortation is matched by Anthony's (1991) where, referring to how even the most group-centred group 'never quite surrenders its adoration of the therapist' suggests that the need for leadership thus becomes 'a symptom of the group that is curable only by a therapist who does not lead'. (p. 86). Of course, as Nitzgen (2001) notes, this is not an abnegation of leadership since groups 'need the very exercise of leadership in order to overcome it' (p. 333). Nevertheless, it underlines an essential democratic spirit in group analysis and a recognition that the conductor requires 'an essential affinity to education according to the concepts of a democratic way of life' (Foulkes, 1964/1984: 64).
4 Schlapobersky (2016) notes that these terms have often wrongly been attributed in their origin to Pat de Maré. This misattribution appears to have arisen because in later editions of the Foulkes and Anthony text (1965/1984) the passage where structure, process and content is discussed in the original (1957) is omitted.
5 Dynamic Administration is a Foulkesian term though not actually committed to print in this precise collocation until Pines, Behr and Hearst (1982).
6 The table, for Foulkes, provides a focal object, reducing the empty space. It can also become a transitional object (Kosseff, 1975).
7 This was something that was clearly evident from the demise of the aborted first wave of the Northfield Experiments led by Bion (see Chapter 1).
8 Citing Hinshelwood (1994), Weinberg describes 'reflective space' as 'that aspect of the group in which members link emotionally and from which the personalities can emerge' (p. 96).
9 Enactments describe 'entering into the grip of repetitive and unmentalized self-states' (Grossmark, 2007: 479); in short, unconscious re-plays in the group of relational activity inherent in early trauma. The conductor needs to be able to achieve a balance that allows the enactment to unfold without risking damaging trust in the group that too long an experience of an enactment is likely to produce. This is a challenging position for a conductor to maintain since it involves being (willingly) susceptible to the 'grip' Grossmark describes though not inescapably so.
10 As Weinberg notes, the conductor does not act in a void. It is his/her secure presence in interactive combination with the 'invisible group' (Agazarian, 1981/1995) – the real, visible group's shared fantasy of a group that is safe enough

– that co-creates the 'multi-unconscious-fantasy' that allows a group to thrive even in 'leaking containers' (Weinberg, 2016: 18).
11 Modelling is itself an important type of intervention (Kennard, Roberts & Winter, 1993) and can include not only modelling 'an analytic, enquiring and concerned attitude' but a whole range of behaviours such as 'coping adequately with distressing events' (Roberts, 1993: 8)
12 I have followed Roberts (1993) here, who classifies conductor interventions of the following types: maintenance, open facilitation, guided facilitation, interpretation, no immediate response, action, self-disclosure, modelling.
13 For a full tabular account of the types of interpretation Foulkes both encouraged and warned against, see Schlapobersky (2016: 448–450).
14 Brown (1998a) remembers how Foulkes often left questions and suggestions 'hanging in the air to be responded to and developed' and how he 'died halfway through an interpretation' (p. 391).
15 Among group-analytic blind spots, Prodgers (1991) suggests 'a tendency to emphasize the constructive, holding capacities of the group at the expense of its destructive, enmeshing or isolating potential' (p. 400).
16 Related to this is the intersubjectivist understanding that there is no 'objective position' from which the conductor is able to approach the group and what is crucial is 'the ability of the analyst to be reflective in a way that includes an awareness of the values and theoretical frameworks which guide him/her' (Weegmann, 2001: 527). Citing Lichtenberg (1983), Weegmann (2001) notes that though 'the analyst can never become value-free (or theory-free) . . . he/she can become more value sensitive' (pp. 527–528).
17 Mermelstein (2000) suggests that most therapeutic impasses can be explained as therapist denial of negative countertransference that is misinterpreted by the patient (and the therapist) as a lack of empathy.

Chapter 5

Core concepts
What does the conductor do? (Part two)

Nick Barwick

Conductor as therapist (continued)

Facilitating communication

The prime reason for the conductor to intervene is to facilitate 'working towards an ever more articulate form of communication [which] is identical to the therapeutic process itself' (Foulkes, 1948/1983: 69). Thus, *'Foulkes's clinical recommendations to the conductor can be summarised as a responsibility for promoting discourse'* (Schlapobersky, 1994: 228). In what ways the conductor attempts to facilitate the development of such discourse – of shared, free-flowing, articulate communication (i.e. communication that is understandable and *is* understood) – depends on the level of maturity in the group and whether or not communicational activity appears to be fluid or blocked.

Early in a group's life, the conductor may focus on encouraging individuals' presentation of narratives ('monologues'). From these, group members begin to orient themselves in relation to each other ('dialogues'). Gradually, as such narratives interact, group themes emerge which in themselves become the communicative focus of the group, leading, over time, to discourse; an exploration about what is inside the group in the here-and-now as well as what is outside and in the past. This brings live, sometimes dramatic, sometimes playful communicational encounters that promote the group's capacity to 'listen to the voice of the symbol' (Schlapobersky, 2016: 282): a capacity for and interest in meaning-making.

A group capable of attending to its own life in this reflective way is one that is moving beyond cohesiveness to coherence. Accordingly, the conductor shifts focus from communication that enhances safety to that which encourages exploration: of fluctuating moods, of differences, of configurations in which certain members find themselves playing roles that, unreflected upon, can restrict their own and the group's psychic unfolding. In all such efforts the conductor seeks to promote, maintain and develop communicational fluidity.

Communicational fluidity enables greater articulateness and provides the raw material for greater coherence. This is so because it ensures all parts of the communicational network remain part of the whole. Its development requires the conductor to hold in mind and, over time, to educate the group to hold in mind, the gestalt of figure and ground, the principle of interconnectedness and the indivisibility of the life of the individual and of the group. It also requires attending to the four levels of communication described by Foulkes (1964) – current, transference, projective and primordial (see Chapter 3).

Nonetheless, despite the best efforts of both conductor and group, characteristic of a network is that parts can and do, temporarily at least, become 'mouthpieces' for broader dynamics at play. This becomes problematic, however, only if the communicational current becomes blocked, leaving individuals isolated from social context and their symptoms 'autistic' in that isolation. Such blocks are disturbances in the communicational matrix 'that prevent a free flow of communications or their reception and thus the sharing of them' (1975a: 131). The conductor must help the group to address these blocks, utilising his understanding of location and translation to do so.

Working with resistance to communication

Another way of describing such blockages is 'resistance'. This re-casts, what otherwise might be construed as accidental, as meaningfully, if unconsciously, motivated. Where there are communicational resistances that the group seems tardy, reluctant and/or unable to address, the conductor must more actively intervene. Even so, the constructive function of resistance – a means of defending against overwhelming anxiety – must be kept in mind. This helps alert the conductor to the pace and manner of intervention: a matter of timing and tact.

Working with resistance to shifting conversations in time-and-place

Group communications may focus on the 'here-and-now' (the present inside the group), the 'here-and then' (the past inside the group), the 'there-and-now' (the present outside the group) and the 'there-and-then' (the past outside the group). Without guidance, therapy groups often focus on 'outside' communicational modes. Here, problems are aired, personal narratives shared and strong resonances evoked. However, experience is, of necessity, at one re-move. It is *re*-called. By contrast, conductors often draw on such narrative experiences both to fuel and shift the focus to the 'inside', particularly the 'here-and-now'. Here, narrative gives way to drama as the group struggles to work in the transference. In this often turbulent arena, much interpersonal learning may be achieved, since problems brought become recognisable in the immediacy of interpersonal encounter and a corrective recapitulation of early family life becomes possible.

At times, however, the nature of the communicational blockage prompts the conductor to turn the usual interventional focus on its head. For example, if there has just been a bombing nearby and the group focuses only on the here-and-now,[1] the absence of narrative regarding the wider social matrix alerts the analyst to a de-cathexis – a withdrawal of emotional energy from the 'there-and-now' – about which the conductor needs to alert the group (Hopper, 2003b; Bhurruth, 2008).

Working with resistant conversations

All groups have conversations aimed at ensuring 'nothing beneath the surface is disturbed or exposed' (Roberts & Pines, 1992: 486). If persistent, the conductor may need to draw attention to these. Nevertheless, 'phatic communion' – 'a type of speech in which ties of union are created by a mere exchange of words' (Malinowski, 1923: 314) – can help provide necessary levels of safety and social bonding and should not be lightly dismissed. Further, language's metaphorical nature naturally affords room for the unconscious, even in communication that appears mundane; for example, a long and laboured discussion about a dearth of parking spaces as a metaphor for concerns about finding room in the group. As Foulkes notes, 'Depth is always there . . . It depends who is looking, who is listening; one need not jump from what is going on to what is behind it' (1974/1990: 280).

More problematic may be conversations which appear probing but focus only on one individual. Although taking the guise of therapeutic endeavour, the conductor must keep in mind what is located in the individual – need, vulnerability, inadequacy, suffering – which may more productively, at some point, be redistributed across the broader matrix of the group.

It can be entirely appropriate, at times, for an individual's narrative to take precedence in a group. Monologuing is part of a group's communicational diversity. Unrelenting, however, it monopolises resources, breeds resentment rather than empathy and can be a form of resistance to dialogue and discourse. Some reasons for such behaviour are referred to in Chapter 3. High levels of anxiety and/or the monopoliser's conviction that they are neither heard nor understood may also prompt this form of communication (Behr & Hearst, 2005). In Chapter 10, I describe one member who monopolises the end of a group on several occasions. My failure to address this contributed to a conflict between her and another member at a time when neither she nor the group were strong enough to contain it, leading to her leaving the group.

Particularly early in the life of a group, it is important that the conductor is prepared to intervene when the group appears unable to do so, in order to maintain what Brown (1998b) calls 'Fair Shares and Mutual Concern'. However, it is also important to consider motivations emanating from the group when the particular configuration of monopoliser and disenfranchised appears to bed in. For example, is the monopoliser going unchallenged because thereby other members of the group evacuate their own greed? If so, any intervention must stimulate thought about what interpersonal dynamic is being (re)enacted rather than simply challenging, or even analysing, the individual or enforcing a conversational rule.

Similar motivating forces may be at work in a group that adopts turn-taking. Although perhaps appearing helpful, turn-taking quickly proves a stultifying way of interacting (or not interacting). If adopted unconsciously, an intervention bringing it to the group's attention may be enough either to make the process available for analysis or prompt diversity of opinion with regard its merits. If arrived at by more-or-less unanimous conscious decision, a more interpretative intervention (about the anxieties against which turn-taking might defend) may be required.

In the context, say, of a group discussion about whether group therapy really provides for individual needs, turn-taking might be understood as a 'restrictive solution' to a 'focal conflict' (Whitaker & Lieberman, 1964) – for example the conflict between a desire for 'me' time ('disturbing motive') on the one hand and a fear of rejection ('reactive motive') on the other. In an effort to resolve tensions aroused by this focal conflict, a mechanistic, turn-taking model of exchange might evolve. This circumvents the problem, allowing contact to continue, though without any further exploration of the original theme. Since the manner in which groups resolve such conflicts is key to developing group culture, and since turn-taking is counter to the group-analytic culture of free-floating discussion, the conductor may need to intervene to stop the restrictive solution and promote a more 'enabling' one. Enabling solutions – those which reduce anxiety but allow thematic explorations to continue – produce enabling cultures more in line with that of group analysis. Nonetheless, restrictive solutions may be necessary, at times, to reduce tensions enough to continue at all. For this reason, the conductor may refrain from intervening, waiting instead to see if the restrictive solution runs its course.

Perhaps most problematic – and certainly among the most challenging moments – are conversations between two sides (either individual or sub-groups) locked in confrontation. Confrontation is important. Potentially, it provides different perspectives, feeding an acknowledgement of difference. Further, it can help develop group confidence in its capacity to survive, contain and integrate aspects of competition, aggression, conflict and the expression of complex and diverse needs. However, where confrontation has a marked lack of tolerance and marked presence of contempt and/or disgust and the group, other than the 'pair', appear voyeuristic and/or paralysed, the conductor must intervene.

The manner of intervention will depend upon the maturity of the group. In a relatively new group, it may be necessary to stop the interaction with a comment such as, 'This is a very important fight. But not now'. This, of course, may well draw aggression onto the conductor. Alternatively, if the conductor has a good enough understanding of the nature of the 'malignant mirroring' at work (see Chapter 3), a direct interpretation may be of use. More useful, if the group seems robust enough, is to invite other members to comment on *their* experience. This is to re-open the wider communicational processes in the matrix and may lead to deeper understanding not only of mutual projections between the main protagonists but also of the likely projections at work in the group-as-a-whole which have become located in this specific relational conflict.

Working with resistance against being 'Independent'

Dependence is an essential foundation for the development of independence. Without a cherished experience of dependence there can be no basic trust and without basic trust there can be no real intimacy. In the intimacy that is dependence we learn most deeply, and in the loss inherent in separating from that upon which we have grown dependent, we make what we learn, our own. Such painfully, hard-won, inner resources are what give us our so-called 'independence' or, from a group-analytic perspective, our 'inter-dependence', since this reflects better the reality in which identity grows.

In a group, particularly early in its life, individual members often seek support from the conductor. For example, questions addressed directly to the conductor are not uncommon. Sensitively frustrating these by asking what prompted them or re-directing them to the group usually quickly helps contribute to a culture of inter-dependence. However, even though careful selection may temper such dynamics, intense, primitive dependency needs can emerge at any time, either at an individual or group level. Such dynamics are considered more fully in Chapters 6 and 7.

Working with resistance to joining the matrix

Von Faunhoffer (2008) notes that few new members relish the prospect of joining a group, the experience often being 'perceived as a loss, long before they appreciate it as a gain (p. 278)'. Brown (1998b) suggests that underlying many people's reluctance to join is a 'hatred of sharing' – informed as it is by 'overlaying memories or fantasies of parents together in the primal scene, or the sight of a sibling at the breast' – and that this is one of the most powerful motors driving anti-group forces (p. 396). Indeed, sharing and loss go hand in hand, being core to the early oedipal situation that entry into a group inevitably re-evokes. This is so because, particularly in the context of intense need – the need for comfort, relief, help – the shift from dyadic (conductor and prospective member) to triadic (conductor, the new member and other members of the group) relations readily re-stimulates primitive anxieties and their attendant defences related to separation anxiety (from the primary care-giver), the successful negotiation of which demands we bear the knowledge that 'when our desired, dreamed of object is absent (and thus lost to us) . . . it may be understood to be elsewhere – that is, with a third' (Barwick, 2003: 63). Although a degree of triadic aversion is thus likely to be common to all, when early oedipal negotiations, particularly with reference to separation from the primary object, have been especially complex and/or compromised, the developmental transition required in the act of joining a group has the potential to reignite trauma.[2] Thus the conductor needs not only to prepare new members carefully for such transition but also to monitor their developmental progress, intervening more actively, where necessary, in order to 'hold' them (see Chapter 6) until they are more able to experience and appreciate both the demands/frustrations and the holding/gratifications proffered by the group itself.[3]

Most new members' responses to the tricky, developmental transition from dyadic to triadic relations might be better described as degrees of hesitation than resistance. For some, however, resistance best captures the type of anti-group behaviour that can be particularly frustrating for both group and conductor and can even appear as purposefully intransigent.

Almost every group, suggests Ormont (2004), has its 'isolates' – 'individuals who rarely . . . make an effort to understand and attach themselves' (p. 65). Isolates do not have the capacity for 'transient identifications' – the ability to identify with others, without losing themselves entirely to and in others. Since those with this capacity are better able to understand, learn from, reveal to and be enriched by others (Scheidlinger, 1964), drawing the isolate into the group flow becomes an essential therapeutic task. While some analysts see isolation as dissolving naturally 'in the temperate mix of group communication' (Behr, 2004: 76), for others, the conductor needs to be particularly active in drawing the isolate in.

Understanding communicated by some members towards group 'isolates' (either spontaneously or at the conductor's invitation) is an example of how such vital connections begin to be made. Further, invitations to isolates to contribute what they understand about another member's predicament or feeling state can also be beneficial since not only does the member in question feel understood, but the isolate experiences something of what it is to understand. However, there will be compelling reasons for an isolate's resistance to connecting with others, and unless these are understood, simple invitations to connect in understanding are unlikely to be very productive.

'The driving reason for isolation is always the disowning of a feeling . . . "If I avoid others, I won't have to feel this or that way"' (Ormont, 2004: 69). In Ormont's model, the conductor works both through the group and with the individual to bring these unwanted feelings (and the communicational patterns adopted to protect the isolate from them) to their attention. The resulting conversion of isolation into loneliness can be a painfully slow one. This is particularly so when isolates, rather than experiencing their isolation as an impediment, present in 'contained guise', 'devoid of emotional colouring', bearing their relational state with 'relatively passive acceptance' and equanimity (Behr, 2004: 79). Further, vital to the therapeutic process is that 'not only does the group enter the world of the isolate, but the isolate [by means of re-location and acknowledgement, by the group, of unacceptable feelings] enters the world of the group' (p. 80).[4]

Sometimes, one or two group members appear to engage with the group, but in role as (co)therapist rather than equal participant. Of course, group therapy encourages members' capacity to be therapist to others. This capacity may even, appropriately at times, emerge through the offering of consciously proffered interpretations. Such offerings can be valuable not only for their content (which can be mutative for the recipient) but also because they may help consolidate a growing sense of insight, authority and worth on the part of the interpreter. However, they can also be more imitative than authentic; a defence against deeper communication, perhaps rivalling the conductor, perhaps competing with siblings for special 'married' status as 'assistant conductor' (Foulkes, 1975a/1986: 117), perhaps projecting vulnerability and need into those proffered their interpretative gifts. Should this be the case, an initial intervention might be one that both values the contribution *and* invites a personal response. If this fails to shift the communicational pattern, a more challenging intervention might be required. Most helpfully, this will come from the group which is unlikely to tolerate such an approach for long.

Collective resistance to joining the matrix can be particularly destructive (Pines & Roberts, 1992) and is likely to indicate anti-group forces at work (see Chapter 7). Understanding the source of such resistance must become a prime focus for the conductor. Although the conductor's 'feather-like' intervention – a lightness of touch – can favourably tilt the process along more developmental lines (Roberts, 1991a), more robust interpretative interventions may be required.

Working with resistance to integrating difference

Not only may those who feel isolated resist joining the group, but the group may resist integrating the isolated. Such resistance may be symptomatic of a collaborative quarantine in which a disturbance in the group is not only located in an individual but also, by means of projective mechanisms, locked there. Although an individual so identified may fit the role assigned them, the conductor needs to think not only in terms of the individual's history (their personal matrix) prompting them to take up such a position but the way in which the dynamic matrix of the group may also be using the individual to avoid integration of unwanted aspects of itself.

Though there is often a psychological 'fit' on the part of a scapegoat, there is not necessarily so. An identifiable 'difference' that threatens the fantasised integrity of the group can be enough to elicit abuse. Foulkes (1964) suggests scapegoating results from displaced aggression – a group member being chosen, unconsciously, as a stand-in for the conductor. Consequently, the conductor needs to draw the aggression towards himself. Causes of scapegoating, however, are likely to be more diverse. Neither are they uncommon, particularly in the early stages of a group when the group-analytic culture has not yet been established. Certainly, groups experiencing high levels of threat are particularly vulnerable to the temporary relief afforded them by this phenomenon. Conformity provides safety for the majority by demanding the eradication and/or expulsion of that which is 'bad', humiliating, shameful, different. Whatever the conductor's responding intervention, he cannot afford to remain silent for long.

When there are socially charged differences in a group – for example around ethnicity, class, disability, sexuality and gender – it is particularly important for the conductor to keep in mind not only the usual projective processes but those aspects of the social unconscious which inevitably penetrate the dynamic matrix of the group, including the conductor. Often, rather than leading to overt expressions of prejudice, repressive forces can produce a tacit agreement not to broach the taboo subject – in effect denying difference. The conductor must not shy away from challenging such unconscious 'gagging injunctions' or from foregrounding differences which otherwise might be kept secret. Once the 'secret' is out and the oppressed group members are spoken about, both the individual/sub-group concerned and the group-as-a-whole are usually better able to engage in productive discourse (Blackwell, 1994; Rippa, 1994). Such discourse is rarely easy, however, since we are all penetrated by the social to the core (and thus by the social unconscious) and are not only prey to its forces but may feel deeply ashamed of being so.

Working with silence as resistance

'One cannot not communicate' (Watzlawick *et al.*, 1967: 51). To this extent, silence is itself a form of communication. Its meanings, however, are many. It accompanies moments of deep reflection as well as of isolation and withdrawal, of communion as well communicative resistance.[5] If the latter, and if prolonged, the conductor must intervene.

When resistant silence is pervasive, a simple observation of it, or enquiry about it, is often enough to re-establish connections. If it isn't, an interpretation may help. However, even if the conductor, drawing on their observations of the group and of his countertransference, feels quite confident about his interpretation, it is often preferable to deliver it half-formed (e.g. as a series of observations or as a 'thought-in-progress') than fully so.

A particularly impenetrable, painful form of silence affecting the whole group, Wood (2016) identifies as 'opaque'. Primordial and inchoate in nature, it conveys '*intense rejection coupled with profound helplessness or paralysis,* of being in the presence of people who are completely unwilling or unable to even recognise that you exist, and that there is absolutely nothing that can be done about it' (p. 234). Wood suggests that underlying opaque silence is the basic assumption incohesion: aggregation/massification ((ba)I:A/M) (Hopper, 1997), itself prompted by fears of utter helplessness in the face of annihilation, of loss of identity either through engulfment or abandonment. (For a fuller discussion of (ba)I:A/M see Chapter 7). When fear of engulfment dominates, communication threatens each individual's defensive retreat into their own universe (aggregation). When fear of abandonment is prevalent, to acknowledge the very need for explicit 'ever more articulate forms of communication' threatens the group's defensive state of undifferentiation, of merger (massification).

The conductor's primary task in such instances is to address group safety – a sense that though feelings of helplessness may be experienced, a reliable, helpful object is at hand. Fundamentally, this means ensuring the stability and predictability of group boundaries and includes not only attending to group structure but to group context – other parallel groups, the institution, the wider community. For example, are any changes happening in the context that might prompt attachment anxieties within the group? What is being projected into or out of the group?

The feelings of helplessness and the fear of communication that opaque silence indicates is likely to be experienced strongly in the conductor's countertransference.

It is vital, therefore, 'to hold on to the hopeful belief that by bearing it, gradually the patient(s) will become able to bear it too' (Wood, 2016: 245):

> Eventually words may be found for it but not too quickly . . . To these patients, 'plunging' interpretations . . . feel like intrusive attempts at taking over their minds, and nearly always result in increased withdrawal.
>
> (p. 246)

When resistant silence is located in an individual, it can be particularly difficult for the conductor to enquire directly. Not only can doing so develop a group culture of depending on the conductor but such enquiries are also often experienced as particularly penetrating and it is always better if other members of the group are moved to engage instead. Further, since the conductor cannot hope to attend to each individual all the time, helping the group develop its capacity to 'hold' its members is preferable to the conductor always attempting to do so. If the group appears to ignore the individual, this observation is itself worth making, prompting thought perhaps about what connections the group is wary of making. In effect, what is the individual not communicating on behalf of the group?

Working with resistance to staying

In the wake of sudden drop-outs, there is little a conductor can do other than help the group process that wake. Staying alert to the premonitory signs – late-coming, irregular attendance, withdrawal from interaction – and intervening earlier is likely to be more beneficial. Even if such intervention does not prevent drop-out, it is more likely to protect the group from a sense of impotence, failure and persecutory guilt. Often, enabling the individual concerned to speak openly about their thoughts is enough to prompt resonances in the group, so helping the potential drop-out feel less isolated.[6]

Resistance to ending

In a slow open group, where patients leave gradually and hopefully with good notice, group members experience several endings during their time in therapy. Since 'the failure to negotiate endings effectively is one of the key causes of intrapsychic and interpersonal difficulties' (Barnes, Ernst & Hyde, 1999: 96), such experiences offer important opportunities for reparative work.

Nevertheless, the intense, primitive feelings provoked by endings (in those who leave and those who are left) make regression common. Old symptoms/ behaviour patterns often re-emerge, mourning processes come into play and the value of the group may be idealised (as if without it, nothing good will remain) as easily as it may be denigrated (as if nothing good has ever been achieved). The conductor must help the group talk and think about these recapitulations. In so doing, he may find it helpful to remember that such regressive dynamics, though transferentially and countertransferentially powerful, are usually temporary and an important part of the work (Maar, 1989; Wardi, 1989). (For a fuller account of working with endings, see Chapter 12). Of course, the group will have had plenty of rehearsals for such explorations in response to absences and breaks.

In a time-limited group, the conductor, not the patient, makes the final decision about ending. It is particularly important, then, that he retains responsibility for alerting the group to it by encouraging the sharing of thoughts and feelings about ending, noting aloud when the group appears resistant to exploring its meaning, and verbalising, if necessary, some of the conflicted feelings that may be evoked, including possible concerns about the future. In effect, the conductor often becomes more active, emphasising the shared nature of the process and usually offering more group-as-a-whole observations. This tends to evoke recollection, reflection and an intensification of feedback. Some conductors actively elicit evaluations – a consideration of what has been gained as well as what has not been addressed.

Sometimes, final sessions are characterised by concrete offerings and acts of sharing. Someone brings cake, another drink, others cards, gifts. These run counter to the classical psychoanalytic principle of abstinence. There is little point, however, in launching into interpretations – at least not immediately. More productive may be an initial accommodation of them before engaging in reflection. The desire to go on sharing, to give and receive, whether there will be any sustaining food once the group ends – these are some of the reflections that might be usefully encouraged in a context of social tolerance rather than analytic austerity.

Conclusion

Somewhat tongue-in-cheek, group analysis has been described as 'therapy for grown-ups'. This refers to the fact that, as we grow older, although turning to wiser, older, stronger figures at times of high anxiety is a natural attachment pattern, we must nevertheless learn to relinquish our fantasy of finding a 'parent' who, attending to our needs with fine empathic attunement, will make it all better. Instead, we must learn how to share resources creatively; to discover, indeed, that new and unexpected resources become available to us when we find ourselves engaging in the communicational processes inherent in such sharing. In a group, the conductor too must relinquish the omnipotent fantasy of providing each individual with the crucial therapeutic intervention. If such fantasies are not relinquished, both conductor and group are destined to be wedded to an impossible, ultimately dispiriting task.

The conductor builds, develops and maintains the group as both therapeutic medium and agent of change. Engaging freely in the processes of resonance, mirroring and exchange, such a group associates at all communicational levels and develops, over time, greater coherence, confidence in its authority, outsight and insight, and capacity for translation. The conductor guides such development, carefully selecting and preparing its members and managing and guarding the group's boundaries. Within the boundaries of the therapeutic frame, he takes a position that is both different from and similar to his patients, utilising his observations of self-in-interaction (including the countertransference) and others-in-interaction (including the transference) to offer a presence that 'intervenes' (holds and contains) as well as an actively intervening presence. Together, these encourage the generative momentum arising out of a creative tension between integrative and analytic forces, enabling the group to progress through constructive, deconstructive and reconstructive experiences (Schlapobersky & Pines, 2009), fuelled by the increasingly complex and meaningful web of communication that is the dynamic matrix of the group. As Barnes, Ernst & Hyde (1999) note:

> The group exists for the benefit of the individual members, yet they can only benefit by giving up aspects of themselves to the group.
>
> (p. 124)

And this is exactly what the conductor must do if, by dint of what he or she is, as well as what he or she does, they are to 'foster an understanding of the group as an entity that is more than the individuals' (ibid.), that is 'different from the sum of its parts' (Lewin, 1951: 146).

Notes

1 Hopper offers just such a striking clinical example.
2 Alternatively, for new members who have, for example, experienced an invasive relationship with a primary care giver, or a loss of the primary object that was successfully ameliorated by an experience of belonging in a new group (for example, a bereaved child sensitively 'adopted' by the wider family), the feelings experienced on joining a group might be, predominantly, those of relief.
3 It is also important to be realistic when considering a prospective member's likely tolerance of 'sharing'. For some, whose experience of separation and neglect has been particularly traumatising, membership of a group might not be appropriate, at least not until some prior therapeutic work has been engaged in a one-to-one setting.
4 Behr (2004) also recognises those experiencing culturally determined isolation; 'a sense of not belonging which stems more from the foundation matrix . . . than from the individual's psychopathology' (p. 81) This form of isolation, built around racial, ethnic, religious, language or gender differences, requires, he suggests, active work on the part of the conductor in drawing attention to it and helping the group find words to explore it.
5 Urlic (2010) refers to many forms of silence (and quietness): repressive, regressive, progressive, transitional, transferential, countertransferential.
6 In response to a sudden drop-out, a conductor may offer one or more individual sessions in an effort to bridge the communicational gulf between individual and group.

Chapter 6

Developments in group analysis

The mother approach

Nick Barwick

An appreciation of the mother-infant paradigm – of how the infant mind forms in interaction with the primary care-giver (for reasons of culture and simplicity, often referred to as 'mother') – though never elaborated by Foulkes, is implicit in group analysis from the start. Referring to the 'group-as-mother', Foulkes (1948/1983) expresses an essential optimism about the group's capacity to nurture; an optimism nicely captured by Pines (1978):

> At a very deep unconscious level this group, an entity greater than any one member, on which all are dependent, which all need to be valued and accepted by, which nourishes them with its warmth, which accepts all parts of them, that understands pain and suffering, that is patient yet uncompromising, that is destroyed neither by greedy possessive primitive love, nor by destructive anger, that has permanence and continuity in time and space, this entity is basically a mother.
>
> (p. 122)

Foulkes's group-analytic model challenges Freudian, one-person psychology; a psychology that construes the individual mind, dominated by innate drives, as a relatively closed system. However, as post WWII psychoanalysis itself underwent radical change, developing along far more relational lines, the emerging two-person psychological perspective, with its appreciation, enshrined in the mother-infant paradigm, of the fundamental significance of the interaction between external and internal in the formation of intra-psychic structure, offered group analysis analytic allies with rich theoretical veins to mine. This chapter explores the mining of some of those veins.

Containment and projective identification

Containing is a psychic activity linked with projective identification. The latter, initially formulated as a primitive defence in which unwanted, unmanageable aspects of self are evacuated into another (Klein, 1946/1988), Bion (1962a/1984) developed to include its function as primitive form of communication. The newborn infant, no longer held within the all-providing intra-uterine environment and lacking cognitive capacities to make sense of unfamiliar, often alarming, 'raw experience', projects the resulting psychic disturbance into mother, eliciting a mirroring anxiety within her. Ideally, out of something frightening, forever (the baby has no sense of time) and formless, mother, in 'reverie' (Bion, 1970) – a relaxed condition where meaning is not made prematurely but arises out of the full, often uncomfortable evidence of experience – makes a thought: you are cold; you are hungry; you are lonely. Acting on this thought, she responds to baby's needs. Baby, in the wake of repeated attuned responses, thus experiences both *being* understood and *trust* in being understood. Building a lexicon of experience based on mother's meaningful responses, baby introjects not only thoughts – I am cold, I am hungry, I am lonely – but also the mental apparatus for thinking. Indeed, from experience, baby learns that new, disorienting experiences, even when prompting disturbing anxieties,[1] can be tolerated and, in the end, made sense of; that is, they can be contained. Thus, though the containing process becomes an intra-psychic activity, it is learnt through, and remains embedded in, a relational context.

Much of our experience, however, is never adequately contained. This may be because of the inadequacy of the container – a primary care-giver distracted, preoccupied, depressed, intolerant, abusive and/or rejecting – or because of the virulence of the projections. Whichever the cause(s), where containment fails, problematic feeling states remain unintegrated, aspects of 'the unthought known' (Bollas, 1987). Consequently, still prey to psychic disturbance, we resort to intensified projective identifications to gain temporary relief, even if no longer hopeful of containment. All this is to recognise that the need for containment fits well Foulkes's own conviction that 'the real nature of the mind lies in each individual's need for communication and reception, in every sense of the term' (1974/1990: 278).

The therapist works to contain the as yet uncontained, projected aspects of the patient, re-presenting them in more digestible (thoughtful) form in an effort to develop the patient's capacity to contain himself/herself. In the face of patient projective identifications, the therapist 'invites invasion but resists capture' (Segal, 1977). This challenging, intra- and inter-psychic work can be understood in terms of working with the countertransference (Ogden, 1979).

In groups, the conductor uses countertransference to contain not only individual but also sub-group and group-as-a-whole projections. The impact of this work can be considerable:

> ... the analyst in the group is at the receiving end of ... projective identification, and ... this mechanism plays a very important role in groups ... The analyst feels he is being manipulated so as to be playing a part, no matter how difficult to recognize, in somebody else's phantasy ... I believe the ability to shake oneself out of the numbing feeling of reality that is a concomitant of this state is the prime requisite of the analyst in the group: if

he can do this he is in a position to give what I believe is the correct interpretation.

(Bion, 1952/1961: 149)

Still greater complexities arise from the fact that all members and the group-as-a-whole engage in projective identification not only with the conductor but also with each other. This can be a mixed blessing. Early in the formation of a group, such projections can lead to antagonism and disproportionate distrust. Alternatively, they may bring about a narcissistic 'fusion' with, and idealisation of, the group and/or conductor. Although the latter is problematic long-term, initially it can help provide necessary (and developmental) cohesion (Battegay, 1994).

Projective identification offers 'endless possibilities for the open expression of denied feelings' (Rogers, 1987: 100). Yet when these projections over-accumulate and petrify, they can also be immensely destructive. Scapegoating and malignant mirroring exemplify this. In scapegoating, for example, the 'sins' of the group are projected into the 'goat'/'other'. The 'other', with apparent justification, is then ousted/sacrificed for the good of the now 'cleansed' in-crowd. As a variation on this, in malignant mirroring, shameful, detested aspects of self are mutually projected into the mirror of the other, cementing a perverse psychological fit.[2]

The capacity to contain not only one's own psychic contents but also those of others (at some level, essentially indivisible) is an important psychic achievement and one usefully learnt in groups. Yet the container also needs robust support attuned to the level of their containing capacity. That is to say, the container needs containing. In groups, this may necessitate speedy intervention by the conductor, if not to contain, to prevent abuse. Ultimately, however, the conductor seeks to facilitate the development of the group's containing function. To this end, the very notion of developing evermore articulate forms of communication and at ever deeper levels – that is, 'putting it into words' – becomes a form of containment; containment that helps develop the group's faith in its capacity to contain (see Zinkin, 1989).

We are all projectors and containers. Even mothers, especially when poorly contained, project aspects of themselves, be they idealised, denigrated, feared or longed for, into their infants. The conductor thus needs to be alert to his own potential (ab)use of the group. Although training and personal analysis should minimise such intrusions, they are also inevitable. What makes the difference is how self-reflection, supported by supervision and other containing relationships, help the conductor work creatively with such containment 'failures'. To acknowledge this intersubjectivity gives new meaning to Foulkes's (1964) comment that the conductor's personality has an 'overwhelming influence' on the group.

Holding, surviving, playing

'Holding' describes mother's attuned response to infant need. Such dependability implies mother's love and it is within this 'total environmental provision'

(Winnicott, 1960a/1990) that the infant, largely protected from the grosser impingements of reality (and of accompanying anxieties) develops a growing sense of 'continuity of being'. In effect, mother acts as baby's 'auxiliary ego' while baby, relatively unperturbed, is left to discover its primitive, coherent, authentic identity/ 'True Self'.

As the infant self coheres, the holding environment loosens. Emerging from a state of attuned 'madness' called 'primary maternal preoccupation' (Winnicott, 1956/1992), mother begins to rediscover her own (separate) mind and the infant begins to experience the 'impingement' of small 'doses of reality'. Not everything happens when he wants it; between a need and a satisfaction, a gap appears.

Gaps resulting from brief, well-timed impingements help the infant gain a sense of separateness and develop psychic muscle. However, impingements that are too early or too intense provoke not the experience of a loosening hold but of being 'let down', 'dropped', forever 'falling'. Defending against such 'drops', the infant reactively holds himself. The formation of a 'False/Caretaker Self' is just such a 'reactive' self-holding (ibid.; 1960b).

Developing psychic muscle, he tests out his environment to see if it can withstand his growing strength. Only when he discovers that the 'object mother' – the mother who, in the primitive infant mind, being distinct from the caring 'environmental mother', is the one against whom he directs his aggression – can 'survive', can he be confident of his own separateness and begin to develop concern for the other (1963/1990). Indeed, through the non-retaliatory, boundary-enforcing survival of the object, he finds not only confirmation of the mother's loving resilience but also 'proof of [her] . . . ability to hate objectively' (1947/1992: 199) – that is, to hate his relentless, 'ruthless' demands and still 'hold on'. Only then, when he is wholly known, can he begin to believe in being wholly loved.

Although recognition of separateness makes available the riches of relatedness, it is not an easy transition to make. To help, the baby develops a 'transitional space'. This space arises out of the infant's creation/use of a 'transitional object' (Winnicott, 1971/1974); objects imbued with 'good-mother stuff' (Deri, 1978: 52). For example, a bit of blanket may seamlessly become, through sensual links with breast, infant's tongue and sucked thumb alongside which it slips, almost an extension of him (and his fantasised unity with mother/breast) and yet is not him/mother/breast. This 'intermediate area of experiencing' – of a 'world' neither entirely inner, wholly subjective and omnipotently ruled, nor entirely outer, wholly objective, impotently inhabited, offers both consolation and challenge and is, for Winnicott, where imagination begins; the 'as if' of play.

Play is a resource not only for infants managing the tricky, conflicting demands of internal and external (shared) realities but also one to which we all must return, at times, if we are to negotiate, creatively, the demands of reality (its separations, losses and frustrations) without undue loss of spontaneity, of 'continuity of being'. Further, play proffers temporary relief from the full demanding force of external reality; a space in which to renew and reinvigorate connections with the 'True Self', whatever form they take, in the service of creative living.

The capacity to play is thus a developmental achievement. Further, it is a precondition for therapeutic work which takes place in the '*overlap of two areas of playing, that of the patient and that of the therapist*' (1971/1974: 44). If patients cannot play, cannot engage in play, therapy's first task is to ensure they can. This requires addressing the developmental need for both the holding of an empathically attuned 'environmental mother' as well as the availability of an exciting, frustrating, challenging 'object' one.

The analytic setting provides the holding environment which, in individual therapy, the therapist communicates by being preoccupied with the patient and placing himself at his service, being reliably present, making an effort to understand, refraining from imposing his own needs/agenda, expressing love through interest and (by keeping boundaries) expressing hate, not being hurt by fantasies, not retaliating, surviving (Winnicott, 1954/1992). In a group context, such holding is communicated first by the conductor, then by the group.

Drawing on James (1984, 1994), Nitsun (1989) highlights parallels between early infant-mother relations and early group formation. The 'infant-group' inhabits a relatively unintegrated state: individuals without a sense of connectedness, continuity, cohesion. This stimulates 'archaic' anxieties about physical and psychic survival. Attuned – even to the point of 'primary maternal preoccupation' (see Doron, 2013) – the conductor adopts the role of auxiliary ego, of holding environmental mother whose empathic responsiveness protects both individuals and group-as-a-whole from gross impingements and whose very presence must speak of 'reliability taken for granted' (Winnicott, 1965/1989).[3] Without such holding, anxieties may feel intolerable and early drop-out, precipitous 'False Self' formation (e.g. rigid, rule-bound, self-holding which keeps the group together at the expense of spontaneity) or even group disintegration may ensue. Nitsun (1989) recommends the conductor be present 'in a tangible way to help the group feel safe, to define boundary issues clearly' rather than maintaining 'a position of determined therapeutic detachment' (p. 253).[4] Careful attention to dynamic administration also helps provide holding sufficient for the group to begin to cohere.

Coherence takes time to develop. This is particularly so when a group first begins. A beginning group has no real history, only that constructed by the pooled fantasies and projections of the new members; fantasies which, on the whole, are likely to be determined by the early intrusions and/or neglects/abandonments that have brought these patients to therapy in the first place (Foguel, 1994). Nevertheless, the conductor cannot and should not seek to hold the group in a 'preoccupied' way forever. Indeed, drawing on both Winnicott's (1965/1989) notion of the mother's, developmentally appropriate, 'gradual failing of adaptation' to the infant's need (thus exposing the latter to manageable 'doses of reality' and an experience, as described above, of flexing its own psychic muscle) and Bion's 'Theory of Thinking' (1962) (where out of manageable frustration – in effect, a contained experience of absence – rudimentary thought emerges), Sargeant (2011) describes the group's experience of 'imperfection and disillusionment' in relation to the conductor. From this perspective, 'failures' in environmental provision, of holding – for example, conductor absence, change of start time or change of room – may become opportunities[5] for fuelling the shift from dependency on the conductor to the development of a thoughtful reliance on the interdependent, sibling connections characteristic of a more mature, coherent group.

Conversely, however, even in a relatively coherent group, the import of holding should not be underestimated. Untoward events can provoke archaic anxieties at any time. Further, as Yogev (2008) notes, patient improvement often comes as much through 'the expansion' as 'the challenging, of the emotional space' (p. 376) and it is exactly such expansion – of the capacity to be and be with – in an environment suitably protected from 'aversive stimuli from his surroundings' (ibid.), that holding in a group provides.

In group-analytic groups, holding is a mutual activity with multiple axes. Although modelled by the conductor, each member finds him/herself in a position of holding as well as of being held. The individual's and group-as-a-whole's growing capacity to hold others is indicative of psychological maturity.

A quality necessary for holding others is the capacity to withhold oneself; holding back (though never losing touch with) one's own subjective experience in the service of meeting another's needs, even when those needs include what can be quite aggressive explorations. Paradoxically, such withholding promotes individual expansion. This is so, not only because it strengthens self-efficacy but it also helps develop the capacity to tolerate difference, that essential ingredient in the development of identity. Further, the group that manages to hold, withhold and 'hold on' (i.e. survive without retaliating) in the face of turbulent elaborations of identity – aggression being an integral part of appetite, motility and creativity (Winnicott, 1964/1991) – helps allay fears of relational catastrophe in the face of such turbulence and develops the group's confidence in, and capacity to, play.[6] Schlapobersky (2016), following Winnicott, goes as far as to say that the conductor's primary task is to equip people to 'play safely with human experience and do so across its wide range of emotions' (p. 7).

Winnicott played a game with young patients called the 'squiggle game' (1968/1989). The child drew something, then Winnicott added something of his own. This to and fro 'communication' continued until something emerged that was satisfying and recognisable to the child, though it was a shared creation, coming into being within a transitional space. This describes well an analytic group at play: multiple, interacting squiggles (free-floating discussion) from which both highly personalised and shared meanings arise within a uniquely personalised yet shared space. Co-created language with frequent references to aspects of group history and myth and the elaborate construction and use of co-created metaphor is often characteristic of such play. Such play loosens, frees, partly because play is less prey to the feared catastrophic consequences of action that characterise the external world; a sense that the world of play is not wholly 'real', even if the feelings are. All this can lead to a great deal of experimentation in the service of living (Jacobson, 1989), including living (through playing) with others:

It is largely through play, in which the other children are fitted into preconceived roles, that a child begins to allow these others to have independent existence.... Play provides an organisation for the initiation of emotional relationships, and so enables social contacts to develop.

(Winnicott, 1964/1991: 144–145)

Within the 'mutual sphere of creative illusion' created by a therapy group, 'gently, and little by little, the group helps the individual to alter his subjective perception of reality as his individual transitional space becomes more interactive with the group space' (Schlachet, 1986: 47). In other words, the group generates 'an intermediate territory' (Winnicott, 1951/1992) for all. The shared, overlapping experience of play that takes place within this intermediate territory, one which allows transference-based experience to be 'played out' – that is, not simply re-enacted but elaborated, challenged and reparatively transformed – a patient tellingly describes:

It is all, it is nothing.
It is real, it is pretend.
Family – father mothers, sisters, brothers, they are all here, yet they are not.
Lovers, friends, husbands, wives, companions, enemies, they are all here, yet they are not.
Joy, pain, love, hate, understanding, confusion,
communication, conflict, they are all here and they are not.
...
And so, we will all, in our way, profit by it, learn
from it, live better from it.
Because, you see, it is painful, but it is not.

(Schlachet, 1986: 51)

Attaching and exploring (in security)

To explore and discover more of oneself, of others, of the world is, potentially, a fundamental life-enhancing activity. Yet explorers, unless driven by self-destructiveness, require two sets of related beliefs/expectations if they are to set forth: first, that there is a good chance that what they find will enrich and enliven them; second, that if threats or experiences which prove too difficult are encountered, there will be somewhere safe and reliable to return to. Attachment theory (Bowlby, 1969, 1973, 1980) calls the first set of beliefs an 'internal working model'; the second, a 'secure base' (Ainsworth *et al.*, 1978; Bowlby, 1988).

More broadly, an internal working model describes a set of beliefs about ours and others natures and a set of expectations about the way these natures are likely to interact. Hypothetically, any working model is provisional, open to revision. However, internal models established early in life tend to resist modification. This is because early attachments – in effect, emotional bondings, for example with mother – being the relational contexts in which the first internal working models are forged, tend to be dominant, even exclusive. Further, attachment patterns (behaviours) developing out of these attachments tend to provoke further self-other interactions that confirm rather than challenge the accuracy of the original model.

Attachment patterns may be 'secure' or 'insecure'. Secure attachment patterns develop through experience of relational safety: of sustained, reliable emotional connectedness. The infant, seeking, for reasons of survival, 'proximity' to the caregiver, wards off threat to that proximity either by 'proximity promoting' (e.g. calling, smiling) or 'proximity aversive' (e.g. crying) behaviour. The emotionally attentive caregiver, responding in a timely, sensitive fashion, instils in the infant/child an internal working model characterised by positive expectations in terms of care, a belief in the efficacy of open communication and a fundamental trust that there is, in the world, a reliable 'place' in which sufficient safety and satisfaction can, in spite of periods of anxious uncertainty, ultimately be found and re-found; that is a 'secure base'.

The secure base, over time, becomes internalised as a feeling of security and worth – worth being a product of sustained experience of caregiver responsiveness to the communications of an emerging self-in-interaction. The care-giving system need not be, however, without lapses in 'interactional synchrony'. Indeed, as long as such lapses/'ruptures'/separations are, in a timely way, 'repaired', they serve to promote resilience: a capacity to manage creatively the rhythm of attaching and parting integral to all intimate relations and to sustain realistic hope in the face of some of life's inevitable challenges and disappointments. However, where interactional synchrony is significantly, and for extended periods, ruptured, the child acquires not 'secure' but 'insecure' attachment patterns.

Following Ainsworth and colleagues (1978) and extrapolating from studies of early attachment behaviours, several ways of formulating adult insecure attachment patterns have been developed (e.g. George, Kaplan & Main, 1985; Brennan, Clark & Shaver, 1998). Briefly, individuals with hyperactivating attachment patterns – also known as 'ambivalent' or 'preoccupied' – responding to inconsistent and/or over-stimulating caregiving, develop a sympathetic nervous system that dominates the parasympathetic (Schore, 1994),[7] become highly anxious about abandonment/rejection, overly focused on the affective life of self and other at the expense of exploration and overly engage in strategies designed to secure others' affection and attention, even though the attention they gain may be experienced as ultimately unsatisfying. Such individuals, often described as 'clingy', can, over time, elicit in others feelings of emotional suffocation/depletion, leading to those from whom they seek comfort, pulling away. Conversely, those individuals with deactivating attachment patterns[8] – also known as 'avoidant' or 'dismissing-avoidant' – responding to 'brusque care-giving' (Holmes, 2010), develop a parasympathetic system that dominates the sympathetic and, denying fears of abandonment, appear self-reliant. Affect is minimised, dependency needs dismissed and, deflecting intimate contact, often with an air of superiority, individuals with deactivating attachment patterns actively push others away.

Lastly, those with 'disorganised' attachment patterns (Main & Solomon, 1990) – also known as 'fearful-avoidant' – responding to caregivers who are not only unreliable but also frightening, find themselves unable to develop a coherent set of expectations about self-other interaction or organise reliable attachment repertoires. Consequently, haphazardly alternating between hyperactivating and deactivating patterns, they may disassociate, self-harm and/or engage, often aggressively, in excessive manipulative control of any attachment figure available. This particular attachment pattern has come to be understood as describing borderline personality disorder.

Both deactivating and hyperactivating patterns, being 'organised', seek relational security through controlling the degree of proximity their internal working model indicates works best. In this way, they establish forms of secure base, even if sub-optimal ones. Individuals with disorganised attachment patterns, however, find difficulty achieving (and sustaining) even a compromised secure base since they remain unclear whether relational proximity or distance best proffers the security they seek.

In individual therapy, the therapist is the attachment figure whose task it is to provide sufficient security for insecurity to be explored – an insecurity that the therapist's presence, paradoxically, also evokes. Through the medium of a responsive care-giving system – the therapeutic relationship – opportunities not only for insight but also reparation become slowly available. In effect, unfolding interactional synchrony inherent in the developing attunement of therapist-patient interaction makes available for internalisation, a more resilient secure base – an 'earned security' (Hesse, 2008) – that becomes a resource for the patient's further exploratory and creative living.

Glenn[9] (1987), drawing attachment theory into group-analytic thinking, explores the link between matrix and secure base. She describes the matrix as:

> ... a kind of belonging, a secret awareness hardly expressible in words: it seemed to signify that which I missed (which was not lost but which I carried within me, indescribably yet palpably *there*) when the group did not meet.
> (p. 109)

Linking matrix with mother (see Chapter 3), she suggests the group's dynamic matrix serves as a 'secure base'.[10] By remaining, at a fundamental level consistent, available, predictable, responsive, accepting, safe, stronger than any individual or relational sub-systems that are part of it, the 'good object' of the matrix becomes available 'to carry one over the cracks and fissures – 'ruptures' – in human relationships' (Holmes, 2010: 6); ruptures that are, inevitably, characteristic of some of the interactions *within* the group.

Marrone (1994) extends Glenn's links with attachment theory, proposing that eliciting, exploring and modifying members' internal working models is *the* essential group-analytic task. Concordant with this are the conductor's four subsidiary tasks:

(a) facilitating group cohesiveness and 'affiliation' so the group becomes the secure base from which exploration occurs (most effectively achieved as members relinquish 'false self' presentations and reveal, for intimate contact, the needy, authentic, emotionally-ridden core);
(b) helping members explore current life situations including the relationships they chose, or habitually find themselves in, and subsequent correlations with attachment behaviours observable within the group;
(c) assisting members in finding out how they interpret each other's behaviour (including the conductor's) and exploring the quality of responses they expect to receive;
(d) assisting members make links between past and present in terms of how their 'internal working models' influence their behaviour, their interpretations of others' behaviours and their predictive blueprints both in the group and the outside world.

To achieve these tasks, Marrone suggests the conductor takes an approach of 'informed inquiry': asking questions about the past in an effort to make attachment patterns and their origins more explicit. Also modelling this approach, he/she encourages detailed recall accompanied by appropriate affect, while identifying incongruities between 'semantic' and 'episodic' memory – the former more likely to be a narrative coloured by the person's internal working model; the latter more likely to capture authentic experience. The empathic response of the group to such authenticity provides a corrective emotional experience to the member being responded to.

Although Marrone insists the conductor pays due heed to resonance as a mechanism binding the group and prompting free associative discussion, the deliberate pursuit of internal working models portrays the conductor as active archeologist. Indeed Brown and Zinkin (1994) indicate Marrone's approach as having 'technical problems' that do not fit comfortably the Foulkesian tradition of a conductor's light touch, of coherence (as developed by Pines) or of discussion (as developed by Schlapobersky, 1994). Further, they note:

> Not all group analysts would agree that behavioural systems are an object of study in group analysis and would not accept the epistemology implied by such a term.
>
> (Brown & Zinkin, 1994: 235)

Attachment theory's influence on group-analytic thinking is, though identifiable, also limited. This may relate to psychoanalysis's own historical resistance to it, Rutter (1995), indeed, noting how Bowlby was at one time effectively ostracised by the psychoanalytic community. Among group analysts, a similar wariness can be discerned:

Basically, though subjectivity is acknowledged, the whole thrust of the theory is biological and behavioural, and the notion of the working model is simply not the same as what most analysts mean by the internal world . . .

(Brown & Zinkin, 1994: 235)

Nevertheless, though a hot pursuit of internal working models might compromise a conductor's group-analytic stance, it is difficult to think how an awareness of an attachment model can do anything other than enhance a conductor's capacity to attune to the personal and interpersonal dynamics at play in a group. Indeed, greater attention to attachment patterns in pre-group assessment/preparation (utilising, e.g. Adult Attachment Interview (Main & Goldwyn, 1995) or The Social Group Attachment Scale (Smith *et al.*, 1999)) could prove helpful not only in alerting both conductor and prospective member to likely attachment hopes, fears and expectations but also perhaps even as an aid to composing 'balanced treatment groups' (Weber, 2016: 459).[11] Further, it could also help the conductor develop the dyadic alliance necessary for facilitating a new group member's entry into a group. Mallinckrodt *et al.* (2005), for example, suggest successful therapy requires an initial partial acceptance of the 'pull' of the patient towards certain relational configurations: engaging more at an intellectual level with a patient with deactivating attachment style; being more flexible with boundaries and gratification with someone with hyperactive patterns.

Markedly absent, however, from most attachment group-oriented literature, is consideration of the role attachment patterns play in the group-as-a-whole. One notable exception is Ein-Dor and colleagues' (2010) hypothesis that there may be an evolutionary advantage in having insecurely attached people in society, namely that those hyperactivating may act as 'sentinels', warning the group of potential threats, while those deactivating may catalyse the group's avoidance of danger by moving on. Such insights might prompt conductors to utilise concepts like resonance and location to help all group members gain a deeper understanding of their and others interactive affective life when faced with profound issues of attachment, separation and loss.

Reflecting

Building on Bowlby, (and drawing, in particular, on Bion's notions of reverie and containment and Winnicott's notion of the mother's eyes being a mirror in which the infant first finds itself), Fonagy and colleagues (2002) offer a compelling argument: that the 'mentalizing' caregiver – one who shows interest in what the child is thinking and feeling, speculates about it and communicates that speculation to the child – soothes the infant not only by confirming the attachment as reliable, attentive and secure but also by making available to it a dyadic emotional regulatory system (Schore, 1994; Sroufe, 1996; Sroufe *et al.*, 2005), one which, over time, through the constant giving of meaning to the child's bodily experience, becomes internalised.[12] Indeed, over time, the 'mind-minded' caregiver (Meins, 1997) introduces to the infant not only a sense of their (the infant's) own mind but also the minds of others, reflecting, for example on how 'mummy's tired now so let's both have a rest' or 'your friend looked sad when you wouldn't play with him, so he's playing on his own'. In this way, the child learns to distinguish between feelings in self and others and to express what he/she distinguishes in ways that are both effective and socially adroit. Further, by means of empathy, they learn how others' behaviours link to mental states about which, though they cannot know, they might also reasonably speculate.

The caregiver's capacity to provide a 'reflective function' (Fonagy et al., 1995) for the child, however, is often less than optimal. Persistent parental misunderstandings of the child's internal states ('misattributions') – for example, the caregiver misperceives the frightened child as angry or the child showing a normal level of need for attention as demanding – severely impair the child's own capacity to mentalise or develop a stable, realistic concept of self, promoting instead an attitude of mistrust, not only with respect to the availability and empathic responsiveness of caregiving, but also with regard to the possibility of potentially enriching intersubjective interactions (Marrone, 2014).

From a mentalising perspective then, where there is reflective deficit – a capacity to utilise left brain cognitive understanding together with a full range of right brain emotional activity – the therapist must maintain the role of sensitive and responsive caregiver facilitating experiences that promote left-brain-right-brain integration and its accompanying capacity for greater affect regulation (Cozolino, 2002; Schore, 2002; Fonagy & Target, 2008).

Marrone argues that reflective function emerges not only out of the dyad but also the whole family system (and indeed all interpersonal dialogue). Group analysis thus proffers 'an optimal context for the development of reflective capacities' (1998: 173). This claim is in line with Fonagy et al's (1995) observation that:

> as the philosopher Hegel taught us, it is *only through getting to know the mind of the other that the child develops full appreciation of the nature of mental states*. The process is intersubjective: the child gets to know the caregiver's mind as the caregiver endeavours to understand and contain the mental state of the child.

Although Marrone addresses the applicability of mentalisation to group therapy addressing a mix of psychopathologies, mentalisation-based therapy (MBT) (Bateman & Fonagy, 2006, Allen, Fonagy & Bateman, 2008) has developed in the context of treating a particular psychopathology: borderline personality disorder (BPD); that is, people with disorganised attachment patterns. Although originally a dyadic treatment, Bateman and Fonagy (2006) argue that 'group psychotherapy is a powerful context to focus on mental states of self and others' (p. 145). Consequently, Karterud (2011, 2015a, 2015b), a group analyst working in collaboration with Bateman, has helped to develop mentalisation-based group therapy (MBT-G).

Acknowledging some patients with borderline personality disorder may be helped by group analysis, Karterud suggests that, when working with more severe personality disorder, a modified approach is required. Noting that such patients frequently report feeling neglected by their therapists, difficulties in calming down after meetings and often withdraw from group-analytic groups, he argues that it is difficult to create a secure base, let alone a 'mentalizing matrix'/'mentalizing group culture' – the experience of minding and being minded by others – out of eight individuals, all of whom are 'very sensitive, aroused at the outset, distrustful, having trouble cooperating successfully with others, [and] easily losing their mentalizing capacity' (2011: 363).

MBT-G, a conjoint therapy, has been described as a modified group-analytic approach since, though retaining an appreciation and use of many fundamental group-analytic phenomenon – the matrix, location, resonance, mirroring – jettisons the fundamental principle of free group association. Noting that free association's psychoanalytic function is to loosen the barrier between conscious and unconscious, making the repressed more available, Karterud comments wryly, 'it is a long time since someone has claimed that borderline patients suffer from repression' (ibid. p. 367).

Karterud argues for deliberately 'constructing the matrix', making sure certain processes are favoured and others inhibited. This entails the therapist playing a much more active care-role (he drops the term 'conductor') to create a group that serves as a 'training arena for mentalisation' (p. 367) – MBT-G's equivalent of 'ego training in action'. The authority the therapist assumes thus runs counter to the group-analytic motto: 'trust the group'. Indeed the group is given an explicit task: to bring stories of difficult personal encounters to be explored by a mentalising stance, an understanding of this stance being supplemented by a psychoeducational group paralleling therapy for the first 3 months. Other differences include the therapist actively inviting the adoption of 'balanced mentalizing turn taking', directing reflection on past events, 'building bridges' between sessions by starting the group with references to the last meeting and practising, wherever interpersonal events become available to the group to mentalise, 'stopping and rewinding'. In effect, taking a 'firm hand', the therapist makes sure 'issues of relevance for the therapeutic project are attended to' (Karterud, 2015b: 141). However, though highly active and at times directive, the MBT-G therapist counteracts patient passive dependence by 'rapidly introducing group level metacognitive questions . . . being careful not to do the mentalizing work on behalf of the patients . . . being very cautious with interpretations that suggest that . . . therapists have a special kind of insight' and above all being 'genuinely "not knowing", but with a curious interest in "finding out together"' (2011: 370).

Potthoff and Moini-Afchari (2014), offering a slightly different take, suggest integrating MBT with a group-analytic approach not only in the treatment of BPD-focused groups but also with groups of mixed pathology. Appreciating that the group-analytic phenomenon of multiple mirroring is congruent with the mentalising process, they note that in groups composed mainly of borderline patients, group members need, through projective identification, to externalise their 'alien selves to maintain their own coherence and . . . even survival' (p. 7). This results in mirroring processes that are often 'malignant' (Zinkin, 1983) rather than developmental/benign. Such malignancy leaves the conductor confronted with entanglements in the face of which evenly suspended attention (characteristic of standard group analysis) can prove counter-productive. On the other hand, more active MBT-interventions can 'too frequently disturb the flow of group associations and prevent the group from discovering itself or developing its creative potential' (p. 14). Thus the authors suggest utilising an oscillating 'binocular perspective', one eye focusing on mentalisation levels (is mentalising capacity being overtaxed? is there evidence of pseudo-mentalisation?); the other on conflicts, transferences and countertransferences. When mentalising capacity appears over-stretched, the conductor proffers interventions that slow the pace of interactions and help modulate affects: for example, asking questions that foster self-reflection, seeking clarifications that challenge assumptions that everyone thinks in the same way and actively directing individuals or the group-as-a-whole to look back and reflect on what they think happened in a particular problematic interaction or set of interactions. However, when mentalising capacity stabilises, then standard, less directive group-analytic practice can predominate. Even so, interactive techniques derived from infant observation and developmental psychology – those that have been shown to promote mentalisation (e.g. marked and contingent mirroring, validating and tactful self-disclosure – the conductor's disclosure about what they feel and the reasons for their reaction) can be employed at any time, as should modelling the mentalising process itself by maintaining a 'basic stance of interest and curiosity foreclosing precocious 'knowledge' of motivations that are still to be explored together' (p. 8).

Empathising

Empathy, a therapeutic quality attachment theory clearly endorses, has long had a significant role in therapeutic encounter. A cornerstone of person-centred therapy (Rogers, 1957), its history in psychoanalytic therapy, though initially less ambitious, is noteworthy nonetheless. Fleiss (1942), for example, refers to it as 'trial identification' (the therapist's capacity, with one half of his ego, to step over the boundary between self/analyst and other/patient) while Winnicott (1970) notes that:

> A sign of health in the mind is the ability of one individual to enter imaginatively and accurately into the thoughts and feelings and hopes and fears of another person; also to allow the other person to do the same to us.
>
> (p. 117)

Over the last few decades, however, empathy's perceived therapeutic import has grown: from being a sign of mental health to being a contributing factor in the therapeutic alliance to, particularly through attachment theory, self-psychology, intersubjectivity, developmental psychology and neuropsychology, having a role equal to, if not greater than, interpretation in eliciting psychological transformation.

Empathy's raised significance arises out of a recognition of its fundamental contribution to the development of self; a self-in-interaction. From a self-psychological perspective, 'empathic resonance' (Kohut, 1977) – dependent upon a parental capacity to empathise with the child (i.e. to adopt a mode of observational encounter Kohut (1959, 1971) refers to as 'vicarious introspection') – provides the medium in which narcissistic needs (referred to as selfobject needs since they relate to various experiences of merger with the object) can be satisfactorily met. These needs – to be mirrored (in the gaze of the parents), to idealise (the parent imago: 'You are perfect; but then, I'm part of you'. (Kohut, 1971: 27)) and for twinship – if met, proffer, respectively, a sense of self-worth, of purpose/self-control and of belonging. (Later, Wolf (1988) adds 'adversarial need': the need to engage with a benign adversary in order to test and develop strength and enjoy healthy competition.)

Just as empathic resonance allows robust development of self organised around satisfying selfobject experiences, its absence self-psychology identifies as the root cause of most psychological disturbance. Without an ambience of empathy, unmet needs leave the relatively incohesive self floundering in chaotic, narcissistic immaturity, desperately seeking relational contexts which might provide what is lacking or, fearing further traumatising disappointment, avoiding relational connection altogether.

Although unmet narcissistic needs are traumatising, given a foundation of adequate selfobject experiences, the self's maturation is furthered by conditions of 'optimal failures' since 'tolerable disappointments . . . lead to the establishment of internal structures which provide the basis for self-soothing' (Kohut, 1984: 64). It is, it could be argued, the creative use of empathic failure within a field of mostly sustained empathic resonance, that often gives therapy its momentum (Chused & Raphling, 1992).

Empathically born selfobject experiences are readily available in group-analytic groups. Under the '"me-in-you, you-in-me" rhythm' in a group, experience of mirroring helps develop self-worth (Stone & Whitman, 1977). Further, as group cohesiveness develops, the group itself comes to represent a 'powerful, calming resource' (Roberts & Pines, 1992: 476) – an idealised selfobject (Harwood, 1983) in which the experience is of being held safely – with comments such as 'I can relate to that' articulating the meeting of twinship/'alterego' needs (Stone, 1995). Further, as Stone (2009) notes, as therapy deepens, the search for relief from the crippling experiences of shame, embarrassment and guilt are found not only in the cathartic experience of sharing but also in the realisation of the 'hoped for experience of similarity' (p. 41). Lastly, adversarial needs may be more readily met in a group than in a dyad, owing to greater diversity in power relations and consequent increased freedom/safety to experiment.

Developmental psychology research shows infants, from the earliest weeks, engaging in 'evocative behaviour' designed to obtain empathic responses necessary for development. Devoid of maternal 'emotional availability' (Emde, 1980), they become distressed (more so than during physical separation) (Field *et al.*, 1986) and their own affective, social and exploratory behaviours are significantly inhibited (Source & Emde, 1981). In contrast, reciprocal positive emotional sharing provides a vital context for nurturing positive development (Bretherton, 2000, Lovas, 2005). Framing these findings in the language of self-psychology, it follows that an infant whose environment includes extended family may have a greater probability of obtaining the responsiveness and the selfobject functions it requires. Indeed, several consistent selfobjects may 'enhance the diversity of the symbolic structure [of self] being organised' (Harwood, 1986: 294). This is particularly important if the primary caretaker is disturbed, since availability of alternative intersubjective matrices helps supplement otherwise restricted mental repertoires for living. Potentially, a group offers just such a bolstering diversity of selfobject experience.

Certainly, early in the group's life, the individual member's experience of the conductor's empathic resonance and capacity to fulfill some of the essential selfobject functions is likely to be crucial. It is to the conductor that members of the group will, initially, be seeking a degree of attuned responsiveness in order to build a secure attachment relationship. In self-psychological terms, for example, the idealising selfobject transference will most likely be dependent on each individual's experience of the dyadic relationship with the conductor. Once this is reasonably secured, it can become the model upon which the more diverse, mutual and reciprocal idealisations that facilitate greater group cohesion can be developed (Stone, 2009).

As group cohesion grows, a clearer sense of 'group-self' (Kohut, 1976) grows with it. Conceived of as 'a deep-going structure, a portion of the self that represents a collective project focused on achieving the goals and ideals of the group' (Stone, 2009: xx), the group-self is that aspect of self in which the norms and values of the group have been internalised (Karterud and Stone, 2003). Nevertheless, representing as it does a 'project', the group-self is neither static nor complete and is inevitably prey to experiences of empathic failure just as, as a sustaining object, it is nurtured by the experience of empathic resonance and attunement. Hence, comments such as 'nobody cares' and 'the group doesn't respond/listen' addressed not at any individual but the group-as-a-whole may be understood as an experience of a lack of sufficient mirroring in the group-as-a-whole and the presence/development of a depleting or fragmenting rather than growth-enhancing sense of group-self. An experience of the former, together with its roots in a lack of mirroring, is something the conductor will need to address. Unattended to, such therapeutic ruptures can all too quickly lead to loss of therapeutic momentum and, worse still, precipitous departure.

With the maturation of self, comes recognition of 'the relatively independent centre of initiative in the other' (Ornstein, 1981: 358). Individuals aware of both self and other in this way are able to engage in 'reciprocal empathic resonance' (Wolf, 1980), leading to greater availability of satisfactory selfobject experiences. Indeed, 'one of the therapist's most important functions will be to facilitate reciprocal empathic resonance as a coordinate of the spontaneous reactiveness that comprises the vitality of the therapeutic group' (Bacal, 1985a: 499; see also 1991, 1998).

The conductor promotes empathic resonance by adopting and modelling an attitude of 'optimal responsiveness' (Bacal, 1985b) – a view in line with contemporary infant research into the nature of the relational environments best suited to psychological development. Indeed, exploring 'non-interpretive mechanisms' in therapy, Stern *et al.* (1998) refer to those 'special moments' of 'authentic person-to-person connection' or 'moments of meeting' involving 'implicit relational knowing' and complex 'affect attunement' that are as mutative as any interpretation (see also Boston Change Process Study Group, 2010).

In group analysis, such moments are not limited to those between group member and conductor. Brown (1989, 1994) recounts how one man's dawning recognition that he, like others, had an internal world that was understandable to others, was inextricably bound up with the empathic gestures aroused in the group in response to him. Likening this to the 'development of the nascent self calling for a responsive selfobject' (p. 91), he refers to the process as 'intersubjective validation':

> the person's sense of themselves in relation to others is confirmed by those others' responses in a mutual process of self-discovery.
>
> (p. 92)

Within a group culture where levels of empathic attunement are dependable and mutual self-discovery consequently enabled, empathic failures which, though difficult are, after all, also inevitable, elicit not traumatising re-enactments but opportunities for a 'fuller *discovery* of our inner world . . . to *discern* the difference between old internal object relationships and new ones, and . . . to *learn* to attune ourselves to *other* people's experience as well as our own'. Brown concludes:

> On the way to more mature, intimate and reciprocal relationships with others, we mitigate the effects of earlier empathic failure and ossification of internal object relationships.
>
> (p. 98)

This essentially reparative process has sometimes been referred to as a 'corrective emotional experience' (Alexander & French, 1946). However, as Pines (1990) suggests, it might better be described as the emerging experience, common to group-analytic groups, of 'the appropriate response, the good-enough gesture, which enables the patient to move from an embedded defensive position towards intersubjectivity' (cited in Brown, 1994: 89). For Brown, the process is one of '*self-development in interaction*' (p. 98).

Although, in a mature group, it is the group that acts as therapeutic agent, the conductor's own empathy can significantly promote a milieu of empathic reciprocity characteristic of a mature group. This is of course communicated by what the conductor says certainly, but more so, perhaps, by the way he or she looks and listens. Ofer (2013), for example, suggests the 'ability to look and listen' (p. 307) is a vital transformational leadership quality; that is a quality in the leader that facilitates transformation in those led. As Bion comments:

> If the analyst is prepared to listen, have his eyes open, his ears open, his senses open, his intuition open, it has an effect upon the patient who seems to grow.
>
> (1974/1990: 131)

Ofer draws on Frogel's (2008) three types of listening/attention: epistemological, ethical and aesthetic. Facility in all three types of listening contribute to a conductor's therapeutic efficacy, yet it is ethical attention – 'attention whose goal is to make more room for personal freedom' – Ofer (2013) identifies as being particularly transformative. Focusing more on the speaker than what is spoken, ethical attention demands the listener's emotional involvement with the speaker's subjective self, their existential experience, an involvement that facilitates emotional expansion. In effect, this form of listening/attention offers a corrective emotional experience; an experience capable of modifying earlier formative experiences of being listened to, ones which, being 'controlled by fear' (in the listener) and 'mired in . . . rigid beliefs' (p. 310) have led to limitation and contortion of what might 'become' rather than its elaboration and expansion.[13]

To compliment such empathic listening (and again drawing on Frogel (2006)), Ofer (2013) notes that, in contrast to 'looks' that limit (Sartre, 1943), there are 'looks' that enable freedom (Levinas, 1982) – the process of becoming. Once again associated with the communication of 'empathy and emotional involvement' (Ofer, 2013: 311), the enabling look is rooted in a profound understanding of ethical responsibility for the 'Other' (Levinas, 1982). Just such a look – the way, for example, in the film *As It is In Heaven* (Pollack, 2004), the choir conductor Daniel looks at Gabriela, an abused wife, who is consequently transformed under his gaze – Ofer (2013) describes in some detail:

> His eyes are fixed on her, carefully accompanies her all the way through her song, taking every breath with her, raising his eyebrows at the same time she does and opening his mouth at the exact moments that she opens hers.
>
> (p. 312)

This, Ofer points out, is the gaze of an attentive mother.

Drawing on neuroscientific and psychological studies, Nava (2007) speculates on the nature of empathy at work in the analytic process. Again, like Ofer, focusing mainly upon the therapist's response to the patient, she suggests patients' emotions 'are mirrored through the mirror neuron in the neuronal circuits that codify the same emotion in the analyst' (p. 20). Such affect-sharing, achieved naturally if not defended against, is communicated through the mirroring of affect in our faces. Affect-sharing, however, can cause 'emotional contagion' (Preston & de Waal, 2002: 6) – a type of merger between empathising subject and object empathised with. This prevents the former maintaining sufficient separateness to be able to offer help. Thus the conductor utilises training, supervision and personal analysis to 'resist capture'. Lastly, mental flexibility and auto-regulation come into play. These involve using personal knowledge, beliefs and experience (in other words, 'self-perspective') to step into the other's shoes while, at the same time, regulating/inhibiting that very same self-perspective.

Where, in the group, defences against affect-sharing are evident, where emotional contagion threatens to consume or, where forms of colonisation of the other (because self-perspective is not sufficiently regulated) dominate, the conductor will need to draw the group's attention. Helpful will be the conductor's own capacity to maintain fairly sophisticated levels of empathic engagement and, when not able to, to reflect upon, be open to and even prompt discussion about, empathic failure. For group members, observing and imagining this is likely, by means of mirror neurons (Rizzolatti et al., 2001), to lead to significant learning – a type of 'empathy training in action'.

The 'curriculum objectives' of such a training, might be to develop empathic ability, both verbal and non-verbal, along three continuums (Yogev, 2013):

- the resonance continuum: the ability to observe and recognise (often unconscious) emotional information transmitted
- the comprehension continuum: the ability to determine what belongs to oneself and what belongs to others
- the identification of needs continuum: the ability to prioritise between needs both within oneself and in relation to others

A group offers ample opportunity to observe empathic sensitivity, addressing 'developmental deficiencies in empathy' (p. 73) where necessary. Further, the effect of such empathy training is to help establish a group culture in which new members, perhaps less empathically developed can, according to principles of 'perception-action liaison' (Prinz, 1997), learn from the normative interpersonal and intersubjective interactions of the group. As Schulte (2000) states:

> The ongoing process of the group, with its standing invitation to dialectical engagement with others, facilitates development of the individual members' intersubjective capacity, the opening up of oneself to the inner life of others.
>
> (2000: 541)

Drawing on Fairbairn, he adds:

> The authentic engagement with others allows ... the goal of therapy, the breaking into the closed world of the patient through the real presence of another.
>
> (ibid.)

To acknowledge both being empathic and being empathised with as core aspects of development is to appreciate the deeply, mutually creative, intersubjective nature of the mother-infant paradigm. For the mother who bears a child with whom, empathising, she feels compassion (the latter being 'an expansion of the capacity for empathy' (Segalla, 2012: 137)) is herself re-born within the mother-infant, intersubjective field. To put it another way, 'finding the other through empathy and compassion is the way to find the self' (p. 136). Along these lines, philosophers Buber, Gadamer and Levinas all conclude, suggests Orange (2009, cited in Segalla, 2012), that concepts of individuality have served us badly over the years and 'so invite us to develop a therapeutic culture in which generosity, care and protection of the other become our central values' (p. 11). After all, as Gadamer notes:

> It is the other who breaks my self-centredness [and so my prison] by giving me something to understand.
>
> (Orange, 2009 cited in Segalla, 2012: 148)

The 'other' mother

Foulkes emphasises the group as 'all embracing mother'. Prodgers (1990) suggests this neglects the negative transference to the 'group-as-a-whole'; transference based on subjective *and* objective experiences of frightening and/or deficient mothering. Denial of this essential ambivalence may be necessary initially in a group, counteracting mistrust that would otherwise inhibit cohesive forces vital to collaboration. Long-term, however, it leads to splitting; an idealised group-mother and denigrated/feared conductor, for example, or 'castrated' group-mother and powerful, protective conductor-father (Gibbard & Hartman, 1973; Raphael-Leff, 1984).

Drawing on analytical psychology (Neumann, 1963), Prodgers (1990) elaborates the notion of the feminine, differentiating 'elementary' and 'transformational' characteristics, each of which has positive and negative aspects. An elementary characteristic of the mother is the 'Great Round': the vessel/group that 'contains and holds fast onto everything within it' (p. 22); protecting, sheltering. Yet that which it contains is dependent upon it; 'utterly at its mercy'. Such a mother may, therefore, also restrict, ensnare, devour. In contrast, the transformative mother is characterised by movement. Again, however, she is two-sided. Symbolised as bearing and releasing seeds from the pod, she encourages change, development, individuation as well as abandons, deprives, rejects.

The experience of the negative mother (in both elementary and transformative guises) appears particularly prominent in larger groups. However, though less foregrounded, she may still be evident in smaller ones:

> The most intense group-induced anxiety – recapitulating early developmental sequences of psychological differentiation – is the annihilation of self, either through engulfment and fusion with collectivity at one extreme, or through isolation from abandonment by the group at the other . . .
>
> (Green, 1983: 4)

Prodgers (1990) suggests Foulkes's (and most subsequent group analysts') idealisation of the mother is a professional 'blind spot' rooted in a relationship to mother inherited perhaps from Foulkes or indeed from Freud (see Rycroft, 1985). Prodgers offers not only a Jungian-influenced redress but also a Bionian one and it is to Bion's work, and group analysis's relationship with it, that we now turn.

Notes

1 Any new experience of which it is not yet possible to make sense evokes anxiety because it re-awakens a primitive sense of absence. This resonates with early experiences of absence of the good, nurturing breast. The good breast's absence not only prompts understandable survival anxieties but, according to Kleinian thinking, leave us in the presence of the bad breast, a depository of all our hatred and aggression. The capacity to bear a state of 'not knowing' characteristic of absence, change and loss, thus demands considerable psychic resilience. Bion referred to this resilience, a prerequisite for creativity, as 'negative capability': the capacity to dwell in 'uncertainties, mysteries, doubts, without any irritable reaching after fact and reason' (Keats cited in Bion, 1970: 125).
2 Indeed, the group itself may be projecting into the protagonists psychic aspects which it feels unable to resolve or hold together. In other words, malignant mirroring can be understood in terms of the location of a group disturbance within the malignantly mirroring couple.
3 Doron (2013) adds that such preoccupation is also needed when new members join the group. Further, when thus 'preoccupied', just as the mother relies on support and containment from her environment, the conductor will need a containing place to 'calm down', in particular, supervision.
4 I am reminded of Guntrip's recollection of a session with Winnicott where, having spent some time exploring Guntrip's experience of an early mother who failed to relate, Winnicott said, 'I've nothing particular to say yet, but if I don't say something, you may begin to feel I'm not here' (Guntrip, 1975 cited in Symington, 1986: 308).
5 See, for example, Grossmark's (2007) discussion of disruption of the group and its mindset as an opportunity for growth.
6 Ashbach and Schermer (1987), drawing on James (1982), describe the therapy group itself as a transitional object. First, the group gradually replaces the therapist as a source of succour and security. Second, though imagined into being, it is also a pre-existent reality. Third, 'under the proper circumstances it allows the membership to develop their cultural potential' – to play (p. 61).

7 The sympathetic system mobilises resources in response to stress – the fight-flight response; the parasympathetic facilitates rest. Schore (1994) suggests a balance between the two is optimal and the outcome of care-giving that is sensitive to the infant's coping capacities, thus facilitating 'optimal arousal'.
8 The hyperactivating and deactivating attachment pattern nomenclature is derived from Mikulincer and Shaver (2007).
9 Marrone and Glenn, both group analysts, invited Bowlby to take part in seminars at the Institute of Group Analysis in the 1980s. Marrone (1994) reports a lively group-analytic engagement in these discussions.
10 In traditional societies, family and tribal groups provide the secure base rather than any single care-giver (Van Ijzendoorn & Sagi (1999). A more recent, telling example of the group acting as a secure base is given by Ornstein (2012) who describe children in a concentration camp, having lost their adult caregivers, developing intense mutual attachment as a group; one, she suggests, that saved their sanity.
11 For a useful exploration of the use of attachment theory in the screening, placing and preparing of group members, see Marmarosh *et al.* (2013). Indeed this book, though not overtly influenced by a group-analytic approach, provides a useful guide to the application of many attachment-oriented concepts and perspectives within the context of group therapy.
12 Schore and Schore (2008), weaving together attachment, object relations, self-psychology and contemporary intersubjective relational theories informed by neuroscience and infant research, describes 'modern attachment theory' in terms of affect regulation. Since the process of developing a resilient self has shown itself to be an intersubjective process, therapy can, he suggests, be conceived of as a 'growth facilitating social environment' that promotes not only earned secure attachment but the expansion of right brain human unconscious.
13 Ofer's reference here is to Bion's 'O' – 'the truth of any object' (Symington & Symington, 1996): O does not fall in the domain of knowledge or learning save incidentally; it can 'become', but it cannot be 'known' (Bion, 1970: 26).

Chapter 7

Developments in group analysis
The 'other' approach[1]

Nick Barwick

Bion's basic assumptions

Wilfred Bion's initial interest in groups ran roughly concurrently with Foulkes's own (see Chapter 1 and the Northfield experiments). For Bion, as for Foulkes, 'the group is essential to the fulfilment of a man's mental life' (Bion, 1961/1989: 53). Unlike Foulkes, for Bion, this inseparability is fundamentally problematic:

> The individual is a group animal at war, not simply with the group, but with himself for being a group animal and with those aspects of his personality that constitute his groupishness.
>
> (p. 131)

In response to such conflict, argues Bion, the group deploys collaborative defences. These defences undermine the group's capacity to think, to function as a 'work group' (W), cultivating instead a primitive 'group mentality' that manifests itself in the form of basic assumptions (ba) – shared, unconscious beliefs about a group's function/purpose, characterised by shared behaviour. Bion identifies three such assumptions.

Basic assumption dependency (baD)

In baD, the assumption is the group meets to make the group feel safe. To this end, it invests omnipotent and omniscient qualities in its leader. In such a dependency 'culture', where a timeless quality allays separation-anxiety, the remaining membership becomes de-skilled. Sometimes, particular members become identified as especially inadequate and in need of care.

Basic assumption fight-flight (baF)

In baF, the group meets to preserve itself. This is done by fighting the enemy – an idea or person(s) usually identified as being outside the group – or flight. Profoundly anti-intellectual, all introspective behaviour is eschewed lest awareness of internal differences (within self and/or group) leads to conflict and feared destruction. Any member challenging this culture is vulnerable to attack. This includes the leader whose role is to identify dangers and lead the charge/flight. A leader refusing this role may be replaced by one more responsive to the group's paranoid demands.

Basic assumption pairing (baP)

In baP, the group invests hope in two or more people 'getting together' and coming up with the 'solution'. In this way, the rest of the group protects itself from anxieties related to thinking and working. In particular, it protects itself from change (with all its potential losses, conflicts and catastrophes), since what is achieved is hope of a solution rather than the solution itself. Indeed, a pair/working party that proffers a solution is rarely welcomed. Thus Bion refers to baP hope as 'Messianic'; hope that 'must never be fulfilled' since, 'Only by remaining a hope does hope persist' (ibid.: 151–152).

Bion/Foulkes, Foulkes/Bion: a brief study of difference

Bion's essentially pessimistic, Thanatos-driven group (Schermer, 1985/2000) contrasts strikingly with Foulkes's essentially optimistic, Eros-driven one. For Bion, in the face of group regressive pull, the individual's capacity to contribute creatively is severely limited. Group pressure provokes individual 'valency' – a person's propensity for picking up and acting out particular types of projections (e.g. aggression or dependency) and a consequent 'readiness to enter into combination with another in making and acting on the basic assumptions' (Bion, 1961: 116). Said individual thus soon becomes 'trapped, and has a fight on his hands to achieve being an individual' (Hinshelwood, 2007: 349). Indeed, the only individual with a fighting chance of springing the trap is the group 'leader'. Offering group-as-a-whole interpretations, the therapist/leader strives to make conscious the forces preventing learning and change, enabling members better to manage their 'disharmonious experience of being group animals' (p. 353).

The fact that so much power resides in the leader evokes a political analogy, namely, whereas Bion's group-thinking develops within a somewhat authoritarian, hierarchical paradigm, Foulkes's develops within a paradigm marked by a more democratic, equalising vision. This description, however, though helpful in capturing an essential difference between the two approaches, is also an oversimplification. After all, it was the very lack of attention that Bion gave to the authorities at Northfield (see Chapter one) that led to the speedy demise of his experiments there. Further, in fairness, unlike Foulkes, who was concerned with the therapeutic group and helping the burdened individual within it, following Northfield, Bion became more interested in training/learning groups than therapy groups and himself remained unconvinced about the therapeutic efficacy of his approach (Bion, 1952/1989).

The application of Bion's group-thinking to group therapy continued to be developed nonetheless and, closely associated with Ezriel (1950, 1952, 1973), became known as 'the Tavistock model'. Highly 'group-centred', it demonstrated itself to be a powerful way of understanding primitive processes at work in groups. However, as a therapeutic approach, outcome studies (Malan *et al*., 1976) revealed high levels of patient dissatisfaction, especially concerning perceived 'therapist detachment' – a seeming lack of interest in individuals which many patients found (re)-traumatising. This study helped prompt modifications; for example, Horwitz's 'inductive approach' (Horwitz, 1977).

The Groups Book (Garland, 2010) describes further recent modifications of the Tavistock model: a 'pragmatic' approach and 'a flexible integration of Bion's theory of group process and his psychoanalytic approach to understanding the material, with a clinical style that owes more to Foulkes' (Hume, 2010: 126). This means greater sensitivity to individual needs (described elsewhere by Hinshelwood (2007) as 'narcissistic' needs) and a willingness to move between individual and group interpretations. Indeed the group itself is recognised as having 'great value as a therapeutic medium' so that:

> when the group is getting on with its task and the individuals in it are facing their problems and allowing themselves to know and be known by each other, we do not seek to dig out and identify basic-assumption activity.
>
> (Hume, 2010: 126)

There is evidence here of a less familiar, more optimistic Bion; a Bion who, contrasting his view with that of Le Bon (1895) (see Chapter 1) – that 'the group never thirsts after truth' – concludes that, 'despite the influence of the basic assumptions, and sometimes in harmony with them, it is the work group that triumphs in the long run' (Bion, 1952/1989: 169).

Deeply rooted differences (and rivalries) between Tavistock and Group-analytic models have made integration difficult. Nevertheless, coming from the Tavistock camp, *The Groups Book*, though clearly contrasting Bion's 'magnificent contribution' with Foulkes's 'lesser' input (Garland, 2010: 1), is a significant step in an integrative direction.[2] Even so, despite the 'pragmatism' described, despite a statement of hope in the group's own capacity to be therapeutic, evident in the focus on the therapeutic impact of therapist interpretations – interpretations that, more often than not, are transference interpretations – there is a sense that the creative power for initiating change remains in the therapist/leader rather than the group. Given the residual basic premise upon which even modified, more group optimistic 'Tavistock' approaches are built – a view of 'group mentality' wedded to Thanatos – this is not entirely surprising.[3] With this in mind, it is now time to look at group analysis's own efforts at integration.

Behind Bion's basic assumptions

Brown (1985/2000) suggests ba phenomena are common in hierarchically structured groups. The Tavistock model, with its locus of power in the 'sphinx-like' leader (a reference here to Bion's analogy of a leader perceived as 'the enigmatic, brooding, and questioning sphinx (in the Oedipal myth) from whom disaster emanates' (Bion 1952/1989: 162), is just such a group. In contrast, in a group-analytic group, the conductor, encourages 'spontaneous interaction and communication at many levels' – that is not just at the level of projection – and offers a 'flexible attitude which conveys . . . a democratic spirit' (Brown, 1985/2000: 210). Indeed, the conductor's interpretative restraint, coupled with efforts to transfer expert authority to the group, helps promote 'mutuality and joint endeavour' rather than hierarchy. This promotes a culture, Brown argues, less prone to ba activity.

Nevertheless, basic assumption theory has much to offer group analysis. Since all basic assumptions may be expressions of, or reactions against, some primary state 'springing from an extremely early and primitive primal scene' (Bion, 1961/1989: 164) – that is, the child's traumatising real or fantasised witnessing of parental intercourse – Brown (1985/2000) notes that such a scene is the 'archetypal provoker of feelings of exclusion' (p. 201). Hence, 'if the reality of belonging to a group does involve facing up to jealousy, envy and the frustration of dyadic dependency, it is not surprising that primitive fantasies and anxieties of this type are stirred up in an analytic group' (ibid.).

By relating ba activity to the dynamics of exclusion, Brown offers a less Thanatos-driven take on ba states. BaD is reframed as regression into mother-child merger as a defence against frustration and loss arising from the presence of others; baF becomes a way of denying rivalries for the good object by mass(ive) projection of aggression on/into objects outside the group; and baP idealises longed-for coupling while, because of its forever-in-the-future nature, protecting the self from envious feelings and the idealised object from envious attack. Such relational re-framing allows the conductor, faced with ba activity, to focus less on group-as-a-whole interpretations of primitive defences and more on encouraging communication about relational anxieties and struggles.

A note on the oedipal situation

In classical psychoanalysis, the primal scene is a precursor of the Oedipus Complex. Indeed, a post-Kleinian take sees both Oedipus Complex and primal scene as part of a broader 'oedipal situation'. The infant/child is confronted with the reality of loss – of the loved object's undivided attention. The question then becomes, 'Will our love survive knowledge?' (Britton, 1985/1992: 45). If we trust it will, we can look, with hope, towards the shared social world. If our doubt is greater, however, we are likely to take refuge in the 'cultivation of illusions': a retreat into the neuroses of individualism, predicated as it is on hallucinatory capacity to satisfy self.

Nitsun (1994) considers the 'primal scene' to be 'metaphorically, humanly ... at the centre of the group' (p. 129). For example, when, following one-to-one assessments, a group begins, all members face the reality of sharing. Such sharing, echoing the loss of exclusive possession of the loved object, may re-evoke attendant anxieties, including paranoid fears of annihilation. Similar anxieties/fears re-emerge throughout the group's life. For example, each new member/baby born out of the therapist's coupling with that which is outside the group may re-evoke them. As Foulkes suggests, 'Coping with the arrival of an infant activates regression on the part of all family members' (Foulkes, 1972/1990: 238). Hence the group may experience both the threat inherent in such events *and* the opportunity to work through unresolved issues within the transference situation. Further, because the group may be unconsciously associated with the mother's body (a view with which both Foulkes and Bion concur), the very process of enquiry into the group's dynamic activity may stir anxieties related to the primal scene – the paranoid-schizoid fear of discovering part of father inside mother (a reference to the terrifying combined parent figure (Klein, 1929/1988)) with its associations of retaliatory attack.

Drawing on an object relations understanding of oedipal configurations in this way deepens the group-analytic understanding of the intra-psychic drama played out in groups. Some would suggest that this has important implications for practice. For example, Halton (1999), identifying the central emergent conflict in group therapy as being one 'between the desire for (or the fear of) an exclusive one-to-one relation with the therapist, and the maintenance of a link with other group members' (p. 86), suggests the psychic disturbances thus generated, and the intrapsychic and group defensive phantasies deployed to manage them, mean that a classical Foulkesian conductor (he or she of the 'light touch') not only 'places a burden on the group members which they are often ill-equipped to carry' (p. 83) but also elicits a therapeutic journey where 'the reality of generational differences and the oedipal situation is evaded' (p. 77). Halton thus calls for the therapist to be 'active interpretatively' and to recognise the need to work in the transference (in particular the Transference – i.e. towards the therapist) with underlying paranoid anxieties (p. 80). He also suggests associated criteria for selection, commenting that those best suited for a group will 'have some capacity to bear the rage and envy aroused by exclusion' (p. 88); in other words, drawing on Britton (1989), 'people for whom an awareness of the primal scene, and of the link between the parents, produces a "psychic trauma" rather than a "psychic catastrophe"' (Halton, 1999: 88).[4]

Many group analysts would, to some extent, be sympathetic with Halton's criticisms. Yet most would also see the intra-psychic drama described here as an existential and social drama too: *existential* in that it embodies essential human notions of belonging and longing, inclusion and exclusion, the hope of creativity and the painfulness of loss; *social* because it deals with our efforts to come to terms with the nature of group/social processes, the developmental differentiating sequence of which group-analytic therapy seeks to promote. As such, though there are times for the conductor to take a more robust, active, even interpretatively active stance (including working actively in the Transference), for most group analysts, the Foulkesian objective of a gradual, overall decrescendo in the expert authority of the conductor remains both a viable and vital part of the group-analytic venture.

Beyond Bion's basic assumptions

Following Bion, three other basic assumptions have been posited:

- *Oneness (baO)* – where individuals 'surrender self for passive participation ... lost in oceanic feelings of unity' (Turquet, 1974: 357–360);
- *Me-ness* (baM) – 'a culture of selfishness in which individuals appear to be only conscious of their own personal boundaries, which they believe have to be protected from any incursion by others' (Lawrence *et al.*, 1996: 100);
- *Incohesion: Aggregation/Massification* (baI:A/M) (Hopper, 1997) (see below).

The first two are from the Tavistock stable, the latter from group analysis. Our focus, then, is on the latter. However, BaM has also been of particular interest to some group analysts and warrants brief mention first.

Basic assumption me-ness (BaM)

BaM – referred to by Lavie (2007) as a 'group-analytic basic assumption' – is a socio-culturally specific form of group mentality arising out of a crisis of faith in the reliability of the big, hitherto containing structures/institutions of state and religion. In baM – a state of 'socially induced schizoid withdrawal' (Lawrence, 1996/2000: 99) where the only thing trusted is the self – the emergence of group identity is feared, threatening as it does the defensive sanctuary of individualism. Consequently, 'groupishness' is denied, shared issues are replaced by private matters and emotional engagement (dangerous because who knows what interdependence might result) by detached objectivity: 'If I were angry I would say X'. This type of exchange, Lawrence refers to as presenting a 'photograph' rather than speaking from experience. Group culture 'is ordered, calm, polite, and androgynous' (p. 110). It is also futile.

Basic assumption incohesion: aggregation/massification (BaI:A/M)

(Ba)I:A/M (Hopper, 1997) combines characteristics of baO and baM in an oscillating configuration[5] but with an underpinning model of mind derived from the Independent rather than Kleinian tradition. Here, envy (and the forces of Thanatos), rather than being primary, are re-framed as defensive derivatives of the virtually universal human experience of helplessness provoked by interpersonal environments that fail to provide adequate security and developmental succour. In short, (ba)I:A/M describes a group state arising out of shared traumatising experiences that have, at their centre, fears of annihilation, of falling apart, of fatal 'incohesion'. Such fears arise out of the experience either of absence of holding/containing contact or of highly invasive/engulfing contact. Both experiences threaten identity's roots, giving rise to 'contact-shunning' (where the experience has been invasive) or 'merger-hungry' (where the experience has been abandoning) behaviours.[6]

A group's contact-shunning behaviour Hopper calls 'aggregation': 'a collection of people who have absolutely no consciousness of themselves as being members of a particular social system' (2009: 220). Characterised by 'too much individuality', the group may fall into uncommunicative silence, failing even to engage each other's gaze. In contrast, 'merger-hungry' behaviour, Hopper calls 'massification': cohesion achieved through lack of differentiation; a pseudo-cooperation or 'pulling together' motivated by inability to endure difference rather than commitment to creative connection.

Oscillation between the two states occurs because both aggregation and massification, though providing temporary relief from fear of annihilating incohesion, also give rise to it. Thus, though individuals experience identity protected when the group functions as an aggregate, they also experience threats of annihilation rooted in trauma of abandonment and/or neglect.

In (ba)I:A/M, some group members may adopt certain roles. For example, the 'lone wolf' (typical of aggregation) is adopted by those with crustacean (contact-shunning) character structures. Such members 'personify' aggregation processes, just as those with amoeboid (merger-hungry) structures may personify massification processes by adopting roles such as 'cheerleader'. Both roles draw on group aggression: the lone wolf manifesting this in cold, over-contained behaviour; the cheerleader through attacks on that which is 'other', calling for 'fatal purification of that which is different'. For this reason, 'The personification of this basic assumption must not only be met with containment and holding forever, but also subjected to understanding and interpretation' (p. 227). In the context of the Bionian tendency to interpret and the Foulkesian tendency to 'hold', this exhortation reflects Hopper's efforts to integrate at the level of theory *and* technique.

The anti-group

The anti-group is a group-analytic construct encapsulating all 'destructive processes that threaten the functioning of the group' (Nitsun, 1996: 1). Heavily informed by object relations theory, in particular basic assumptions and the concept of container-contained, it is a construct intended to counter-balance Foulkes's 'sometimes blinkered optimism' (Nitsun, 2015: 3).[7] A product of multiple, toxic, uncontained projections provoked by the universal, conflicted experience and concomitant annihilatory anxieties around belonging – the fact that the individual is a 'group animal at war' (Bion, 1961/1989), anxious about surviving in a group, about the group surviving and about the environment containing the group surviving (Nitsun, 2015) – it is an expression of Bion's group mentality. Basic assumptions, being a product of such mentality, are thus seen as specific forms of anti-group resulting from a failure of containment:

> Through projective identification, the failed group becomes impregnated with chaotic and persecutory elements of the uncontained, leaving the membership floundering in a morass of unprocessed and unresolved experience.
> (Nitsun, 1996: 66)

Indeed, suggests Nitsun, basic assumption groups do not really function as groups since coherent intra-group relatedness is absent. Rather, primitive, illusory dyadic relationships prevail; ones that are 'linear' (characterised by reaction and projection) rather than 'spatial' (characterised by reflection and integration) (Barwick, 2004). In baD, the undifferentiated group mass looks to its leader; in baF, it looks away from (or against) its enemy; in baP, gripped by bemused and/or expectant paralysis, it looks on.

In drawing on Bion, Nitsun does not, however, turn away from Foulkes. For example, in contrast to the Bionian emphasis on group-as-a-whole interventions, Nitsun advocates addressing all levels of the interactive system: individual, subgroup and group-as-a-whole. Further, while Bion's approach emphasises the 'unending cycle of regression and destructiveness' (Nitsun, 1996: 68), Nitsun, though noting these potentialities, emphasises the opportunities successful anti-group containment presents for mobilising group creative processes.

In considering how to successfully 'handle' the anti-group, Nitsun considers two forms of anti-group manifestation – pathological and developmental – and re-visits the conductor's influence upon these.

Handling the pathological anti-group

Nitsun cautions selecting members likely to contribute to pathological anti-group developments. For example, contra-indicated are highly aggressive individuals, particularly within a borderline personality constellation, and isolated, schizoid individuals who, in repressing rage and envy, may inhibit expression of these feelings in the group. Such inhibition encourages the anti-group to fester rather than find containment in articulation. Nevertheless, Nitsun recommends assessment according to principles of 'group membership and commitment' rather than conventional diagnostic and personality categories. Of particular relevance here are:

- *bonding capacity*, for which Adult Attachment Interviews (George *et al.*, 1985) provide a useful assessment instrument

- *passion for proximity* (Mendez *et al.*, 1988) as opposed to 'aversion to proximity' in interpersonal situations
- *group-object relations* – Nitsun's (1996) own term describing how individuals perceive and relate to groups.

The conductor's capacity to handle anti-group manifestations depends greatly upon his attitude *to* the anti-group. For example, a conductor unattuned to negative group processes is likely to prompt repression rather than expression of them, leading to potentially more insidious, pathological anti-group activity. Linked to a conductor's capacity to attune will be his attitude towards aggression. Is it seen as potentially creative or simply destructive? Such attitudes are rooted in both personal history and theoretical stance.

Acknowledging contradictions, limitations and complexities inherent in groups[8] helps members *reflect on* rather than *react to* them. 'Maintaining the group position' (p. 176) – that is, resisting the anti-group tendency to focus simply on individuals – is also crucial. So too, given the anti-group's propensity for 'attacks on linking' (Bion, 1959/1984) – a fragmenting, defensive mental activity that splinters connections between thought and feeling and between people – is the conductor's capacity to maintain his own 'linking function' (see Gordon, 1994; Hinshelwood, 1994).

Making meaningful connections is, essentially, an interpretative activity. Distinguishing between the conductor's 'broadly interpretative function' (e.g. making connections between non-conscious aspects of group communication) and 'focused interpretation' (addressing unconscious phenomena related to deeply rooted anxiety-defence constellations), Nitsun (1996) notes the former is widely valued in group analysis; the latter, less so. However, in the context of the anti-group, traditional interpretative reticence needs modifying since 'sensitively judged' focused interpretations congruent with the language, themes and metaphors of the group can ameliorate anti-group forces. Addressing individuals, prior to offering group-as-a-whole interpretations of underlying traumas prompting the anti-group, is an aspect of such 'sensitivity'. This approach can be deeply resonant and have a 'groupifying' effect (Anthony, 1983).

Overall, in the face of the anti-group, especially when latent challenges to and conflicts with authority appear present, the conductor needs to take a robust, interpretative stance in order to bring these dynamics to light before they erupt into the manifest level in ways that 'derail the group and leave the members and the conductor, reeling' (Nitsun, 2009: 329). Even so, Nitsun strikes a cautionary note:

> The anti-group is a sign that the therapeutic alliance in the group, often in relation to the conductor, has broken down, and with it, the capacity for reflection and insight. Making an interpretation in this context. . . . may therefore be counterproductive, fuelling rather than assuaging some of the primitive forces that generate the anti-group.
>
> (1996: 180)

The anti-group, being characterised by an accumulation of aggressive responses springing from a variety of sources, requires the conductor to work towards a deconstruction of such 'defensive agglomerations'. Utilising the concept of 'location' helps trace aggression's concealed sources, making them more available to communicative process. Understanding aggression in terms of the developmental stage of the group (Gans, 1989) – for example, the aggressive response that results from 'stranger anxiety' in the early part of a group or when new members join as opposed to aggression related to the struggle for control characteristic of a later stage – can also be helpful in working out how to draw hostile feelings into the communicative process. So too can an appreciation of how aggression defends against anxiety, or against the vulnerability experienced in the face of loss or intimacy or against the painful frustration of relationship needs (Rosenthal, 1987). Often, to bring aggression within the field of communication, the conductor usefully draws it towards himself. This can provide a useful containing and modelling experience for the group (Tuttman, 1994).

The anti-group is an 'autistic' aspect of the group, saturating primitive levels of communication. The conductor relies heavily, therefore, on his counter-transference when working with it; that is, he must be sensitive to and containing of the resonances evoked and provoked in him. Although this containing capacity is, in ordinary group development, a function of the group, when the anti-group dominates, it is the function of the conductor. However, the anti-group also challenges a conductor's capacity to contain, in part because he is likely to identify himself with the group – it is his baby – and narcissistic over-identification can, in the wake of anti-group fragmentation, provoke devastating loss of confidence in both himself and the group.

Handling the developmental anti-group

The anti-group may also be construed as developmental phenomenon. For example, certain individuals/subgroups may adopt a contrary position that aggravates the rest of the group. To re-frame such anti-group activity as projections of the group-as-a-whole and to encourage acknowledgement and integration of them can be an important developmental step. Indeed, the capacity to 'survive' the anti-group may itself be transformational. Not only does it lead to a more realistic evaluation of destructiveness (i.e. aggression is containable and not necessarily catastrophe-inducing), it may also lead to shared responsibility for the group and desire to make creative reparation (Klein, 1952/1988). Further, in promoting confidence in the container's robustness, the group becomes available for object usage (Winnicott, 1971/1974), paving the way, within the group transitional space, for 'freer use of imagination, thought, and feeling, and, in particular, the exercise of play' (Nitsun, 1996: 63).

More broadly, the anti-group can be framed within a dialectical perspective: a perspective that sees tension (between opposites) as the basis of transformation:

A dialectical imagination invites us to embrace contradiction and flux as defining features of reality . . . encouraging us to recognise that the parameters of organisation define the rallying points for disorganisation, that control always generates forces of counter-control, and that every success is the basis of a potential downfall.

(Morgan, 1986: 265)

Drawing on Ogden (1992a, 1992b), (who describes psychopathology as a collapse of this dialectic in one direction), Nitsun (1996) describes anti-group and 'pro-group' as 'two poles of experience that define the development of the group' (p. 204). It is not the presence of the anti-group that is pathological but a collapse of the dialectic in the direction of destructive processes. Similarly, a collapse in the direction of pro-group cohesive forces, leaving destructive forces denied, split off and projected, also threatens development. Thus, from this dialectical perspective, the matter is no longer Bion versus Foulkes but Bion *and* Foulkes as group analysis becomes 'a way of dealing with Eros and Thanatos in an endless ebb and flow' (Cortesao, 1991: 271).

Other 'other' approaches

For reasons of both brevity and bias, any overview is prone to omissions. Among the most significant in this 'mainly theory' section of this book is the limited reference to contributions from outside psychoanalysis. For example, historically, a fuller account would include the influence of systems theory (Bertalanffy, 1968; Miller, 1969; Bateson, 1972) and particularly its continued elaboration in the work of Agazarian (Agazarian & Peters, 1981; Agazarian & Gantt, 2000). Although the 'systematic dialogue' with systems-oriented group therapists that Foulkes hoped for (see Durkin, 1983) never emerged, the influence of systems thinking, being present from the start in Goldstein's work on the neuronal network, though rarely explicit, has been pervasive. Readers interested in pursuing these ideas are directed to Blackwell's (1994) useful introduction as well as more recent discussions (Brown, 2003; Gantt & Hopper, 2008a, 2008b; Schermer, 2012a, 2012b).

Two radicalising challenges to mainstream group analysis also demand brief reference, namely Dalal's post-Foulkesian perspective (1998, 2001, 2002a & b) and Stacey's theory of 'complex responsive processes' (2000, 2001, 2003, 2005).

Radicalising Foulkes

Some of Dalal's important contributions to a group-analytic understanding of the social unconscious have already been mentioned (see Chapter 2) as has his distinction between orthodox and radical Foulkes. Allying himself with the latter, Dalal draws more deeply upon the work of Elias (1939/2000, 1989/1991; Elias & Scotson, 1965/1994). Thus the 'individual' mind is construed not only as being formed by the social nexus in which it develops (an Eliasian idea Foulkes readily adopts) but that social nexus is characterised by social power relations (an idea that Elias emphasises but Foulkes does not). It is these power relations that profoundly influence how we think about, experience and relate to ourselves and each other.

The social unconscious, in which power relations are both enshrined and denied, feeds our assumptions about difference, allowing groups to use power to reinforce their dominance over other groups. A central, radical, post-Foulkesian task then is to pursue awareness of the dynamics of the social unconscious: 'progressively to stand outside the context we are inside in order to scan it, to enter another context, ad infinitum' (Brown, 2003: 159). In response, however, Hopper (2002), though appreciating the need to 'be sensitive to the constraints of the external world' suggests that:

> We must not adopt an overly socialised model of man without instincts, drives, sensations and physiology, not to mention passion, who is merely a figment of the imagination of powerful others. I would not like to be a patient of a group analyst who regarded people in this way.
>
> (p. 334)

Complexity theory

Stacey draws on complexity sciences (Nicolis & Prigogine, 1989) as a 'source domain' for analogies and, translating these into human terms using the work of social psychologists Mead (1934) and Elias (1989), and 'language psychologists' Bhaktin (1986) and Vygotsky (1962), elaborates the Foulkesian idea that individual minds and social relationships arise together. Again, in accord with radical Foulkes, there is no room for 'internal' (the inner world of the individual) or the 'external' (the outer world of society) – not separately. However, while Foulkes appears content to modify internal world psychoanalytic concepts such as the unconscious, transference and countertransference to meet a more socially contextualised perspective, Stacey recasts them as forms of 'complex responsive processes'. Projective identification, containment and even the matrix share the same fate.

Behr and Hearst (2005), though broadly appreciative of this 're-working' – foregrounding as it does the importance of communication, of evolving patterns of interaction, of the illusory nature of separating inner from outer – question its absolutism and suggest its unrelenting translation of psychoanalytic theory into the more elaborate language of complex responsive processes potentially diminishes, rather than revitalises, the processes it describes.

Conclusion

The journey this brief theoretical introduction to group analysis has taken, from its conceptual birth in Goldstein's neurological post WWI studies, to its recent radical twenty first century elaboration in the wake of complexity sciences, has been a long, winding, though necessarily, adumbrated one. Characterised by a spirit of eclecticism, group anlaysis's efforts to 'accommodate' theoretical diversity can, at times, threaten cohesion.[9] Yet, despite this diversity, a fundamental coherence remains; one rooted in the principle of interconnectedness, in a profound, shared understanding that group and individual are inextricably entwined.

Notes

1 This slightly mischievous subtitle is not intended to suggest there are only two therapeutic approaches to groups or indeed only two psychoanalytically-informed approaches. (For a brief and informative summary of the latter see Schlapobersky (2016: 205–217). This includes a useful digest of Rutan, Stone and Shay's (2014) systematic comparison of leader activity and focus across models.) Nevertheless, in the UK at least, two psychoanalytically based group approaches do predominate: group analysis and, based on the work of Bion, the Tavistock model. In this context, the term 'other' intimates a complex historical rivalry between these two 'schools', one which, though having its source in real and significant differences has also, I believe, been complicated by the dynamic processes of splitting and projection. I have also made brief reference to this rivalry elsewhere (Barwick, 2015).

2 Garland is herself an interesting figure in the context of the rivalries described. A group analyst and author of a seminal group-analytic paper still widely referred to (1982), she later trained as a psychoanalyst and became a significant figure at the Tavistock. In *The Groups Book*, however, there is no mention of her group-analytic background.

3 The Tavistock's own group psychotherapy training requires of its trainees personal individual psychotherapy rather than group. This alone, perhaps, says something of a fundamental suspicion of the group; a lack of trust in its capacity to be a good enough therapeutic object.

4 Halton (1999) adds to his selection criteria those for whom a facilitated self-help model is appropriate and those whose difficulties are much more severe and for whom 'one-to-one relationships threaten to evoke terrors of engulfment, dismemberment, and profound loss of ego-identity.' In the latter instance, the group acts as 'a mediating factor against the terror of a mad internal primal object, or horrifying combined objects' (p. 89). Such patients often present as severely phobic, schizoid or borderline.

5 Cano (1998) also suggests baO and baM function 'alternately and indifferently'. She thus re-formulates baO and baM as one basic assumption: basic assumption Grouping (baG). A group in the throes of baG fantasises total union or total self-sufficiency instead of wrestling with the painful, risky business of trying to achieve realistic interdependence.

6 The emphasis on forms of 'environmental deficit' as the essential ingredient in traumatising experience does not necessarily deny the contribution of the particular 'sensitivity' with which some people are born. As Wood (2016) notes, recent developments in neurobiology and genetics have demonstrated 'certain genotypes, in combination with certain kinds of intrauterine experience, lead to some people being predisposed to experiencing as overwhelming and traumatising what to others might be normal and manageable degrees of frustration and threat' (p. 238).

7 The view of Foulkes as over-optimistic is one that has gained considerable ground since his death, even to the point of becoming mainstream. Recently, Schermer (2012b), assessing Foulkesian thinking in the light of complexity theory, suggests

it offers 'a one-sided view that emphasises orderly patterns and wholeness at the expense of the chaotic, entropic and destructive aspects of living systems' (p. 490). Nitzgen (2013c), however, challenges this, emphasising Foulkes's acknowledgement, uncomfortable though it was, of Freud's death instinct and 'the truth and usefulness of the concept of a primary self-destructive force' (Foulkes, 1964: 138–139). For him, any neglect of 'the darker, more destructive and chaotic aspects of group life with its ubiquitous failures of translation, continuous breakdowns of communication and imminent collapse of meaning' (Nitzgen, 2013: 323) is the product of Post-Foulkesian group analysis, not Foulkes himself.

8 Smith and Berg (1988) note that it is well nigh impossible to have a group devoid of conflict since contradictory processes of progression and regression, individuality and belonging, attachment and alienation occur in tension in most groups. In therapy groups, where members are more likely to experience relational difficulties, such conflict may be even more acute. Nitsun (1996) also identifies ten group-analytic group characteristics that can aggravate tensions and stimulate the anti-group: the group is a collection of strangers; is unstructured; is created by its members; is a public arena; is a plural entity; is a complex experience; creates interpersonal tensions; is unpredictable; fluctuates in its progress; is an incomplete experience (pp. 48–54).

9 That two prominent group analysts, Vella (1999) and Stacey (2000, 2001), bridging the millennium, envisage very diverse approaches to group analysis – the latter challenging its psychoanalytic foundations, the former arguing a return to Freud – nicely captures the strain on group-analytic cohesion that diversity brings. Nitsun (2015) also notes how creative theoretical expansiveness, especially when 'not adding ballast to clinical practice' can 'attenuate the fragile fabric of group analysis' (p. 64).

Part II

Mainly practice

Chapter 8

Working with(in) groups
A dialogue

Martin Weegmann and Nick Barwick

MW: I'd like to start with the question, what do you think are the essential qualities that are required to be an effective group analyst?

NB: Empathy, authenticity, trustworthiness. I'd start with these. There's a clear correlation between group members' experience of such qualities in their conductor and 'therapeutic success'. However, experience is co-created. Qualities such as these are only realised when discovered. This reminds me of a colleague's story of a particularly challenging, rejecting, grudge-ridden group with which he'd been struggling for some time. Then, one day, as the group reviewed their work, a consensus formed: that though the group members had made little progress, the previously inadequate therapist had become much warmer, more available and better at his job!

The qualities of a group analyst are clearly important then, but I think we need to keep thinking of them within the relational context within which they are 'realised' – the wider membership of the group. Indeed, research suggests (Vlastelica *et al.*, 2003) that, in the end, most group members identify their peers as being most helpful, and not their therapist alone. To me, this fits perfectly a group-analytic perspective; that is, it's the group, not the analyst, that's the principle agent of change. If this is so, then any qualities that help make a group analyst effective must be ones that help him cultivate a therapeutically effective group.

How does this fit with your thoughts Martin? Do you agree in principle?

MW: Yes, absolutely. I'd say, for me, that the following are essential qualities for a conductor in helping create an effective group. First, that acquired competence and confidence in being able to 'lead' – we would rather say 'conduct' – in bringing a group of people together in a meaningful activity, in this case psychotherapy. They need to be able to 'look after' the group as a whole while keeping each member in mind, and value the vast diversity of contributions. To use an optical analogy, one can say that one needs a wide angle lens and a close focus. Being able to cultivate a 'culture of inquiry' is central too, which means nurturing the group so that its members are able to engage independently with the work.

The expression, 'distributed empathy', comes to mind. Another way of putting it is that the group conductor needs to have an encouraging, supportive presence, and to balance an active interest or involvement with an ability to know when (and for how long) to 'stand back'.

NB: And how would you characterise a therapeutically effective group then?

MW: Any group, even a single-session group can be effective if there is a shared confidence in the setting, the therapist and the ability of the members to relate well with each other. Of course, clarity about the purpose of the group is the framework within which all this comes together; groups need cohesion, which is the equivalent for groups that the good therapeutic alliance is for individual therapy. In a long-term group, the situation is somewhat different, insofar as people need considerable time and trust to fully bring themselves into the unfolding group dialogue, the 'life of the group'. I am reminded that 'trust' is related to 'touch' in etymology, and that both require 'tact' and 'timing'. If the group can get those elements 'right', then a great deal is accomplished.

More often than not, however, the process is gradual and faltering: one step forward, one step back. People simply need familiarity with each other, and the conductor, and the conviction that the group is a safe and effective place for exploration to take place. If it is, then good 'resonance and reciprocation', to use Dennis Brown's terms, are built. I have written of the progressive unfolding of communication and the need to encourage a richly layered, 'populated' matrix that replaces the thinner narratives and caution that is usually there at the beginning. This is perhaps another way of saying, as Schlapobersky has put it, of movement away from monologue, into the more established and confident dialogue and discourse. Even so, even the hypothetical beginning is where and when the work already starts. To this degree, I was amused and surprised to learn that the great Renaissance humanist, Erasmus, in producing new translations of the Bible, substituted the phrase, 'In the beginning was the conversation', as distinct from the usual, 'In the beginning was the Word'!

Nick, does this notion of an effective therapeutic group tally with yours?

NB: I just wanted to say first, I like this reference to Erasmus, Martin. Creation springs from dialogue and discourse, from interdependence, from intercourse; not from omnipotent monologue! Even if, in a group, monologue is often where we start from.

As for your description of an effective group – yes, I agree, though I'd like to add cohesion as a fundamental here; the group's capacity to stick together, to experience and depend upon its interpersonal bonds.

Foulkes's advice for conductors was 'trust the group' and this works equally well for group members. Such trust grows through the activity of sharing personal narratives (monologues even), vulnerabilities and through a growing sense of commonality and empathy as these are shared. For a therapeutic group to be effective though, there needs to be more than cohesion. To put it another way, cohesion isn't the whole house but the foundation upon which the house is built. If the group is founded on a robust, resilient trust that is synonymous with cohesion, what can be built is a capacity to tackle difference. In this way, the motto of the group shifts to include not only, 'we're sticking together because we're safe and feel a lot in common' (cohesion) but 'we're sticking together because we value the meaning we make with each other: the insights we gain when we work together, even when that work is difficult, painful, troublesome.' It is the latter motto that motivates the group as it ventures towards greater coherence.

An example:

> John, a man in his late thirties, had dropped out of two universities and several jobs. In the group, he re-enacted this tendency by dropping out either literally – through lateness and unplanned absences – or metaphorically – through communicating disinterest by means of bored demeanour, physical restlessness, dismissive comments and contemptuous air. Over a period of a year or so, the group held on to him despite frequent rebuffs, slowly helping him to give voice to feelings of inadequacy and fears of humiliation, rejection, shame. Such communications resonated in the group, finding an understanding among its members which was reparative, transforming his contempt-ridden, depressive isolation into a moving articulation of loneliness and eliciting in him a sense of both belonging and longing, the latter expressed in his desire for friendship with some group members beyond the therapy group.
>
> With the arrival of a new member, Ceri, he tried hard to tolerate her uncontained anxiety which showed itself in her tendency to dominate the group with talk, seemingly oblivious to others' needs. However, under the relentless current of her monologues (and occasional dialogues), John's efforts to remain engaged wore thin and, once more withdrawing, the presence only of his slow fuming silence remained. Prompted by the conductor's intervention – a wondering about the dynamic in which two members (Ceri and another) excitedly engaged in conversation while the rest said nothing – John exploded, attacking Ceri with accusations of self-obsession and insensitivity to others' needs. He simply didn't like her. And the prospect of working with her in this group felt impossible to imagine. However, as the exchange within the wider group unfolded, though his opinion of Ceri did not immediately change nor his despair about working with her, he added: 'But I'm also 90 percent sure it will get better'.

What I'm reminded of here is the hope that gets engendered in an infant as a consequence of repeated experiences of containment; the hope that experience, even when painful and disquieting, can be made meaningful. But this hope has to build over time and is vulnerable, particularly early in its development, to being overwhelmed. So, when you refer to the conductor acting with 'timing' and 'tact'

Martin, I take this to mean acting in a reasonably attuned way: attuned to the group's development of hope and capacity to make meaning, and measuring the strength of that hope and that capacity against the weight of difference it is asked to bear: difference that is therefore at once a threat to, and potential source of nourishment for, both individual and group.

MW: And do you have an example of a group which stopped being effective, or when reflective space was undermined? How so?

NB: In the context I've just outlined, my generalised example of an ineffective group, would be one whose sense of trust and cohesive capacity (a capacity and willingness to 'stick together') is inadequate to the weight of differences and associated anxieties/conflicts – real and fantasised – that it's required to bear. This leads either to a retreat into a defensive form of cohesion where communication becomes restricted and the group stagnates, or to a level of incoherence where the flood of difference and conflict ruptures bonds leading to the group falling apart.

For John, initially, it could be argued that the group was therapeutically ineffective. One could also argue that this was because he had insufficient trust in the group to find a way of voicing, rather than acting upon, his feelings. Yet, though John had insufficient trust, the group did not. It stuck with him and drew him into the dynamic matrix of the group.

When absences are widespread, the group itself can be seen as being ineffective, faltering. Here the anti-group reigns. This might be seen as happening in the group I describe in Chapter 11 where, after a particularly virulent form of malignant mirroring between Punya and Abisola, unplanned absences grew rife. Yet even here, though the group seemed near collapse and incapable of engaging in any reflective process, something about the absences and the intimate pairing they gave rise to, suggests the group unconsciously chose an 'enabling solution' (Whitaker & Lieberman, 1964); one which offered a degree of greater privacy in which vulnerabilities could more safely be exposed, explored, reflected upon. Only then were these vulnerabilities gradually woven back into the fractured fabric of the group-as-a-whole, as group members began to return in states of mind that allowed a wider reflective and, indeed, reparative engagement to take place.

As you can see, I'm having trouble finding an ineffective group per se, only periods of ineffectiveness which themselves, within an environment of sufficient trust (hard won by the work of the group, including its conductor) can become fuel for the growing creative resilience and psychic muscularity of the group. In the end, it's a matter of tension and release – at the heart of all compelling music and drama. Nevertheless, as I suggest in Chapter 11, in a group, as in music, tension unresolved leads to more tension and a sustained absence of resolution (the absence of a move to something more harmonious and coherent) can give rise to musical incoherence so extreme, no conductor or orchestra/group, be they ever-so post-modern/mature, can bear it.

So let me try once more for an example of an ineffective group, where reflective space is truly undermined:

> Some years ago, at an interview for the post of conductor of a self-reflective group (part of a psychotherapy training), one of the interviewers told me about how the previous year, one group, complaining the room was too cold to work in, exited on mass, leaving only the conductor behind. She then asked me how I might have dealt with such a situation.
>
> From what I gleaned, the group's complaint was not entirely without foundation. For some weeks, there had been a heating problem. Nevertheless, I suspected that there was much more meaning to be had in this 'acting out' than a response to faulty heating. Was there an overwhelming experience of lack of care, of holding? By the institution? By the conductor? Was the conductor experienced as cold, impervious to their needs? Had they themselves been feeling abandoned?
>
> All such aspects of curiosity, however, had no forum in which to be articulated. For that week at least, there was no real or reflective space to explore such possible meanings, to translate the symptom through 'the progressive unfolding of communication', since the analytic setting itself had been destroyed by 'strike action'. I could only suspect that this was because, at some profound level, the group-as-a-whole had lost hope in the efficacy of communication, which, as Foulkes suggests, is synonymous with the process of group therapy. Where there is insufficient hope that one can make oneself heard and that what is heard will be understood, strikes against self or other are inevitable.
>
> As for the bottom line of the interviewer's question: how might I have dealt with such a situation? To this, I had nothing to offer, only the hope that, at an earlier point in the group's unfolding, before hope itself had been lost, drawing upon my understanding of location and translation, I might have found a way of making some useful intervention.

I wonder what you make of the balance I describe Martin: between sameness and difference, between trusting the group and the importance of actively intervening when the group's capacity to trust and its cohesive properties appear to be overwhelmed/threatened by unresolved tensions in the group – by, to re-coin a Foulkesian phrase, 'an intolerable imbalance'? And could you give any examples of such imbalance, tolerable or intolerable, and how you gauge when and how to intervene or not?

MW: I like your emphasis on the balance, an essential tension as it were between 'group cohesion' and the 'further exploration' that is always in the offing and which may threaten established levels of comfort, security and predictability. This is the inherent paradox of any attachment process, that therapy offers to explore the insecurity that brings people for help in the first place. But then one hopes that, eventually, group members create a space in which they can 'explore in security', a phrase I borrow from Jeremy Holmes. Shakespeare puts it another way, pointing to our tendency to, 'bear those ills we have than fly to others that we know not of'.

Manageable tensions occur all the time, under our noses, insofar as every meeting of the group is a 'new time', and the space of communication that occurs therein is unique – even with a repetitive or 'stuck' dynamic there are small variations and micro developments. By contrast, whether a development is 'intolerable' or not is only known in retrospect. In this way, I agree with points made by the philosopher, Gadamer, who said that 'understanding' as an event happens in stages with an 'after time' – it catches one up, like a speaker 'gets' what is being said only during the course of a conversation. Many a situation or conflict appears catastrophic or irreparable when it first arises, like the situation in which two members of a group took a violent dislike to each other and hurled words of insult and offence. People, including myself, were worried this would lead to actual violence and one of the protagonists walked out, which I took to be a protective measure. However, both returned the next week, studiously avoiding eye contact or further exchange, at least for several groups. I had to remind them of a basic group norm – no violence. I have encountered many similar conflagrations, particularly in working with those with substance misuse and personality disorders, and particularly in groups where the members are very new to each other (e.g. a short-term group on a detoxification ward) or new to a setting that is frightening (e.g. someone with borderline personality disorder joining a residential therapeutic community). Sometimes there is a kind of 'joining crisis', with all its potential for hostility, storming out and fear-based reactions to or from peers. One witnesses emotional disregulation in live form.

A brief example:

> In a group for those in recovery from substance misuse, John increasingly pitched himself as an alternative leader, challenging every therapeutic aspiration of the group (including his own) and inviting members into a grim and aggressive fantasy of group destruction. What it would be like if they all jumped off an adjacent building and what would happen to me as a result? It would amount to my professional death as the therapist who presided over the group that committed collective suicide. This proved very challenging and there were many variations on the theme. John found it hard to bear his despondency and fear of relapse, and so wanted to bring others down with him. Ian, who had an actual history of suicidality, surprised the group when he retorted, "You jump if you want to, but fucking leave me out!"

So, even a group whose coherence and rationale is provided in a shared aim of recovery, can face enormous challenges when faced with feared or actual set back, such as relapse or despondency. I intervened when I judged that such fears needed to be re-stated, and realistic safety, or hope, re-established. That included re-stating group boundaries, such as a 'no violence' rule. But during the storm, when any reflective space does seem under attack, this is easier said than done. There are two therapeutic risks for the therapist: one is to over-react to what are really strong emotions and hot eruptions and which usually do not get out of hand (CBT therapists might call this 'catastophising') and the other is to minimise the situation and let it gather without comment, in which case it might *really* explode.

Thinking of a contrasting aspect, when, Nick, do we know a group is thriving and its members are getting what they need?

NB: First, I want to respond to your comment that the conductor only knows when a development is tolerable or intolerable in retrospect. You're right of course. To think otherwise is for the conductor to succumb to omniscient and omnipotent delusions – a component of the 'temptation to play God' that James Anthony (1991) warns against. Indeed, I can think of many occasions when my experience of a group 'event' being intolerable was, with hindsight, less to do with accurate therapeutic assessment and more to do with being a group member, penetrated and temporarily overwhelmed by fears and phantasies populating the matrix. Often, on returning to the group, I would find that, despite fears of fracture, the group-as-a-whole remained, at some profound level, capable of holding faith, of trusting its own capacity to contain, even when individuals (including myself) faltered.

Even so, experience as a therapist prompts me to make judgements about what is tolerable or intolerable. I find this so particularly early in a group's life. For example, in the group I describe in Chapter 10, fights broke out before the group itself had developed adequate cohesion to contain them. I believe that early dropouts may have been in part caused by such conflict, since they constituted, at least for some, an 'intolerable imbalance' rather than a 'tolerable' one. Certainly I was fascinated to hear a senior group analyst recall her own experience of such conflict and her own intervention in response to it along the lines of: 'I feel sure that this is a very important fight, not only for you [the two involved] but for the group. But not now.' A potent if not quite 'divine' intervention!

A more active, one might say, robust intervention is also called for if scapegoating appears to gather pace. For example:

> In a generally thoughtful, mature but rather 'well-behaved' group, Jack spoke with increasing virulence about the group's continued lack of direction, its lack of leadership in particular and, ultimately, a lack of genuine human care. The group responded initially with silence – the kind of awkward silence that involves gazing down at shoes, hoping that a spot of bad behaviour will go away. Sufficiently provoked, however, members finally began to counter with judgements regarding Jack's lack of appreciation of others, of insensitivity, and their observation that he seemed to be spoiling for a fight. Maybe he was right, they suggested; maybe he would be better going it alone.

Although, in many respects, agreeing with the group's analysis (Jack's fierce, independent – sometimes bloody-mindedness belied a history of hugely painful abandonment), I resisted the group's seductions and, instead of interpreting his behaviour, offered him an alliance. 'It seems very difficult,' I suggested, 'for us to hear just how uncared for Jack feels; how disappointed, angry and dissatisfied he is, especially with me. It seems we don't want to engage in his efforts to think about such things' (adding, in my mind, 'for fear, perhaps, that to do so might spoil the comforting experience of maturity which the group feels it has gained?').

And now, your question! 'When do we know a group is thriving and members are getting what they need?'

There are often those moments where a change in an individual's behaviour indicates that needs are being addressed, even if the process of addressing them is uncomfortable:

- Janet, a bright, young, middle-aged woman who, prior to the group, had spent three years in individual therapy exploring her relational difficulties (though always in a slightly detached, rationalised way) suddenly explodes at several group members who have been busily engaged exchanging stories about their lives. She manages to articulate some of her fury at what seems the impossibility of claiming a space among their competitive voicings. Moments later, she breaks down in tears saying, 'I don't have stories to tell like you. I just have this [her experience of never getting heard, of never belonging]!'
- George, a driven, extremely able young man who had spent much of his life resentfully trying to organise his 'dysfunctional and incompetent family', his fellow workers and more recently his anxiety-ridden girlfriend, for a while finds himself playing a similar role in the group, until so frustrated and furious with what he sees as the group's lack, he threatens to leave unless they reform. Returning the next week, he apologises for the manner of his outburst and, for the first time, manages to speak of his own need: his longing to be thought about and cared for.
- Aja, a young woman who, despite a recent attempt to kill herself and a series of admissions to A&E, professes a hardened independence – from others and, indeed, from her own affective life – for the first time tells of a gang rape when she was 11 (she had not told those who were caring for her at the time or anyone since) and for the first time, in the presence of others, finds herself shedding a few simple tears.
- Moznu, a man in his thirties, whose deep depression leaves him socially isolated, full of contempt for others whom he watches in judgement despite a desire to belong, begins to find himself listening to another, slightly younger man, even more isolated than himself. He shows concern; a concern that begins to draw him into engaging in an important aspect of the work of the group – helping others – as well as finding a way of tolerating, with greater

sympathy, a part of himself that he sees in this other. Through this, he discovers both an ability to make a difference and belong.

Yet these moments of movement on the part of individuals always occur within the dynamic matrix of the group. They are part of other changes and exchanges, of movement that happens in the relational processes at work. So, for example, Janet's cry of fury and for help is matched by the recognition, by some of those who have been verbally dominant, of how words can hide affective life as well as express it and how perhaps Janet's outburst is in some ways a shared outburst of other aspects of self that are feeling suffocated even within the verbally adroit.

An individual group member getting what they need is part, then, of the group getting what it needs; of the group-analytic process at work. It is difficult to imagine those moments of vital connection and communication happening without working through many difficult tensions within and between individuals and without imbalances within the group that may even be experienced as intolerable at times. Yet there are particularly productive moments when the long gestation of some aspects of the work emerges; moments where there is a shared experience of lives fitting together, of an aesthetic coherence, of community and belonging. At these times, as the group moves, with some fluidity, back and forth from past to present, from stories focusing on the inside of the group to the outside and back again, I find myself intervening, in an active way, relatively rarely. Instead, the group utilises its own 'expert authority', not as multiple therapists might, but as part of an organic process of communication. Although still different from my fellow members, I feel, at such times, as much group member as group therapist and experience the privilege of being part of a very human endeavour: an affectively rich exploration of the relationship between self and other, between other and other, developing within a culture of inquiry and compassion.

Do you have an illustration, Martin, of a group involved in the developing process of communication that Foulkes saw as being synonymous with therapy?

MW: Yes, and before offering it, I appreciate what you say about a long process of 'gestation' in groups and the importance of fluidity; that creative 'in between' where there is, to use the words of Gadamer again, a 'fusion of horizons' – not as an end point of group dialogue but as a part of many further, incomplete acts of understanding. Understandings and misunderstandings are a constant feature of the dialectic of group life.

The group in question was well-established and those to whom I refer were some of its members over a period of one to three years. It was a group that I particularly enjoyed, a point to which I shall return later.

> In this session, Peter and Claire found themselves in heated exchange, one that had been simmering for several weeks. Claire, 32, spoke, as she often did, of being psychologically crushed by her mother's carping comments, with whom she lived. Perhaps without fully realizing it, she aped her mother's

accent and discouragements, to which Peter, of similar age and depressed, angrily responded, "I'm sick of hearing about your bloody mother! She's not a member of this group, you are!! You play into her hands all the time and nothing will change unless you do. It's all moaning, that's all, and it gets us nowhere!" His voice was raised and Claire quickly retreated, with a look herself of suppressed anger and embarrassment.

To add something more of the context, Claire came into the group with a sense of life-long dissatisfaction and a wish to psychically, if not physically, separate from her mother. Peter, for his part, was stuck in a self-attacking depression, forever believing that others made progress in their lives at his expense. Another group member had previously described him as being at risk of building his whole life upon nursed resentments. He had not raised his voice before, and all were taken by surprise.

Meanwhile, Angela was visibly shocked, mumbling that it was all too uncomfortable. She was even tempted to leave early, but others encouraged her not to. She had a headache. Brought up in the unpredictability and chaos of an alcoholic household, two weeks later she was able to see and to say that the 'row', as she put it, between Peter and Claire, led to physical symptoms in the form of palpitations. She explained that it had reminded her of nasty verbal attacks at home and a fear that strong anger could lead to violence. Claire, by way of reply, said that it had felt awful at the time but that Peter was expressing his exasperation at how stuck and repetitive she must sound. Peter, for his part, said that Claire's position with her mother tapped into his own stuckness in life and temptation to hold others responsible for his own lack of progress.

Finally, the group's youngest member, Norman (25) said, in part-identification with Angela, that he was afraid of the expression of strong emotions, but for different reasons. He joined the group with an issue of long-standing inhibition and lack of confidence and unsureness about his life goals. Studying at the time, he confessed to a fantasy of shouting expletives at his lecturer and shocking the whole assembly with his invective. He expressed some admiration, therefore, that Peter was able to speak his mind and agreed with Angela that he had little ability to trust in angry feelings without them degrading into abuse or complete disinhibition.

So there you have some moments in the life of a mature group who are, I think, developing confidence in their ability to communicate and gaining in their ability to experience and survive major growing pains and sites of distress. I did say that I enjoyed this group, for two main reasons. First, it was a group that I had set up and nurtured, so there was some pride in this being an established, secure resource for group members and for the department in which I was practicing. Second, and perhaps more importantly, I enjoyed witnessing the developing confidence of group members to immerse themselves, explore and the reflect upon their interactions, adding depth and breadth to the matrix of group life.

Any thoughts?

NB: Only that I think this is a nice example of the kind of ordinary enriching interactions that take place in a mature group. By mature, I mean a group that has learned to access, express and meaningfully digest significant aspects of its affective life; to act, in other words both as provoker and container of experience, present and past, as the group works its way through what Schlapobersky (2016) refers to as the three dimensions – relational, reflective and reparative – of psychotherapy.

Your example also reminds me of Caroline Garland's (1982) observations. Group members, she says, bring their conscious 'problem' to the group seeking 'advice, encouragement and support'. The group encourages such 'confessions' – indeed demands them as part of the process of initiation into the group. Perhaps this is the case with Claire. She presents her perceived problem to the group: her mother's treatment of her.

Such disclosures tend, initially at least, to elicit sympathy. Often, other members venture some comparisons and contrasts with their own lives. In this way, through the sympathetic sharing of similarities and differences, the group develops greater trust and cohesion and, for all members, significant learning can emerge. When such narratives are repeatedly presented though, sympathy may wear thin and irritation, frustration, resentment and anger may emerge.

So it is with Peter. He responds to Claire with an angry outburst. This feeling has been 'simmering'. We learn later that he is angry not so much with Claire's stuckness as with his own and the resentment it brings. What he has seen in Claire is a mirror image of himself. We learn also that Peter's anger resonates within the broader group matrix. Both Angela and Norman have associated narratives to share. Without any explicit intervention from the conductor, the group begins to digest the uncomfortable interaction between Peter and Claire, making sense of its affective life within the context of their own lives as well within the life of the group. In what is at once a highly focused yet free floating discussion, the group explores many facets of aggression and its potential for fuelling creative momentum and/or destruction. In this way, as Garland comments:

> the individual's problem . . . is dropped in favour of the passionate discussion of and involvement with the shifting roles, relationships and behavioural communications that make up the system of the group itself.
>
> (p. 57)

Do these reflections tally with your understanding about what is going on? I also note that there is no record here of any explicit intervention you made and wondered whether this was in keeping with my own experience of how often, in a more mature group, the conductor can find themselves saying relatively little?

MW: Yes, I think they do. I'm also reminded of what the late Daniel Stern (2004) said about 'present moments':

> Like a musical interlude, the present moment hovers between becoming the past and progressing into the future. Critical moments . . . are moments in

which the parties are fully in the present. . . . caught in a pivotal space where any action, or even inaction, will change the destiny of the situation and the actors themselves.

(p. 365)

Of course, in a group, this is happening all the time, across multiple planes and parties, rather like an orchestra.

On the question of what I say, or how much I say, I did not have space to illustrate any examples. I'm not sure that I'd agree that it goes down over time, relative to the maturity of the group. I think that this is putting it in too quantitative a way. So I would often say quite a bit, even within a mature group, but it might be more bridging comments or questions of clarification, along the spirit of, 'have I understood you right in that what you are saying is. . . .'. Or I might simply invite someone else to try to capture the essence of what someone else has said, particularly when it is a significant moment in that person's group (and external) life. Earlier on in the life of a group, a different sort of help is needed.

Reading over this dialogue, Nick, I think we have reached a natural ending point. We started with the qualities of the group analyst, moving swiftly into discussion of therapeutic effectiveness and what this means. Conversely, we discussed situations in which interactions can go awry and how a state of threat and potential in-cohesion arises. Quite rightly, you stressed that these are not so much static processes, but 'moments', even when they are prolonged, and that the question then is always one of how to foster growth and cultivate forward movement again. We returned to illustrations of the mature, well-functioning group, noting how such a culture is built over time. I've spoken in other contexts (Weegmann, 2014) of how the expanding horizon of the group is a precondition for the expanding horizon of individual members and, by the same token, the work of individual members changes the scope of the group, in a rich contest of figure-ground relations. In other words, individuals shape group dialogue and are themselves shaped by it, including the conductor.

Nick, thank you for this opportunity engage in a dialogue that I have found clarifying.

Chapter 9

Beginnings
Ted's story

Martin Weegmann

This chapter tells the story of a fictional client, Ted (27), his assessment and decision to join an analytic group, and some group interactions during his first 3 months. There is a considerable writing challenge in describing individuals in relation to groups, insofar as it creates a certain descriptive abstraction – the individual cannot be described in isolation. A further aspect is that although the individual is already changed by and changes the group matrix – as soon as they are a possible or actual member of it – it is of course individuals who join groups, with their own specific history, motivations and therapeutic wishes (Nitsun, 2015). In order to try to overcome this descriptive issue, some other members will be mentioned, including the conductor, albeit it briefly.

Some links to theory are explored, in particular attachment theory, self-psychology and the Winnicottian tradition, as they can usefully highlight some of the anxieties involved at a beginning, as well as the type of milieu that the group conductor seeks to create at this time. Such models help guide the group analyst and the wider use of theory is discussed at the end.

'Ok, I think I've decided now': towards the end of an assessment

When Ted was told during the course of his two assessment sessions that he had a choice between individual therapy or group therapy he was surprised as he had not properly heard of group therapy before. New in fact to any form of 'talking therapy', and increasingly ashamed of his lack of progress in life, he had been prompted to seek help by friends.

Ted was all too aware of repeating patterns in relationships, within social groups and at work, of an inhibition and a reticence that held him back. 'You go all quiet and don't show your talents', one friend said, another commenting, 'You're great and have loads to give, but it's like you clam up when there's more than two or three of us'. Fortunately, he could see connections between his problems and the way in which he was raised. Although his family was caring and consistent, he seldom felt he was actively enjoyed by his parents, and was often told to go off and 'play quietly' in the 'comfortable room' for which, he was frequently reminded, he should be forever grateful.

Instead of the lively, spontaneous family life he witnessed in his best friend's house, his family seemed bound in a routine that squeezed the fun out of most situations. His parents valued conformity above all else, but to what exactly, other than their religious beliefs? The pervasive Calvinism of his parents was unswerving and Ted felt growing guilt at realising that he had no interest whatsoever in matters religious. Worse still, his parents were forever critical about the 'decline in family values' and of 'decent authority' that they saw all around them. On the rare occasion when he challenged his scholarly, articulate father, he felt put down by his father's slur on his best friend's family – 'I see where you get all that nonsense from – a family without guidance goes adrift; no faith – no direction'. Worse still, this was said in earshot of visiting friends of parents. Ted, unable though wanting to reply, blushed, feeling acute anger and shame. He retreated to his room, his mind burning with injustice.

In the assessment, the therapist felt that Ted had formed a good therapeutic bond and was eager to overcome the inhibitions and anxieties that were holding him back. Ted was frustrated that others were always 'overtaking him', while he was overlooked; 'I want a future, not just a "getting by"', he complained. Ted was taken aback when the therapist said, 'Given that many of your difficulties are manifested in your relationships with others, including colleagues, and that there are repeating patterns here, might you consider joining a psychotherapy group, where some of this could be looked at and addressed?'. Ted's immediate, subliminal image was of a group of attractive, confident people, already well ahead of him in life. And yet he was intrigued, trusted the therapist's judgement and came to see that being together with others might well be the best way to address his core problems.

With more discussion, and a week to decide, Ted made a decision to take up the offer of group psychotherapy, assured by the good feeling that he would be seeing the same therapist, to whom he had warmed, but next time in a group context.

Comment

Like any good psychotherapy assessment, the therapist is concerned to evaluate a quality of 'psychological mindedness', to see whether the client can take responsibility, maintain realistic hope and understand something of their symptoms and anxieties as meaningful responses and communications (Coltart, 1993). Can they be mindful, so to speak, of the content of their own mind? (Holmes, 2010). Moreover, although symptoms have an adaptive value, does the client recognise that they have outgrown their use so that the resultant suffering becomes a potent source of motivation for change? And is the desire for change strong enough? Can the difficulties be connected up, at least provisionally, with past relationships? Although much has been written about 'psychological mindedness', there is less on what might be called 'group mindedness', of which an active willingness to learn from and be helped by others is key, as well as an enjoyment of the potential bonds that groups provide.

There were two ways in which the therapist felt that Ted was responsive and would be able to cope with the rigours of group psychotherapy. Thinking in attachment terms, he believed that Ted had internalised a somewhat brittle, conditional, perhaps a lifeless form of reliability that was costly in terms of felt inner confidence and a capacity for safe exploration. There was a pattern whereby Ted felt that his progress was dependent on conformity with the stance of his parents and that straying from this would be experienced by them as disloyalty. Marrone (1998) notes the potential congruence of attachment approaches and group analysis, both being concerned to with identifying repeating relational patterns and addressing the 'internal working models' of care, response and exploration that may underlie them. Through real life interaction of a group, the therapist thought that Ted could benefit from its 'corrective developmental dialogues' (Tolpin, 1971). Moreover, such dialogues could give him, '... the opportunity to look forward and not exclusively backwards and to bring movement' (Pines, unpublished, 1996: 11). This developmental progress would involve the revision of internalised templates of care and response, and allow the emergence of a firmer self, with more confidence in the future and so be better able to pursue ambitions and goals.

The second, favourable aspect, was Ted's obvious responsiveness, which, significantly, was boosted by the interest and care that the therapist had shown. Ted was encouraged by the feeling that someone – and here a person in authority– believed in him. In the terms of self-psychology, it could be said that Ted was suffering along the broad continuum that Kohut and Wolf (1978) call, 'disorders of the self'. The therapist thought that Ted had experienced a lack of emotional validation and mirroring, even if he had all the external trappings of care and a 'good home'. As a result, Ted felt easily belittled and inferior, lacked a certain dynamism of ambition, self-belief and 'go'. The therapist, in line with this, and guided by the attachment and self-psychology approaches, hoped that the group could provide a potentially responsive, confirming milieu, within which Ted could build resilience and vitality of self. In the words of Wolf (1988, p. 169), reflecting on therapeutic aims, 'one may look for a strengthening of the self to the point where the self has become enabled to rely less on defensive manoeuvres designed to protect the cohesion, boundaries and the rigour of the self'. However, for him to experience the group in this nurturing way – to see his group peers as companions in exploration and meaning-making – he would need to challenge his own imagined view of them as eminently more attractive, successful individuals.

The new group member, or member-to-be, brings a set of anticipations, something like a 'part-group' (similar perhaps to a 'part-object' in psychoanalytic terms) that is based on these (Pines, 1979). Similarly, the existing group members will form various images of the incoming person, about whom they may only know his or her name, including rivalry and curiosity. In the process of preparing the group, to which we will now turn, there is a considerable degree of emotional as well as practical, dynamic administration.

Preparing the group

The group analyst in this example gave the group 3 weeks' notice of the newcomer and gave no details other than their first name. Ted himself was given all the practical details and guidance he required, from group times and norms (attendance, holidays, etc.) and the framework of it being analytic in nature and relatively long-term. A process of preparation takes place both for the newcomer and for the group who will receive them. In the group itself, the existing members will be aware (although may have 'forgotten', particularly if it has been a very long time since there was any change in the group composition) that it is a 'slow-open' group, with newcomers taking up vacancies when and as they arise. Inevitable questions, some for information, others exploratory, will arise in the minds of group members, some articulated, others not, such as: What are their problems? How old are they? Will they fit in? Will they challenge me? Will I feel rivalrous? The group analyst encouraged expression of such questions, without supplying the 'answers', rather inviting the group to look at what such questions mean to them.

Further, for the incoming person, clients often fear groups at the assessment stage, unconvinced that they will be therapeutic, that they will be lost in a crowd, and so forth (Bowden, 2002). Fortunately, Ted overcomes this and sees its potential. Second, all clinical decision-making takes place in specific contexts, involving actual spaces and particular services. Suppose in this case that the wait for the group was 3 weeks and the wait for individual therapy was 3 months. This difference could be one factor influencing Ted's choice. He is, after all, wanting help to arrive sooner rather than later, given that he has already taken the step of undergoing an assessment. Finally, the group time happens to suits Ted's job, which is also significant, even decisive.

As regards the group analyst, suppose he wants to build group numbers and ensure a good range of personalities and range of problems. For quite a while he has wanted to enlarge the group. However neutral the analyst will aim to be in his language and offering, his own desires might well be a factor and even transmit in some unconscious way to the client.

Seeing, hearing, joining

'Group space' is more than the place and time of the group, but rather is a metaphor to describe the contracting and expanding envelope of group communications and accommodations – the 'feel' and make-up of the group. Ted is a new member in the life of the group and, whether welcome or not, he changes its landscape and the group matrix evolves. Elsewhere I have described the type of richly layered and varied group space that can arise in time as a 'populated matrix' (Weegmann, 2014).

In his first impressions, Ted felt that the group members were more akin to 'real, every-day people' than he had thought, and were far from the confident people he had imagined, and nor were they like the lively young people he worked with. He was warmed by Sally, of similar age, who smiled at him and noticed Harry, his chair pushed slightly back, untidy in appearance, distinctly nervous and avoidant of eye contact. When Ted acknowledged, half-way through, 'It's going to be difficult, but I'm really glad I'm here', others nodded, and he felt a sense of relief.

What then of the 'joining process'? How do the others respond to the newcomer? As has been acknowledged, group life is difficult to describe in written form, so we will somewhat artificially isolate two fragments from Ted's first group.

Harry's first reaction to Ted was, 'not another youngster! And he looks sure of himself'. Harry, in middle age, was a man who was beset by anxiety much of his life and, with the ending of his long-term marriage, felt more alone than ever, and age aware. This reaction is ironical, in the light of Ted's picture of the group before joining. Harry is an avoidant man (see Chapter 6), who also fears the isolation that avoidance brings, hence his membership of the group. He had two breakdowns in the past and his aim in joining was to learn 'how to be comfortable with people'. It is normal for him to make comparisons, seeing himself in a negative light.

On the other hand, Sally said, in response to Ted's expressed relief, 'It's always difficult at first, but we're an incredibly honest group and it's good to have you on board. By the way, do you always dress in dark colours?'. Sally had been in the group for 2 years, from its inception, and had gained greater confidence in expressing herself. Others in the group called her, affectionately, the 'lightening rod', as she had an uncanny art of seeing what was going on for others. She had been a 'young carer' to a mentally-ill mother and had developed a fine sensitivity to the emotional states of others, often to the neglect of her own. As a result of the group, her confidence and directness had grown, as evidenced in her comment about Ted's clothes, of which he had not been unaware.

Finally, the therapist felt a tinge of excitement at the thought that his group was 'on the move again', after a period of seeming slowness, and was more balanced in gender. He was pleased that Ted was well-received, as the last time he had brought in a newcomer they had not returned after just one session. Liking Ted, he was momentarily reminded of his own struggles as a young social worker in trying to feel socially comfortable with colleagues.

Comment

Mirroring is a rapid process, as is impression formation, and is often subliminal in nature and operation. What do we see in others, including aspects of ourselves? To whom are we drawn? How do we register others in terms of liking, disliking, identification or its opposite? Although there is one group, each person sees and experiences it in their way, and are changed by their involvement and the responses shown. In the words of John Donne, in *The Good-Morrow*:

> Let us possess one world, each hath one, and is one.
> My face in thine eye, thine in mine appears.

Group membership is an inherently exposing process, as we 'show ourselves', are seen, and, as emphasised by Foulkes, this includes the group conductor. As we subject ourselves to the gaze of others, self-consciousness is aroused and with it the risk of shame, embarrassment, comparisons, and so on. As Steiner (2011) notes, 'we are all familiar with the emotions aroused when we are being observed ... both pleasant and unpleasant feelings' (p. 23). In the case of Ted, one can appreciate that his joining would immediately touch upon such anxieties, given his lack of confidence and pre-existing expectation of a confident group of people. Ironically, Harry not only sees Ted as the youngster, reflecting something of his own negative comparison of self and age, but as sure of himself. Harry does not verbalise such feelings, as this would cause him shame. There is encouragement too, as vocalised by Sally. Any joining of a group, be it in a therapy group or one in everyday life, touches upon our human need for affiliation and meaningful association with others, as well as our tendency to hold back and/or avoid situations that might hurt us. The work of this group is already gathering pace, so that in Sally's comment about Ted's clothing, there is an invitation to dialogue, to meaningful conversation. She notices something that he was not aware of, which connects to his fear of visibility, of being seen, which he thinks is masked by dark clothes. These anxieties can be understood in terms of self-psychology and the search for confirmation and positive mirroring. At the same time as the group affords many opportunities for reparative 'selfobject' experiences, including emotional validation, it also provides a reality where fears are tested and actual people replace those of the imagination (Harwood & Pines, 1998). Not only this, but groups are places in which one finds symbolic friends and playmates – one requires 'interesting companions' to borrow a useful phrase from the developmental research of Trevarthen (2005). Interesting companions not only provide us with extended interest and engagement, but also with possibilities of helpful challenge as 'healthy adversaries' (Wolf, 1988), as Sally's response indicated.

Finally, there is the question of the therapist's responses, both inward and declared. Although there is a strong analytic ideal of the opaque analyst, divested, even, of 'memory and desire' (Bion, 1967), in the real world both are present and may even be apparent to clients, even if indirectly. The group conductor, after all, is concerned about the life of the group as a whole, its protection and vitality, and in this example, Ted's joining may help matters. It is, after all, 'his', the therapist's group, the one he started in the department and for whom he has the overall responsibility to nurture. Inwardly too, he can identify with Ted, seeing an aspect of his own, younger self and struggles reflected in Ted's reticence and social awkwardness. With identifications such as these, the therapist continues to work on his own self and professional development through departmental discussions and supervision.

What we carry: 'cultural cargos'

Three months into the group, Ted felt awkward as he listened to two others. As Sally spoke about her excitement of a long, birthday weekend with her young son, Ted felt that the group time was wasted hearing about 'kids play'. Then Terry spoke about 'carefree childhood holidays' of his past. Ted felt annoyed, bit his tongue, then delivered a sarcastic aside, 'Sounds like a bit of an undisciplined scene there!'. Terry and Sally were taken aback, felt criticised, with Sally saying, 'I don't know what your problem is! You know what, you're sounding every bit like that miserable dad of yours'. Ted was also shocked, and embarrassed, knowing that what she said rang true. It was as if his father's voice had come out of his own mouth.

Comment

One of the patterns of human behaviour is how often we find ourselves doing the very thing which we disapprove of, or voicing an attitude we usually despise; we carry the innumerable traces of those influences and others that make us the people whom we are. When Bollas (1987) refers to the 'unthought known' of our unconscious lives, there is equally the 'unthought known' of the social words that have shaped our multiple identifications over many years.

Liesel Hearst (1993) Foulkes' lecture, addresses 'Our cultural cargo'. In literal terms cargo means goods, a consignment, delivery, baggage, and in the metaphorical way in which Hearst uses the term, refers to those symbolic possessions which we 'carry' as parts of ourselves, and which may be burdens, riches or simply those social goods which serve our needs. Through cross-cultural examples, she argues that, 'the small analytic group contains and discloses the historical and cultural self-component of its members' (op. cit., p. 391). The symbolic groups which we carry as individuals might include family, neighbourhood, social class, nation, and so forth, and the work and process of therapy allows both a, 'unique individuality and communality to emerge' (p. 403).

Our cultural cargo may appear as a trace, even a visceral sensation or pre-vocal reaction, as we 'gather up' a position or take a stance in relation to others and what they represent. Ted's inner and then voiced reaction to the talk of play and holidays demonstrates this. This is not only a question of oedipal identification, of, for example, taking the admonishing position of his father, but also includes the familiarity with the cultural dimension of his families' life-world: – Calvinism, certain disciplinary practices, values associated with faith, conduct and the role of families. These are part of what Ted 'carries' within himself. The two run together, as from those values and their transmission, Ted felt his own 'playful self' was insufficiently enjoyed and promoted in growing up. Fun or positive playful recollections provoke reactions in him that he can only see once they are pointed out and 'given back'.

Play is an important area in group analysis, particularly the capacity to play and be free in the safe knowledge that one is enjoyed and appreciated. As Barwick points out (see Chapter 6), in the 'analytic group at play', we encounter something akin to the, 'interacting squiggles (free discussion) from which both highly personalised and shared meanings arise within a uniquely personalised yet shared space'. There is also a counter-reaction of shame when something critical and disapproving within us is aroused, but in spite of this we may gain greater insight into difficult areas within.

'Progressive emotional communication' is the felicitous phrase coined by Ormont (1999) to characterise forward movement in group therapy. The well-functioning group fosters the maturational needs of its participants and deepens the capacity for rewarding relationships and life commitments. In addition, emotional tolerance is increased and social learning enhanced, which includes a capacity for being 'at play' and losing oneself.

The personal uses of theory

It is useful to devote some thoughts to the personal role of theory held by the group analyst. In this example, the therapist draws upon a range of ideas which, let us say, he was influenced by during training, including attachment and self-psychology theories. Therapists work and interpret within a variety of horizons – personal, professional, including our cultural cargo. Of course, therapists are profoundly affected by the 'pre-understandings' of their trainings – formative experiences, values, allegiances, preferred models and so forth. I (Weegmann, 2014) have argued that the therapist's theory can be understood as a 'horizon' within which distance is gained and understanding is formulated. Theory can be understood not only as a model of thinking, but also as an internal selfobject, as it were, helping the analyst to feel secure and coherent in his/her functioning. We gain a sense of coherence and purpose from the models on which we draw, over and above their actual evidential relevance. On the down side, we are all capable of retreating into the comforts and consolations of own prejudices and there is always the risk of the analyst's over-identification with a particular model can lead to dogmatism and a host of anti-therapeutic implications. How then, does the group conductor maintain an openness to experience and a (life-long) capacity to learn? It might be helpful to adopt the broad stance taken by the pragmatist philosophers when they spoke of the importance of holding theory with a 'light touch'. Certainly, encouraging within oneself, as well as in others, a 'spirit of inquiry' is essential. With this in mind, one is in a better position to ensure that the group provides the optimal 'facilitating environment'.

Chapter 10

A group in action
Making room (Part one)

Nick Barwick

> Great hatred, little room,
> Maimed us at the start.
> I carry from my mother's womb
> A fanatic heart.
> (Yeats, 'Remorse for intemperate speech', 28 August 1931)

Introduction

The following two chapters tell the story of working with(in) a group over a three year period. It is about the group's efforts, amidst intense and often despairing conflict, to 'make room' enough to relate, reflect and learn. As a trainee group analyst at the time, it is also a very personal story; about my struggle to make the transition from individual to group therapist in a context – an outpatient psychotherapy department in a psychiatric hospital – that was as yet unfamiliar to me.

Unused to the consistently high levels of disturbance with which some NHS colleagues frequently work, my supervisor aptly referred to this, my first work in such a setting, as 'an initiation by fire'. Yet fire has its creative uses and this fire, together with the containing support of supervision, theory and my own therapy, helped forge for me a type of 'group-analytic skin': a social and psychic robustness both strengthened and made more permeable by means of a more integrated sense of my own aggression, a lessening of omnipotent defences and a securer sense of my own realistic authority. In clinical practice, this led to many changes in terms of timing and technique – most particularly when to focus on the individual and when the group – as well as of approach: a greater firmness, playfulness, spontaneity and willingness to 'shoot from the hip'. It also meant gaining greater tolerance of working in the countertransference, greater capacity to 'face the swirl of conflict in the group as a real person' (Foulkes & Anthony, 1965/1984: 62) and greater awareness of the significance of Foulkes's observation of

> ... how great and deep-going was the influence of the doctor's personality and approach on their group.... Change in him in relation to his group,

particularly on unconscious levels, would alter the course of events in the group.

(1964: 251)

From an intersubjective perspective – a perspective of human relatedness that, in keeping with Foulkes's own, implies 'a permeability of the psyche together with a reciprocal influence' (Friedman, 2014: 194) – how could it be otherwise? After all, as Schulte (2000) notes:

> the nature of the therapist's subjectivity is jointly responsible, together with those of the other participants, in determining the therapeutic process.
>
> (p. 542)

Since what follows is essentially a clinical tale, barely edited since its first telling[1] (Barwick, 2006a & b), the reader may wish to refer back to relevant theory in the first section of this book as a way of elucidating some of the material. I have given occasional indications where I think this might be particularly worthwhile. At its end, I have also invited Martin to offer some further reflections.

It may also be helpful to consider the development of this group story in the light of the three dimensions of psychotherapy: relational, reflective, reparative (Schlapobersky, 2016). A therapeutic relationship (i.e. the relationships in the group) is offered in order to help develop reflective understanding of self and others in interaction, thereby facilitating a reparative experience that promotes psychological growth and change. To achieve a semblance of this process, in the context of a group so riven by primitive anxieties as this one was, is no mean feat for group or conductor. When relations are characterised by massive projections – what I call 'linear relations' – the conductor must accept, for a while at least, the role of auxiliary ego, making themselves available to the unbounded projective identifications at play. In no small way, amidst this 'ring of fire' (Schermer & Pines, 1994), one of the most important contributions a conductor can make is to 'survive' – and to survive 'with hope' (Winnicott, 1971/1974). Only in so doing can the group and its members begin to trust in its/their own capacity to survive: to survive, ironically, an experience of intimacy. Out of intimate exchange, a whole universe becomes available for exploration. Such exploration involves learning to witness feelings, thoughts and behaviours in self and other(s) and between self and other(s). It is this witnessing (see Chapter 3) that is both the basis for and product of reflective activity: reflection rather than reaction, characteristic of 'spatial', rather than 'linear' relating (Barwick, 2004; see also Chapter 7). The shift from linear to spatial relationships is both reparative and developmental. It is the complex, difficult process of making this shift that I refer to as 'making room'.

Gathering

The individual, the group and borderline phenomena

Of the six patients with whom I began my group, four were long-term unemployed. Though two were in relationships, both of these relationships were highly dysfunctional; one being consumed by jealousy, the other by emptiness. Of the remaining four patients, two, following severe depression, experienced very limited social contact and two were chronic isolates.

'Man', state Foulkes & Anthony (1965/1984), 'is primarily a social being, a particle of a group' (p. 234). Since even in the most apparently asocial/anti-social people one can discern the wish to belong, individualism is, they argue, a symptom of neurosis, not a sign of health. A significant sign of health is the capacity to make, and make productive use of, social 'exchange': to participate, belong and creatively relate in a group.

There is a paradox to be unpicked here: that individualism signals a lack of individuation. Only by separating out, by having a sufficient sense of 'skin' (Bick, 1968) – that differentiating psychic membrane that holds together what is within and regulates its relational exchange with what is without – can the individual become effectively social and truly belong. This is so because, although 'the so-called inner processes in the individual are internalizations of the forces operating in the group to which he belongs' (Foulkes, 1971: 212), unless we have enough sense of being separate from that to which we belong, we are rendered mindless; impelled, if we do not abdicate ourselves to a life of compliance, either to colonise the world by means of grandiose illusions/delusions or, prey to a boundariless chaos (where each interaction becomes a potential colonising threat to an incohesive self) to engage, overtly or covertly, in relentless, psychic, territorial war.

I am describing here some of the characteristics of narcissistic and borderline personalities. They were also the characteristics of several members of my group. In itself, the inclusion of borderline patients can have certain advantages (see Chapter 4). Yet inclusion also carries concerns. Pines (1994b) warns that such patients should 'not predominate either qualitatively or quantitatively' and the group to which they belong should have 'sufficient resources to withstand the regressive pulls of their primitive mechanism' (p. 146). For reasons I explore elsewhere (Barwick, 2006a), including inexperience and institutional pressures, this is a warning of which I took insufficient heed.

The universality of some 'borderline' phenomena

Lest the patient with borderline personality becomes the depository of all that is most difficult in the group – the scapegoat – I suggest his/her struggle is one that is, in some ways and to some degree, universal. It is widely acknowledged that the earliest interactions are the most formative and it is here that the immature self is most vulnerable to inappropriate 'impingements'. Since the 'mother's face is the mirror in which the child first begins to find himself' (Winnicott, 1971: 51), it follows that unreflecting, distorting and projecting 'mirrors' (the result of carers who, being preoccupied with their own minds, do not have 'room' enough to establish a reliable level of empathic attunement with the infant) lead, in the infant, to distortions in the maturational development of a coherent, authentic sense of self (what Winnicott calls a 'True Self') and, potentially, a traumatically disturbed sense of 'going-on-being'. Consequently, out of the *con-fusion* between mirror (mother/caregiver) and object (infant), an overly adaptive 'false self' emerges, in which the caregiver's desires (and fears) – or at least the child's experience of these desires and fears – are relocated in the heart of the child. As Lacan (1973/1998) writes:

> Man's desire is the desire of the Other.
>
> (p. 235)

Drawing on a Winnicottian perspective in particular, I have focused here on the mirror metaphor, capturing as it does something quintessential about the way we develop in interaction with those who look at us (Pines 1982/1998, 1985b/1998, 2003a) (see Chapter 3) or, to borrow a line from Rilke (2003), how 'faced with you, I am born, in the eye'. More recently, developing an attachment theory perspective, Fonagy and colleagues (1995, 2002, 2004, 2008) have powerfully conveyed how caregiver reflective distortions (their misunderstandings or 'misattributions' regarding their children's feelings and behaviours) can lead to *con-fused* states in the child and a compromised capacity (in the case of adults diagnosed with BPD, severely so) to reflect on the affective life of their own minds as well as those of others; that is to 'mentalise' (see Chapter 6). As Schulte (2000) notes, if a child's experience of how he/she is held in mind is too threatening, it can derail the child's willingness to be aware of what it is in the mind of others:

> Such a derailing ... will reflexively derail the child's understanding of his/her own mental states: self-understanding ... is mediated through others' understanding of us.
>
> (p. 536–537)

In short, developing, as we do, in a 'hall of mirrors' (Foulkes & Anthony, 1965/1984), we are all composed of myriad reflections. For better or worse, we seem destined to inhabit each other: to dream each others dreams; to live each others lives. This psychic intertextuality can be both a source of succour and trauma, the latter leading to a severely reduced capacity for self-reflection and at once a longing for, and wariness of, engaging fully in the intersubjective field that, inescapably, is our *modus operandi*.

Traumatised (linear) ways of relating: the 'fanatic heart'

Emerging from disruptions of and/or distortions to authenticity, the self's capacity to productively regulate exchange in and with the group – to be sensitive to appropriate and productive degrees of emotional closeness and distance – can be severely compromised. Lacking a resilient internal coherence, intimacy becomes both feared and yearned for, promising, at one moment, succour and salvation, at the next, an annihilation of identity.

A disturbing, sometimes violent oscillation between these poles quickly became apparent in my group and found its countertransferential resonance in me, in the contradictory feelings of being eaten up/possessed and spat out/shunned. This corresponds to 'merger-hungry' and 'contact-shunning' defensive traits (Kohut & Wolf, 1978), two forms of 'fanatic heart' (Yeats, 1931) evident in group members who are particularly likely to personify malignant and malevolent ways of relating/'mirroring' characteristic of incohesive, traumatised groups (Hopper, 1999, 2003c; see Chapter 7).

For my group, then, the struggle to find room enough for nurturing, for reflective contact – a sustainable intimacy free from the fear-inducing dynamic of the 'fanatic heart' – was a particularly fraught one, since at stake was identity rooted in the capacity to separate out enough to belong.

Assessment: initiating the therapeutic alliance

Cohesion is the group equivalent of the therapeutic alliance in dyadic work and is maintained through the relationship between individuals and the group-as-a-whole (see Chapter 2). Inevitably, however, in the early stages of a group, it relies more on the relationship between patient and analyst. I was able to form useful alliances with each patient in assessment. However, despite attending to individual fantasies about what group-life might be like, these alliances may have fed some patients' desires for merger, making the transition to a group alliance more difficult. Experiencing, with each patient, a desire to make deep empathic connections, I suspect both 'patient pull' (Leitner, 1995) and my own omnipotent defences (against the anxiety aroused by a lack of experience of working clinically with groups) and narcissistic needs (to be recognised as a particularly capable therapeutic provider) may have influenced my approach.

My assessment of Tracey was just such a complex encounter. An attractive woman suffering from pathological jealousy, at times high levels of anxiety and prey to impulsive angry outbursts that threatened both her job and her relationship, she had been dubious about joining a group. Inadvertently, I and the administrative staff who were in the room-next-door, had been party to her initial assessment when Tracey's rage had filled both rooms with a stream of accusations. In my own assessment of her for my group, a similar dynamic soon began to emerge, until I reflected back a few empathic comments. The results were striking. Quickly soothed, and having only moments earlier complained that it would be difficult to make the group on time, everything, quite suddenly, became possible – including terminating work with her life-coach to whom, until that point, she had been determined to cling. Though wary of the speed of this 'conversion', my desire to make a viable group within a tight schedule (a product of my training needs) made me take her at short notice and without further individual investigation.

Beginning

Early drop-out

In the first group session, with her coat on throughout the group, Tracey was mostly silent. Mindful of the seemingly ambivalent attachment style she had presented in assessment, I was concerned to offer something to allay the attachment anxiety she appeared to be experiencing in the group. I made a note that if she hadn't spoken by halfway through the session, I would address her directly. Forty minutes in, Jane made an overture, commenting that Tracey had barely spoken. Tracey responded curtly, 'I'm just worn out', adding, 'I'm not going to be bullied into speaking'.

Breathless, Tracey came ten minutes late to session two. Still in her coat, no sooner had she sat down than she said how much she had needed to come, how it had been stressful getting to the group, how there was nowhere to park and how she'd been telling people she 'felt crap' but no one believed her. She then dissolved into tears.

Between session two and three, Tracey took an overdose. The group, shocked, communicated its concern. Part of this concern emerged in the form of the suggestion that she might be better having individual therapy.

Over the next few sessions, a communicational pattern emerged. Tracey would remain relatively, sometimes absolutely, silent for most of the session until, in the last ten minutes, having been addressed directly, often by me, she would deliver a list of anxieties in pressured, uninterrupted speech. I commented on how she left herself very little time to speak despite bursting with things to say.

In the penultimate group before the first break, as if in response to an 'invitation', Tracey began to speak half-an-hour before the end. After ten minutes, I found my interest waning. Her relentless talk became first tedious, then irritating as it took on a manic, religiously inspired, 'preachery' air. Not long before the end of the group, Ed responded with an attack on 'fanaticism', indirectly alluding to her 'missionary zeal'. A brief row ensued in which some members engaged, some panicked and some said nothing. Ineffectually, I 'called time'.

The last session before the break, Tracey did not attend and left no message. Ed, with Christmas cards in hand, had, in Tracey's case, no one to give it to. I wrote to Tracey, who attended the first fifteen minutes of the first session after the break (from which Ed was absent), only to say she was leaving. She complained of making herself vulnerable only to be 'shot down'. 'No one listens'.

Despite the floundering efforts of the group to hold her, Tracey would not be held. Nor would she listen. Further, Jane in particular became quite panicky, talking incessantly and interrupting several of my and other's attempts to address Tracey. Fearing her imminent departure, I entered into a very direct empathic exchange with her that echoed the assessment interviews. As before, this had a calming effect. Jane, however, would not be calmed and, panicking still, interrupted angrily once more. Tracey, as if enraged at the shattering of the empathic mirror I had been offering her, stormed out. She did not return.

I was left with the thought – one not uncommon to this phase of the group – that I could handle this person individually, if only the group, especially Jane, weren't there. In part, this can be understood as a defensive pull, in the face of feeling powerless, towards ground more familiar to me (i.e. individual practice). Yet it is also the articulation of an unhappy coincidence: a negative transference to my personal therapy group – the therapeutic value of which I did not entirely trust at the time – and the countertransference pull of the members of my patient group arising from their intense neediness and desire for merger. Although the conductor needs to attend directly to fragile members at times, at this particular time my attempt to rescue Tracey while neglecting the dynamic matrix of the group proved counter-productive.

The crowded room

This was not the first row in the group as they crowded for attention. With inadequate experiences of early containment in common and a history of gross impingements, many had little sense of room/space either within or between them. Concomitant with this, as if lacking sufficient sense of skin, they found themselves jostling against each others' raw psychic nerves, experiencing contact as painful violation.

I should like, here, to relate a dream; one that visited me, in slightly different forms, several times over the first months of this group. In the dream, I walk into a 'room' to conduct a group. The 'room' has no clearly defined walls. A mass of chairs are arranged at its nominal centre. Several people (my patient group) are seated there. As I take my seat, a sudden influx of more people invade, until the 'room' is crowded and all chairs taken. I recognise some of the newcomers as members of the 'official' group members' families. I feel intensely anxious, distressed at the terrible matter-of-fact intrusion, the thought of fragile intimate exchanges, suddenly and without warning, coldly exposed. Voices are lost in the hubbub and I find myself 'at a loss' as to how to progress.

The real group's mind is thus crowded not only by the neediness of those that constitute it but by all the needy family members who invasively crowd each member's mind. Indeed, each member's mind, the group's mind and my mind (since I am the dreamer and am trying to hold all in mind) is so glutted with the voices of the neglected that there is little room for differentiating one voice from the next. In this cacophony, where the act of gathering offers not containment but unremitting chaos, anxiety runs rampant, phantasies of falling to pieces are pervasive and identity is at risk.

I think this dream tells of massive and unbounded projective identification. It is about my experience of psychic assault and about my floundering efforts to contain all being projected into me. I felt consumed by my patients' fear and rage, and resentful of their relentless crowding of my mind. It was as if, unable to find a place of their own to live, they demanded a place in me.

It was not only in dreams that I was susceptible to my group's psychic struggles. In waking life also, the persistent fear that my group would fall apart and the awful despair and shame this prospect provoked was, I think, deeply resonant with group members' own traumatised internal worlds. Like my patients, I experienced a profound threat to my own identity – as an aspiring group analyst. Further, in supervision, I often felt painfully uncontained and angry (though mostly silently so) at the lack of time afforded me or of any concrete help. And with the time I did receive, I found myself delivering anxiety-ridden monologues of minutely recorded interactions, as if the sheer weight of words might be enough to elicit some understanding, some containment.[2]

Yet the dream was not simply about what was projected into me but about how my own internal world responded to it. Foulkes (1964) notes how the conductor's understanding of his group:

> rests on his own empathy. He can never emerge untouched . . . At the same time he must be free enough from personal problems not to be drawn into the emotional whirlpools of his patient.
>
> (p. 179)

These are difficult, treacherous waters to navigate, demanding a quiet confidence and calm authority of which, not infrequently, I found myself quite incapable. Indeed, a conductor's relationship to authority – and related to this, to aggression – is crucial in effectively taking up a 'leading' role within the group. My own ambivalence in this regard, at this stage of my and the group's life had, I feel sure, a deleterious impact on the group's development – something I have elaborated on elsewhere (Barwick, 2006a).

Early efforts to make room

Monologues characterised this group. Although a valid form of communication (see Chapters 3 & 5) in this group they seemed particularly resistant to development – into freer-flowing forms of exchange. I came to see them as evidence of a lack of experience of early attuned, rhythmical exchanges – the developmental context of reciprocity in which identity develops (Stern, 1985; Fonagy *et al.*, 2002). There was nothing about contact with a separate other here, but rather a tragic muddling of the act of giving, of disclosure, with the act of possession; a deviant social effort to assert identity by colonising the world through speech and creating, for the time of talking at least, the narcissistic illusion of merger.

Yet the illusion could not hold. Others could not bear it and the resulting rejection served only to confirm fears of not belonging. That Tracey held forth in such a way just prior to our first break could thus be seen, at least in part, as a defence against a fear of abandonment, located in her and later in Jane, but belonging to the group-as-a-whole. My failure to facilitate a broader ownership of these concerns and anxieties within the matrix of the group left some individuals to bear the burden and contributed, I believe, to more than one premature drop-out.

Despite my growing determination to keep both 'figure and ground' in mind, countertransference pressures to attend, in detail, to each member, were immense. Such attention is both impossible and 'anti-group'. Though often forgetting this reality in the face of such pressures, following Tracey's dramatic departure, I managed to remember it and in doing so, hold onto a dual – figure/ground – focus.

No sooner had Tracey left, Jeremiah and Ayesha urged me to go after her. I said I understood their concern but thought it important we tried to think together about what had happened. There was much anger with Tracey, especially from Jane. Only Jeremiah came to her defence, agreeing that people didn't listen. Hanna said Tracey's rage reminded her of her mother, adding, 'There's no room to say anything and digest it'. Jane agreed, angrily looking askance at me, 'Not that Nick's interested. You come here, hoping for support and what you get is kicked in the stomach'.

Jane's frenzy picked up pace as did Hanna's distress. The latter began to talk about feeling responsible for her mother's rage, feeling powerless to pacify her. I focused on Hanna's evident struggle with being left with something so very undigested and painful and related it to how the group felt following Tracey's exit. Hanna began to cry.

Without pause, and oblivious to Hanna's tearfulness, Jane launched into another monologue. This was met with a furious return from the usually composed Hanna.

'Will you stop talking!'

Jane, instead of countering (her usual approach) asked, with genuine surprise, 'What's wrong?'

'You never listen! You're always moaning! You never listen!'

A brief, stunned silence followed. I added, 'It's very difficult for people to get the room they need and to get it in a way that is helpful to them and not harmful to others'.

Once more, Hanna wept.

This interaction seemed to bring about a significant change in the final part of the session. Jeremiah, usually detached, was visibly moved by Hanna's distress and offered her the tissues. The group supported Hanna's attempt to reflect upon what Tracey's rage and departure had stirred in her. This led to a 'free-floating discussion' in which all members were engaged: about guilt, about responsibility, about the fear of contaminating others and about how owning one's own distress could bring relief both to oneself and to loved ones.

It had been important for me to protect the boundary/skin of the group in the face of the threat of further rupture. Containing my own anxiety went some way to containing theirs. Consequently, I was better able to utilise the dynamic matrix – the re-presentation in the group of angry need and frustration which had, till then, been evacuated through Tracey – to facilitate reflection. This embryonic containing experience became one upon which the group was able to begin to draw. Yet the room proffered was fragile and, partly as a result of this first major fracture, several further ruptures threatened the collapse both of the group and of my commitment to the training.

Holding on

In these first turbulent months, I found myself needing to be far more active than I had imagined. In being so, I found it helpful to think in terms of securing the infant group's sense of 'skin'.[3] Close attention to attendance and punctuality helped to consolidate this potentially containing boundary. So too did efforts to slow the pace of the group's relentless delivery; a relentlessness mirrored by lack of reciprocity, of basic listening.

Again, I came to think of this lack (and the loss of moments of potential exchange that accompanied it) as re-enactments of unheard/lost gestures and vocalisations from infancy: evidence of disrupted 'dances of reciprocity' (Stern, 1977, 1985, 1999), of neglected 'vitality contours' (Stern, 1999) and of vocal 'turn-taking' gone awry (Trevarthen, 1979). Left in their wake was an impoverished experience of mirroring, of 'empathic attunement' (Stern, 1985) and a perverse and distorted model of social intercourse and interaction.

In the group, highlighting the way that conversations often overlapped and how contributions (and contributors) were, as a consequence, frequently left un-reflected upon, led to much discussion about the skills of listening and the vital importance of developing them. It also led to a growing intimacy.

Further ruptures and a belated lesson in firm holding

As mentioned, for those suffering traumatic early impingements, intimacy is both desired and terrifying. This was so for Jane whose dependency on the group (she hardly missed a session) was equal to her hatred of it. While ruptures in the group – particularly real and threatened departures – provoked anxiety in others, in Jane, echoing early violent and chaotic abandonments, they provoked panic. This panic (in which she perceived herself as helpless victim) was complicated by her own merger-hungry nature which wanted jealously to destroy anything that threatened her possession of the good object. Since she was confused about what constituted the good object (myself alone or the group), her terror of turning up one day with only me there (all the others having been murdered) was both dream-come-true and guilt-ridden nightmare.

Her response to what she experienced as the frightening fragility of the group was to monopolise it with monologues of complaint. Jane's insatiable needs and explosive tendencies posed real challenges to the group's integrity. Indeed, while one supervisor had queried her inclusion from the start, another had suggested she might need to be removed. Yet something about my own difficulty in taking up a sufficiently robust sense of authority, linked to an insufficiently integrated sense of my own aggression, aggravated the situation, inhibiting my capacity to get a firmer grip on her in a timely way. Insufficiently held, she flayed about, frequently filling the room that had begun to open in the group with her unremitting talk.

Where I failed to challenge, Hanna did. Yet Hanna's observation of how Jane presented led not to reflection but expulsion. Jane attacked the group and Hanna in particular. I made several attempts to engage her, interrupting her assault. I also encouraged the group, which had quickly dropped into stony silence, to explore where they were in what was going on. Yet Jane's willingness to be stayed was limited and Hanna's defensively elevated air served to fuel the fire already raging in Jane. Consequently, Jane's rant became so frenzied, so incoherent that I thought she was experiencing a psychotic break. Under this barrage, Hanna, for a while curiously composed, suddenly broke into angry wordless tears and ran out.

Ayesha asked if she should go after her. I nodded. This left only myself, Jeremiah (who by now had abnegated all responsibility) and Jane (Ed being absent). I found myself 'taking hold' of Jane like a parent taking hold of a raging child. Adopting a firm, soothing manner, and drawing on my countertransference, I told her she was frightened of everything collapsing. She was angry at this, I suggested, because it was so important to her. Most of all, she was angry with me. She desperately wanted me to 'protect' her (in fact she had recently written to me a pleading for just this) and yet she felt I had betrayed her, betrayed her trust. All this seemed to still her and, in the stilling, enabled her to begin to digest something of what I had said. Feeling vulnerable and unprotected was something everyone managed to talk about once Ayesha and Hanna returned, though not without the need for me to interrupt Jane, on several occasions, often with some force.

This session was the beginning of a turning point in the group, in large part, I think, because it was the beginning of a turning point in me. Amidst the destructive chaos, I managed – just – to be both authoritative and empathic enough to hold something together, making room for reflection, first in Jane, then in the group. However, this lesson was a belated one, delayed by my continued struggle to own my authority and aggression. Thus, though I and the group survived, Hanna, who left shortly after, be it to another group, did not.

Notes

1 This and the subsequent chapter constitute a slightly edited version of my (clinical) training paper written in 2003 and later published (2006a & b) in *Psychodynamic Practice*.

2 This can be understood in terms of parallel process (Doehrman, 1976) – paralleling the culture of monologuing that characterised the group at this time. In personal group therapy too, similar parallel processes were at play. What progress I made too often felt corroded by simmering resentment: on a personal level, at what I perceived as judgemental rather than empathic responses; on a professional level, at what felt like the lack of a sufficiently robust model for dealing with the aggressively expressed needs of my patient group.
3 I am drawing here on Bick's (1968/1988) concept of 'psychic skin' which is discussed further in Chapter 11.

Chapter 11

A group in action

Making room (Part two)

Nick Barwick

Introduction

As I brace myself for the second part of this narrative about the mutual struggle of trainee analyst and group to make room enough to reflect and learn, I am reminded of some advice given to me when, in a previous professional incarnation, I struggled to manage the psychological impact of working with young adolescents in my probationary year as a teacher in a secondary comprehensive school. 'If you're going to survive', I was urged, 'you need to develop a thick skin'.

Something of my experience of developing such a skin, I have alluded to elsewhere (Barwick, 2001). Not an uncommon defence against the threat of being overwhelmed, of 'falling apart', the psychic skin becomes petrified, renders itself impermeable, while omnipotent phantasises muster false authority at the expense of sensitivity to the internal worlds of other and self. This precocious 'muscularity' relates, perhaps, to what Bick (1968) refers to as 'second skin'.

Such a rallying of defences is, of course, not an option for a group analyst; nor is it advisable, for that matter, in the teaching profession. Yet the forging of a more robust, less hole-ridden skin – around the analyst and, increasingly, around the group – is. Evinced in a growing confidence in the capacity both to survive and contain that which permeates the dynamic matrix of the group, it provides a vital psychic resource for each group member in their efforts to forge their own 'internal space', their own 'room for reflection':

> ... [the] internal function of containing the parts of the self is dependent initially on the introjection of an external object experienced as capable of fulfilling this function ... Until the containing functions have been introjected, a concept of a space within the self cannot arise.
>
> (Bick, ibid., p. 187)

From first to second year

Developing skin

Over Jane's remaining time in the group (she left after 14 months), I and the group became increasingly able to contain her anxieties and threatened outbursts.

More firmly contained, she offered useful insights into important aspects of the dynamic matrix, not so much by acting them out, but by talking about them. As the original members of the group were gradually replaced, Jane became something of a parental figure, giving particular attention to the youngest member, Punya, who was a suicide risk. She also made good sisterly attachments, particularly with Abisola, a forthright woman, herself prey to angry outbursts.

One of Jane's complaints had been how difficult it was to find clothes she could afford and how second-hand shops proffered little which both fitted *and* suited her. In my mind, I associated these references with an absence of skin – of a sense of sustaining and sustainable embodiment – within and by means of which she felt she could properly and safely belong. Towards the end of the first year, however, Jane commented on a change in *my* dress. She suggested I had been told to 'get my act together', that I looked much smarter for it, and that I clearly 'meant business'.

What Jane noted was my decision to don some very expensive, second-hand suits – my father's. Wearing these symbolised a greater integration of more aggressive aspects of me which were present in, but had also been projected onto and into my father, a wealthy, self-made businessman. It was shortly after this, just prior to Jane's departure, that I also grew a beard. In personal therapy, though confessing a nod to Robert De Niro in *Heat*, with some amusement, several group members pointed out that, during the long summer break, I had acquired a characteristic shared with our conductor! Smiling, I recognised that resonant with this observation was the developing resolution of a negative transference to him, and a growing trust in the group and its capacity to contain, which I held inside.

Re-match: the group makes room for gradual re-integration.

Rows arising from 'malignant mirroring' (Zinkin, 1983; see Chapter 3) – a dynamic in which mutual projective identification leads to a hostile relationship between a pair and which may itself be understood as emerging out of the unconscious dynamics of a similar type at work at a group level (Gordon, 1991) – broke out, yet never quite with such force and certainly not with such anxiety on my part again. One such row occurred between Punya and Abisola. As if echoing, respectively, Hanna's and Jane's altercation, Punya, with morally superior calmness, reproached Abisola (who had related an incident where, in the spirit of revenge, she had taken a hammer to someone's car) for her irresponsible and uninhibited violence. Abisola responded to Punya's reprimand with considerable vitriol and, though we struggled to unpick the mutual projections (for example, unknown to the group at this point, Punya, a quiet and thoughtful young man, shamefully carried the knowledge of an act of violence he had himself committed prior to joining the group, while Abisola, though having a history of bullying, as a child had been the victim of repeated cruel and violent abuse), the psychic territorial war enacted was too fiery to make room for mature reflection and both they and the group left feeling bruised.

For several sessions, the group, as if reaching a dangerous impasse, began to stagnate. There followed 3 weeks with only two members present in each session. Had this near collapse occurred a few months previously, I would have felt not only great anxiety but also great guilt. As it was, though frustrated by the way intimacy so often led to recriminations and a shunning of contact, I was also able to recognise these absences as the group's 'enabling solution' (Whitaker & Lieberman, 1964). It was as if, aware of a lack of room and of the fragility of 'intimacy involving openness and contact between people in the field of vision of other people' (Brown, 1985/2000: 217), the group made an unconscious agreement to offer a limited privacy in which first Jane and Abisola, then Laura and Punya and, finally, Punya and Abisola, exposed to each other their vulnerabilities.

When the full group met again, Abisola, in motherly fashion and as if trying to heal a rift that had earlier also occurred between Jane and Punya, related the fact that Punya had cried. (Unbeknownst to the others, crying in the group was one of Punya's greatest fears.) She also said she thought this was very brave of him. Perhaps prompted by the fact that she had initially felt quite unsure how to respond to Punya's distress in what grew, through awkward faltering movements, into an intimate and empathic exchange, she went on to talk about how, because she was so often 'on the defensive', she felt concerned about her ability to be 'open' to the needs of Andrew, her son.

Jane, having earlier had a session alone with Abisola, now re-explored with her – and in front of the group – Abisola's relationship with her own mother. This revealed, for the first time, several disturbing stories, one of which was about her mother bathing her, only to end up scrubbing Abisola so hard that her skin began to bleed. I suggested that, for her, spaces that might promise safety and allow vulnerability had turned into nightmare settings, full of violent abuse. It was little wonder she found it so difficult to trust and be 'open' in the way that she wanted to be, both with her son and in the group.

Abisola said she wanted to be 'broken'. It was as if, though the desire for real contact (beyond her defensive posturing) was genuine, the very language of intimacy had become impregnated with violence. Jane suggested that she wanted to be able to 'fall to pieces'. Abisola's eyes moistened. As if to keep herself 'together', she talked again of her son, complaining how inadequate school, social services and the area in which she lived were in terms of offering care or safety. Her story, though clearly significant, had a monologuing air that irritated me rather than drawing empathy and I noted that both Punya and Laura appeared to be drifting away. Eventually, I said, 'It's interesting how Abisola's son has become a major figure in the room, like a member of the group who has filled the room with his presence. I wonder, though, if his presence is not only in Abisola's story but also in others. I wonder if anyone identifies with him.'

Punya said he did and that, as a child, he had experienced no real physical contact from his parents, though he did remember his mother reaching out to him once, to stop him falling. At this, Abisola laughed. Invited to say more, she simply apologised and said that laughing was just something she did. Jane, however, still curious, soon returned to the issue, pursuing it further. What emerged was that Abisola's laughter was a response to pain. This led to a discussion about muddled communications eliciting disappointing responses and a broader discussion followed investigating the way members communicated with their parents and what they might like to ask them and really say to them.

Noting that Laura still had not contributed, I invited her into the discussion. Laura, whose aunt (for all intents and purposes, her mother) had died recently, said that, just before she had died, she had talked to her about how she had felt overlooked as a child and about how hurt, angry and resentful she was about this. Her aunt, taken aback, had said that she had had 'no idea' that this had been so. I suggested this might happen in the group; that she might feel overlooked sometimes but not speak up until it was too late. Then she might end up feeling hurt and resentful and angry. Punya asked if this was how she did feel. She assured him it wasn't. 'You look like you've switched off though,' remarked Jane, 'sat back in your chair like that. You look a bit out of it, like you're saying, "leave me alone"'.

Engaging Jane in a brief conversation about Laura, I agreed that it did seem like this, but wasn't it a curious message to send for someone who had experienced such a painful lack of care and attention? Laura, annoyed, said she hadn't been feeling very well lately, that was all. Surprised, Abisola asked, with considerable sympathy, 'Haven't you? What's wrong?' Laura, swallowing, began to cry.

As Jane responded with motherly noises, Punya spoke as if *for* Laura, relating something of their intimate 'one-to-one' session 2 weeks before. Abisola added Laura to her list of 'bravehearts' and Punya said it was Laura's willingness to 'go to pieces' in that 'one-to-one' session that had enabled him to 'go to pieces' in the 'one-to-one' session with Abisola. Jane joked that maybe people were upset because she was leaving.

This comment was nearly lost so, a little later, I picked it up, remarking on how striking it was that Jane made light of her departure, particularly since she was a founding member of the group – a bit like a parent in fact – and that the group had been very important to her over a long period of time. Abisola, in particular, said how much she would miss Jane, and Jane, whose attendance had been erratic since announcing her departure, and who, when actually present, had made several attacking comments, complaining of how distant she felt from the group, confessed now that she nearly had not come again. It had been a huge risk to do so, particularly since, having messed everyone around so much, she had feared we (and me in particular) wouldn't want to see her. Then, as the group talked of how 'touched' they felt at sharing in this way, and how precious tears were, as if to complete an intimate *orchestration*, for the first time, apparently for 25 years, and in the most curiously restrained and delicate manner, Jane also began to cry.

A conductor's reflections

That this group felt like an 'orchestration' is an apt sign, I think, of my growing capacity to play 'conductor'. Indeed, this musical analogy prompts another. Having, as a child, had a classical music training, I made the decision, during the second year of conducting this group, to learn jazz tenor sax. Doing so has been a liberating experience. Of particular interest has been to realise that, in jazz, as Art Tatum says, 'There's no such thing as a wrong note'. Not only is a so-called 'wrong note' never more than a semitone away from a 'right note', but also the difference between 'wrong' and 'right' is simply a difference between tension and release. And it is the interplay of tension and release – a 'tolerable imbalance' (Foulkes, 1964: 58) – that constitutes the music of jazz.[1]

The tensions at the start of my group were evident still, if less strident, some 15 months on. An important difference, however, was my capacity (and the group's) to tolerate them and, holding onto a sense of hope, make use of them in the movement towards release. This was not to adopt a naive optimism. I remained very aware that tension uncontained led only to more tension and that a constant missing of the resolution towards a more concordant note would give rise, in the end, to a musical incoherence so extreme that no conductor (or orchestra for that matter), be they ever-so post-modern, would be able to bear it. Nevertheless, what I did find is that I accrued a greater faith in the natural developmental capacity of groups when properly attended to.

This maturing perspective (mirrored by greater tolerance of my own internal discord), better enabled me to hold that group-analytic poise of which I spoke earlier. In turn, this allowed me to attend with greater fluidity to the fluctuations between figure and ground. For example, in response to Abisola and her monologue, awareness of my countertransference prompted me to intervene in such a way as both to hold her as well as open up the possibility of relocating the source of need within the group. Further, I was able to draw upon aspects of the group locked in the silent group members and to reach out to them, almost playfully. Where challenges occurred in the group (as for example, Jane's to Laura) they did so not in my absence (leaving the challenger open to possible rebuff of a type that may have proved overly difficult) but in my presence as 'participant-observer' (Sullivan, 1954). All this facilitated, I believe, a deepening resonance in the group, in which the fractured and malignant mirrors could be reassembled in less distorted, more integrated fashion, and put to good use in a room that encouraged developmental reflections.

The second and third years

Making room for play

In this and the previous chapter, I have chosen to focus mainly upon the first 14 months of my training and of this training group – the point where the last of my original members, Jane, left. Within the group, this was a time dogged by distressing rows and precipitous departures. Material from my second and third years would have presented a group less turbulent, more reflective; one in which the forces of the anti-group, of anti-therapeutic destructiveness, were less prevalent and my capacity to take up the role of conductor, with both authority and sensitive reserve, more in evidence. Also in evidence would have been my capacity to take part in, and elicit, play. I take the import of this capacity, in myself and others, from Winnicott's dictum:

> *Psychotherapy takes place in the overlap of two areas [or more] of playing ... where playing is not possible ... the work done by the therapist is directed towards bringing the patient from a state of not being able to play into a state of being able to play.*
>
> (1971a/1974: 44)

Concomitant with my attempts to elicit play was an increasing interest in encouraging the elaboration of metaphors arising in the group. Metaphor is based, like play, on the notion of 'as if' and its elaboration in the group allows for multiple 'overlappings', thus creating an area of shared 'intermediate experience'. Thus, for example, in a series of sessions half-way through the second year of the group, stories of violent acts (fantasised and real) around the theme of invasion and expulsion were related. One of the less traumatic stories focused on one member's anger (a member who had been identified by the group as being the least aggressive) at having a seat usurped on a crowded train. The opportunity to reflect upon the meaning of this and the other stories was made available not through classical interpretation (something I became far less reliant upon) but through an exploration of the meaning of an empty seat in the group during one of these sessions – a seat that marked the absence of Abisola, herself experienced by some, at times, as quite aggressive and bullying. This, in turn, gave rise to the idea not only of its removal (Abisola was about to leave) but also of the gradual removal of other seats, 'as if' in a game of musical chairs. In this relatively safe, playful space, members of the group were able explore issues regarding rivalry and aggression. In this way, play led not only to new knowledge (Winnicott refers to it as the 'gateway to the unconscious') but also provided an arena in which healthy group relationships could grow (Winnicott, 1942).

This is not to say that there was no fire or fracture during this period, nor that once some room for reflective intimacy had been established, it was never assailed. The very fact that I was unable to expand the group to a full compliment until early in my third year, alone says something about the continuing experience of 'crowding'. Nonetheless, the group eventually did grow in size and, after 3 years, on leaving, I handed it over to another conductor who had joined me as a 'trainee' 3 months before. With him, the group continued its work, certainly for at least a further 3 years (the time of my last communication with my colleague) after my departure.

Leaving

Making room for loss

Loss is integral to living and our capacity to make meaning of it is integral to our capacity to live with ourselves and with each other in hope. To make meaning, we must tolerate the pain of loss, that is, we must give it due room in our minds. Intimacy is inextricably bound to the issue of loss, since it is in the intimacy that is dependence that we learn most deeply, and it is in the loss inherent in separating from that which we have grown dependent upon that we make what we learn, our own. When we are capable of waiting for meaning to emerge out of the unknown that loss heralds, we enter into a benign, if anxiety-provoking cycle, leading always to psychic enrichment. When, however, the mind is so crowded by unprocessed earlier losses – those which have never had room enough to find meaning – the prospect of further loss provokes either panic or a resort to defensive mechanisms that, though temporarily ameliorating fears, prevent the rich symbolic holding of that which is to be lost, inside.

There were many opportunities to make room for reflecting upon loss, in particular when members left. When these opportunities were taken (and often they were not) they made a significant contribution to the development of both group and 'departee'. The fact that Ayesha left (after about 9 months) in measured fashion, for example, allowing due reflection on complex and contradictory feelings about her departure, enabled the group to gain a sense of its own value by recognising the value of what it could no longer have. This process also provided a model for making room for reflecting upon later departures.

Even so, those who left subsequently did not do so with ease. For example, Jane was, I think, prompted to leave as a reaction to her own feelings of abandonment (following a growing sense of belonging) during the long summer break. It took firm and sensitive handling to contain her last-moment attacks (including absences) and to bring her properly into the group so she could properly go.

Abisola too, whose departure (after about a year in the group) marked a successful completion of her studies and an equally successful beginning, outside the city, of her professional life, seemed unable to leave without resurrecting her conflict with Punya; this despite, though I suspect because of, their growing intimacy.

For Laura, who, like the 'good child', had given 3 months notice (she was moving out of the city), the attack she launched before leaving seemed more a sign of hope than a defence against loss, of progression than regression.[2]

Complaining about unsupportive colleagues and an incompetent Managing Director at work forcing her to take on burdens beyond the contractual scope of her employment, a member brought to mind a story she had told previously: of her as a child, struggling to carry her younger 'siblings' home when in fact she so desperately wanted carrying herself. I added how, in the last few weeks, she had taken increasing responsibility in the group and, though this was apt in many ways, wondered whether she wasn't missing something in terms of care *from* the group.

At this, a certain petulance that had been simmering became overt in her open criticism of the group and its blind ignorance of her own needs. Another member expressed surprise at this 'hidden', angry and deprived aspect – a surprise echoing Laura's aunt ('I didn't know that was how you felt. I had no idea').

'That's the problem', snapped Laura. 'People don't know because they don't think!'

Though angry with the group to whom she had given much, she was also angry with herself.

'I need to find out how to ask without leaving it too late!' she said.

I said that I thought this was important. If she didn't speak up, she was likely to bear silent resentment and be glad to be rid of us. This surely would be a terrible loss, since the group *had* helped her and *had* been important to her. Laura said that wanting to get rid of the group was exactly how she had begun to feel.

In her last session (early in the third year of the group), Laura was particularly aggressive, hateful even. Members took umbrage and a brief 'scuffle' ensued. Mindful of the little time left, I drew Laura's aggression towards me. In response, Laura commented on how she could now see 'all the cracks' in me. Andrew, a new member of the group looking for someone to confirm his own pessimism about group therapy, suggested she was saying she had got nowhere in the 18 months she had been in the group.

Irritated, Laura retorted. 'No! That's not it!' Listing the many things that had changed for her, she added, 'And one thing that's really changed is that I'm angry! I mean *really* angry! And I'm only angry because I feel safe enough to *be* angry!' She also said that although she'd got a lot from the therapy, she hadn't got enough. She added that, when her dying aunt had expressed surprise at how overlooked Laura had felt, Laura, consoling her, had told her it was OK. But it wasn't OK! And she wasn't going to pretend anymore.

Laura's final farewell was in fact a fond one. She demonstrated a realistic gratitude that enabled her to take away something that she was losing and keep it inside. She was able to do this only because, I believe, she expressed her 'hate ... in a known environment, without the return of hate and violence from the environment' (Winnicott, 1942/1991: 143); that is, she found room enough to be.

The last farewell

Despite giving 4 months notice of my departure, the group found it difficult to explore its emotional import, except to express some concern about the competence of my co-conductor (who joined us 1 month following my notice to the group). I also found it difficult to address it directly, in part because of a 'competing' death in the form of Thea's father.[3] More than this, however, despite evidence to the contrary – one usually very consistent member's sudden spate of absences, Andrew's suicidal despair around the previous break – I just could not quite believe how important my 'little death' (Kubler-Ross, 1969) might be.

Andrew's response – that one therapist was much like another – was the most dismissive, yet the whole group seemed curiously unperturbed and I began to feel rejected, dejected and smouldering with anger. Although lacking, at this point, the detailed attention of a training-supervisor, I eventually understood these reactions as part of my countertransference – intimations of what the group-as-a-whole found too difficult to contain. Even so, I found myself trapped with these feelings, unable to find a way of offering them back to the group other than by self-disclosure.[4]

During this time, Punya's attendance began to deteriorate, a similar deterioration having occurred prior to Laura's departure. Laura and I were the most significant group members for Punya and I began to see his withdrawal as evidence of what the group found too painful to give room to. On his return near to 'my end', I made it a priority to draw him into the group, so that what was located in him could be redistributed within the matrix of the group. In so doing, it became clear that, contrary to Andrew's summation, Punya feared I was irreplaceable and that, in my going, all that he had gained would be irrevocably lost.

In my final session, Punya was absent. Andrew enthusiastically set a question for the group: 'How can we [depressed people] stop being so depressed?' The group, however, seemed unable to give a satisfying answer. Indeed, Thea, for example, said she feared that her 'new openness' – following the initial grief at her father's death she had seemed to gather a new strength – was disappearing again and Gina remarked that she was feeling less confident once more. Gina then related a dream in which, feeling panicky, she had looked everywhere for consoling support, only to find that everyone she turned to was dead.

The group became silent. After a while I said, 'A dream is sometimes like a gift to the group. This dream seems to be about loss about which there is much preoccupation in the group', and I listed some examples, including Thea's father's death. 'In fact, this preoccupation is one that Tim [my co-conductor] highlighted last week.'

As I had hoped, Tim continued, 'And, of course, the loss of Nick is imminent.'

A shock-wave swept through the group. It was if we had never discussed my departure, or as if, as one member said, till then they had had 'all the time in the world'. A brief but immense sadness followed, mainly located in Gina who admitted how, despite herself (I noted how she kept her chair a little out of the circle), she felt deeply connected to the group and to me.

Andrew began to lead the discussion elsewhere. However, Doug a big, quietly spoken man, blurted angrily:

'We're not talking about it!' Straining not to show too much, he turned to me saying, 'I need to say how important you've been to me. I feel you've given a lot. I'm going to miss you and I feel uneasy about what will happen when you've gone.'

A number of similar comments followed from other members, including Thea who made, at last, an explicit link to the loss of her father. Only Andrew remained untouched by these exchanges, taking on a calm therapeutic role. I mentioned this to him and wondered aloud why.

'Are you suggesting I'm sublimating my own fear of losing you?' he replied. The remark had a dismissive air.

I 'bit' back. 'I don't know what you're sublimating but I did notice that you're picking up the language of 'the therapist' just at a point when you might have some feelings about what is being talked about.'

Andrew said that what he felt was 'disconnected' and 'impatient' to get on with the work. As he spoke, a flood of losses came to my mind, in particular the loss of his mother which he had never found out how to mourn. In my struggle to make some connection with him, on this my last day, I glimpsed something of how despairing he must have felt with his own emptiness and lack of engagement with the world. How very difficult it was, I thought, for such an omnipotently defended and *impatient* man to give himself room to *be a patient*; one who, suffering, needs. I thought too, with sadness, how for me, there was now no more room to explore this with him. These and other issues were now the work of the group with their new conductor, not with me.

As if in response to Andrew's denial, Doug, choking with tears, apologised and left the room. This echoed Punya's sudden departure mid-session a few weeks earlier. Doug, however, returned a few minutes later and, aptly, it was Tim who 'picked him up'. Doug talked of suicidal feelings and, as he did so, I began to feel immense guilt: at being grossly negligent and ill-preparing the group. Yet I also knew that this was not so. We had, to the best of my, my supervisor's and my co-conductor's abilities, been thoughtful about this ending.

'All this,' I said, 'and I'm leaving as well.'
'Yes,' he replied, 'It's not a good time.'[5]

This simple exchange seemed containing – something I noted both in Doug's still distressed but more thoughtful demeanour and in my own less anxious countertransference.

It was only then that the group, at last, addressed Punya's absence and how upset he had been several weeks before. Someone suggested that, knowing how important my leaving was to him, he probably didn't know this was my last session. I simply added, 'Or perhaps he did.'

Despite Punya's absence, I found myself still hopeful that my loss would not be catastrophic but creatively, if painfully, borne. I felt more hopeful for the fact that in my penultimate session, Punya had offered the group a recognition and an apology: it was not just me but the group that he had turned to over the years, and it was work done with the group, including me, that had kept him alive. This did not lessen the pain of my loss, but it gave him reason to hope that he might be able to go on.

Following the group, I wrote to him. Some months later, I received a card dated the day of my leaving. It was of a tiger – a significant image for someone so fearful of his own aggression. It was a long, moving message, from which I offer but one line:

Beyond the confusion, sadness, pain and tears, I know there is light somewhere and I know I am closer to that light.

Conclusion: 'one little roome'

Punya epitomises the struggle of each member of the group, and indeed of each of us throughout our lives, to make meaning out of loss and hopeful and realistic expectation out of frustration and despair. Our capacity to adopt a 'philosophic mind', to 'find/Strength in what remains behind' (Wordsworth, 1804) is dependent upon our experience of having had room enough to thoughtfully bear these losses and, without defensive posturing, make meaning out of what we have left inside. The room that we may productively make use of is the room co-created with others in the context of a matrix of competitors and carers. This is the room with which I found myself engaged in struggling to see into being; a room in which the 'fanatic heart' could begin to relinquish its primitive territorial needs and, in free and frank discussion, negotiate a place, within and without, for all. Making room and negotiating by the light and safety of that room is what educationalists might call a 'transferable skill', what psychologists might refer to as having a high degree of 'generalisability', and what John Donne, the poet, might have seen as being the product of 'love':

And now good morrow to our waking soules,
Which watch not one another out of feare;
For love, all love of other sights controules,
And makes one little roome, an everywhere.

(*The Good-Morrow*)

FURTHER REFLECTIONS ON 'MAKING ROOM'

Martin Weegmann

I appreciate your honesty, Nick, in describing the group and your struggles at that time as a trainee group analyst. It is always illuminating when clinicians 'bring themselves in', in the sense of considering their contribution to the clinical problems which they encounter. The other aspect to note is the way in which clinical *writing* can help as a process of 'working-through', done, as it is, with the benefit of retrospective vision. Mahoney (2001) says that, 'writing is more than just a working medium, it is an organising and creative process', and I am aware, Nick, that you have also called writing a 'developmental process' (in Barwick (in press).

It is difficult to comment in detail on another person's account of their clinical practice, and so I will be brief. First, there is the challenge we all face in the act of establishing a group and creating the culture that feeds its growth; usefully, you use the metaphor of 'finding room', or creating space, throughout. Now psychotherapy has many spatial metaphors, so that we talk about people being in a 'difficult place', of someone not being 'at home with themselves', therapy as a 'secure base', a 'safe space' and so forth. I like the way, Nick, in which you bring Winnicott in to help such discussions, with his emphasis on play and potential/ intermediate space, though of course he speaks as a psychoanalyst, not a group analyst. And, rightly, play cannot be forced, but develops where there is a certain freedom from anxiety – in all parties, including the conductor. We are often stiff and hemmed-in by self-expectations, of a 'right way of doing things', in the beginning; we 'carry' our training ideals and requirements within us. 'Conducting' too, as you note, is a playful craft that requires considerable experience. In this regard, I thought your references to music were most apposite. Some of our skills have an invisible presence, though what we do does give provide character, shape, sometimes momentum to the group. The famous conductor, Sir Simon Rattle, said something along the lines of *one cannot practice in isolation, but one needs the orchestra* – in our case the group – *to practice with!*

Returning to the issue of how to build the right climate. Yes, groups are difficult to join and there is common self-consciousness, inhibitions about exposure and uncertainty about peers. 'Will I get on with them?', 'Will we have enough in common?', 'Will they like me?' are normal reactions. Pre-group preparation and orientation are important, but do not guarantee a smooth passage once *in* the group. And yes, even with perfect preparation, newcomers can take flight or not feel sufficient identification with the others. People naturally behave and respond in a way that protects their self-esteem. And group conductors have to know when to be more active – even providing explanations of processes – as distinct from the adoption of more traditional, analytic reserve. I personally have learned to be active and evocative, in creating a climate for safety, comfort and stability. Validation, in my view, is also important, and not only for those with more traumatic or disrupted backgrounds.

Much of my wider clinical experience has been with those suffering from substance misuse, personality disorders and other, complex needs, and so I have learned a way that places considerable premium on the 'supportive' as distinct for the 'expressive' (or exploratory) dimension of group life. So, for example, I might, initially, emphasise the similarities rather than the differences, between people. This happens to be a saying used in Alcoholics Anonymous ('look for the similarities not the differences') and also at the core of Yalom's more interpersonal tradition. More mundanely, Foulkes, spoke of people, 'being in the same boat'. This, I suggest, is congruent, in the field of substance misuse, with the 'modified dynamic group therapy' as developed by Khantzian *et al.* (1990) and others. I've also learned a great deal from the sensitive ways in which individuals with borderline personality disorder are responded to in, say, DBT groups, with its focus on the development of emotional skills and emphasis on long-term over short-term needs (Linehan, 1993). Both these examples are, however, homogeneous groups with special populations, but some of these principles (e.g. support, validation, building of reflective and regulatory capacity) I would extend to a heterogeneous, slow-open group.[6] Confidence-building simple is an under-stated aspect of the client (and therapist) experience.

In this regard, I enjoyed reading about how you help group members to develop the confidence to reach out one to another, and to experience the efficacy that they *can* help. I guess this is in part about therapeutic siblings, but is also about lateral relations in general – being alongside one's peers. As groups grow, so more experienced peers grow, who are culture carriers and help (provided they remain open!) newcomers to settle.

We all change as our experience grows and time is required in order for group analysts, in this case, to develop their style and clinical judgment – also to grow beyond the dependence and strict identification with supervisors and teachers, which may be appropriate at an earlier stage of training.

Notes

1   In the words of another great jazz pianist, Bill Evans:

   There are no wrong notes, only wrong resolutions.

2   Wardi (1989) refers to 'constructive termination regression', an intense, anxiety-provoking, transient phenomenon that needs to be borne if the phase of separation is to be constructively completed (see Chapter 12).
3   Thea, Gina and Doug all joined early in the third year of the group.
4   The issue of my departure was one which I had hoped, and suggested, my co-conductor might also raise when appropriate. His difficulty in doing so (in addition to mine) and my irritable feelings in response to this reticence, takes me into complex territory of co-conducting which is beyond the scope of this chapter.
5   In my process notes, in error, I originally attributed these words to Andrew. This parapraxis is, I think, particularly apt, since it is through Doug that Andrew's unconscious can be understood to speak in this session.
6   Nitsun (2015) suggests group analysts, particularly when working with people whose severe psychological disturbance is entwined with, and complicated by, relentless socio-economic deprivations and pressures, need 'to construe refuge as a key function and to evolve the notion of the group as refuge.' This focuses concern 'more with fundamental levels of survival and belonging and less with analysis' (p. 110).

Chapter 12

Endings

THEORETICAL REFLECTIONS

Nick Barwick

The impact of ending

On her deathbed, Helene Deutsch, eminent psychoanalyst and one of Freud's analysands, when asked whether she had any regrets, replied:

> I wish I could have finished my analysis with Dr Freud. One day he came in and said, 'This is our last day', and he made room for the Wolf Man.
> (A personal communication with Anne Alonso, 7 December 2000, cited by Shapiro & Ginsberg, 2002: 319)

For therapists today, such an ending seems shocking. Could it really have happened like this? Whether it did or not, this was how Deutsch remembered it. And the memory, with what one might reasonably surmise as a myriad of affective associations – rejection, inadequacy (in the face of a more interesting subject), disappointment, dissatisfaction – stayed with her until *her* very end.

Deutsch's remembered experience appears not to have undermined the remembered experience of the year-long therapy that preceded it. With a more vulnerable, less independent-minded person, one could imagine how it might have done. The psychologist Daniel Kahneman (2011/2012) offers just such a story, though the context is a long way from the consulting room. Following a lecture, a member of the audience approached him with a story of 'listening raptly to a long symphony on a disc that was scratched near the end . . . the bad ending "ruined the whole experience"'. Kahneman notes that:

> Confusing experience with the memory of it is a compelling cognitive illusion – and it is the substitution that makes us believe a past experience can be ruined. The experiencing self does not have a voice. The remembering self is sometimes wrong, but it is the one that keeps score and governs what we learn from living.
>
> (p. 381)

He goes on to argue that two principles guide the remembering self's reconstruction of experience: the 'peak-end rule' and the principle of 'duration neglect'. This means memory is shaped disproportionately by the most intense part of an experience and its ending (particularly when they come together) rather than its duration. And the shape memory takes hugely influences our decision-making process, leading Kahneman to refer to 'the "tyranny of the remembering self".[1]

Kahneman's principles of the remembering self have attracted considerable interest over recent years. Usefully, they have prompted greater focus on the significance of endings beyond the therapeutic field as well as within it. Unfortunately, based on the simplified premise that 'all's well that ends well', they have also prompted a great deal of advice on how to orchestrate, by dint of ritual, celebration and shared positive acknowledgements, a happy ending for all. In such heavily manufactured endings, there is no challenge to the tyranny of the remembering self, only collusion.

In contrast, an analytic approach does not accede to the primacy of the remembering self but challenges it, interrogating its veracity. This is coupled with a sustained curiosity about the experiencing self. What might otherwise be essentially fleeting is *slowed down*,[2] brought into focus and subjected to reflective processes. In this way, it grows ever more articulate, gathering a voice. This double scrutiny – of the remembering and experiencing selves – helps develop a greater congruence between them.

The meaning of ending and the ending of meaning

In analytic therapy, whether individual or group, the significance of ending has long been recognised, not only because of the impact the affective intensity that tends to accompany it can have (Wardi, 1989) but also because of its meaning. Such meaning is likely to be both particular to the individual experiencing it as well as fundamentally universal.

From an analytic perspective, the meaning of ending arises from an understanding that each end signals a separation and a loss. This is so, even if the separation has, for all intents and purposes, been willingly entered into. As Marris (1986) notes:

> Even the bridegroom, by convention, holds a wake for his bachelor days on the eve of his marriage.
>
> (p. 42)

Further, every loss is understood to resonate with every other loss we have experienced. This is what gives the experience of ending its psychological depth. Such depth can, however, prove problematic. For example, if the earlier losses evoked have been insufficiently metabolised (i.e. meaningfully integrated into an adaptive and coherent view of self and world) then rather than enriching the harmonic texture of our experience, they may create such unbearable dissonance that our capacity to process what we feel, that is, to think, is overwhelmed. Of course, what may prove problematic in everyday life, may, in therapy, provide live material with which we may creatively work.

The myriad losses all of us encounter in our everyday lives – disappointments, failures, betrayals, the loss of a job, money, a house, intimate friends – Kubler-Ross (1969) calls 'the little deaths of life'. The term is apt. Existentially it is apt because such losses challenge our casual omnipotence – our best laid plans – reminding us that, in the very end, we have no control over our lives for indeed we are only mortal. Psychodynamically it is apt because the current of loss which flows through our lives and which each new loss re-animates, brings with it turbulent waters from the very source of life – for example, separation from and loss of the womb, the breast. These reanimated currents of loss prompt in us, to some degree, the primitive fears of forever falling, of disintegration and death that, from the outset, accompanied them (Freud, 1917; Klein, 1940; Winnicott, 1962). And all this is before we complicate such currents with potentially traumatising losses such as the recurring failure, in our early years, of significant others to provide sufficient constancy, holding and/or containment or the sudden death of and/or abandonment by early attachment figures.

The sociologist Peter Marris (1986, 1992) argues that when, in adulthood, we lose a significant attachment figure, it is not the loss of the relationship itself that provokes intense anxiety, restlessness and despair but 'the whole structure of meaning centred upon it':

> If recovery from bereavement only involved making good a lost relationship in the context of a life that still made sense, it could be readily accomplished. But how do you make good a loss when nothing seems to matter any more, when the reasons for caring and living are inextricably bound up with what you have lost?
>
> (1992: 18)

This problem assails us because it is through attachments that we make meaning of our lives and that our lives mean something to us. This is so from the very start since attachment:

> ... underlies all our understanding of how to survive in and manage the world we inhabit. Our first and most basic grasp of cause and effect, of predictable order, of how to get what we want, we learn from our attempts to manipulate this vital relationship ... Bereavement, therefore, because it robs us of a crucial attachment, profoundly disrupts our ability to organise experience in a meaningful way.
>
> (1986: viii–x)

In the face of such debilitating loss, if we are creatively to claim life rather than death, we must find a way of relinquishing the past without repudiating it.

We cannot repudiate it for this is where our meaning is invested. We must relinquish it or else we are consigned to a stultifying, ultimately futile existence. In short, we must find a way to transform and abstract the meaning we have made in the context of the lost relationship so that it can become relevant to the future. This, suggests Marris, is the central task of grieving,[3] that,

> slow process of assimilation of loss and psychological reintegration impelled by the contradictory desire to search for and recover the lost relationship and to escape from painful reminders of loss.
>
> (1986: vii)

Marris broadens his understanding of loss and grieving beyond the emotional challenges experienced by the bereaved to include both individual and social responses to change:

> Change ... presents some common features: the need to re-establish continuity, to work out an interpretation of oneself and the world which preserves, despite estrangement, the thread of meaning; the ambivalence of this task, as it swings between conflicting impulses ... and the risk of lasting disintegration if the process is not worked out.
>
> (1986: 42)

In this way, the capacity to make meaning not only despite but out of loss (and out of endings), in a way that is true to the individual's continuity of self, while remaining adaptive to new environments, becomes a key feature of psychological health.

Termination: ending therapy

To end therapy is to end one or more attachment relationships in which meaning, hopefully, has been made. As such, it requires a period of unhurried grieving to best ensure continuity and expansion of the self in the face of such loss. Research (Parkes & Weiss, 1983) suggests several factors can adversely affect the outcome of grieving:

- early unresolved experience of insecure attachments and traumatising losses
- ambivalence towards the present lost relationship
- an overly dependent relationship on what is being lost
- the suddenness and unexpectedness of the present loss

All but the last of these will constitute important work that needs to be engaged with at all stages of therapy. However, it is also likely to require (and provide an opportunity for) careful reworking as the ending approaches. As Foulkes (1964) advises, trying to ensure that the ending is gradual and clearly delineated rather than sudden, helps provide a frame in which such working through can best take place.

Given the impact and meaning of an ending in therapy, it is no accident that the word most often used to describe it is an ominous one – 'termination'. As Yalom (1970/1985) notes, termination 'is the microcosmic representation of some of life's most crucial and painful issues' (p. 373): 'the rush of time, loss, separation, death, ageing, and the contingencies of existence' (ibid.). In both individual and group therapy, these issues can, of course, become very present at any time and not just at termination. Sometimes, for example, they may be provoked by experiences outside therapy – a move, the loss of a loved one, a separation, a divorce – sometimes by experiences within – the end of a session, a break, the physical absence of the therapist or other group member due to illness, the loss of the therapist's and/or group's attention even when physically present. However, as a rule, in terms of terminating therapy, while in individual work the complex and challenging experience of ending a real, here-and-now significant attachment relationship happens only once, in a group, it is part of the warp and weft of group life. As such, it produces plentiful and rich opportunities for working through issues around separation-individuation (Kauff, 1977; Flapan & Fenchel, 1987; Maar, 1989; Rutan *et al*., 2014); of loss, of death, of the experience of leaving as well as of being left (Foulkes & Anthony, 1965/1984).

Scratched endings

Mindful of the affective intensity characteristic of endings, of their tendency to prompt a recapitulation of core themes, conflicts and symptoms as well as contributing so powerfully to the 'remembering self' (Kahneman, 2011/2012), the conductor is wise to ensure proper time and careful attention is given them. Yet, as suggested, it is also important to keep in mind that thinking about endings – about the impact of separations, absences, abandonments, disappointments, disillusionments, frustrations, betrayals – is the staple diet of therapy. Some would say, it is its core. After all, as the poet T. S. Eliot (1942) reminds us, 'The end is where we start from'. Birth itself bears loss. And to explore loss, to reflect upon our and others' experience of it, not only in the 'there-and-then' and 'there-and-now' but also the 'here-and-then' and 'here-and-now' (see Chapter 5), to endeavour to make something creative out of what is always potentially traumatising, is itself to give steady, due attention to the peak-end pulse of our lives:

> We shall not cease from exploration
> And the end of all our exploring
> Will be to arrive where we started
> And know the place for the first time.

This is not a reason for complacency or lax attention in the context of this highly charged phase of therapy. However, it is a reason to trust, sometimes in the wake of considerable countertransference pressures suggesting the contrary, in the robustness of careful, patient, attentive, meaningful work already done.

Michael Balint used to tell a story of how, as a young analyst, he struggled with a male patient over many years, bearing the frustration of stuckness, aggressive passivity, and complaint until one day, finding his patience stretched to breaking point, he said something which, following the session, he greatly regretted but could not remember. He only knew that it had had such an impact on his patient that he never returned. Then, one day, several years later, while walking on Hampstead Heath, he spotted what he thought was his former patient in the distance walking his dog. Suddenly, flooded with terrible guilt and shame, Balint ducked behind a bush, pretending to search for something he had dropped on the ground. A few moments later he heard a voice – the voice of his former patient – and looked up to see him standing just in front of him, looking down.

'Dr Balint!' exclaimed the man.

With as much dignity as he could muster, Balint rose to his feet as the man put out his hand.

'I'm so glad to see you', said the man, 'to have a chance to thank you for all that you did for me. And especially at the end. That thing you said to me at the end. It was so very helpful, so important'.

Balint, whose curiosity now began to outweigh his feelings of awkwardness said he was very glad indeed to hear of how helpful their work had been, but perhaps the gentleman could just remind him of what exactly he had said, at the very end, that was so helpful.

'Why Dr Balint', replied the man, 'you said' 'For God's sake man! Pull yourself together!'[4]

Types of ending: premature and planned

Endings in group therapy can broadly be described as belonging to one of two types: premature and planned. Characteristic of premature endings is a sense of therapy being disrupted, particularly for the individual(s) leaving but also for the group remaining behind. Characteristic of planned endings is a sense of there being sufficient opportunity, both for the leaver(s) and the left, to make something meaningful out of the themes of separation-individuation, attachment and loss that are inevitably provoked by such an event; meanings that better enable members to continue the process of psychological development, whether that be within or, in the case of departing members, without the group. Having said this, it is important to say that 'sufficient opportunity' is not simply a matter of time since even quite sudden and premature endings can, if reflected upon, become important learning experiences, especially for those continuing therapy, just as carefully planned, unrushed endings can, if not engaged with at sufficient depth, remain relatively meaning*less*.

Time-limited groups add further complexity to the neat dual categorisation of premature or planned. Although all group members that end at the pre-appointed termination of a group, end according to plan, not all members will be ready to end. In effect, their planned ending may, and more often than not at some level will, be experienced as premature. It is the experience of the 'premature' – an impingement on the illusion of timelessness – that is an important dynamic to explore in the termination phase of all time-limited groups.

For the purposes of this chapter, our main focus will be on endings within the context of slow open group-analytic psychotherapy groups. Martin offers three vignettes – one describing a premature ending, one an ending which could be described either as premature and/or planned, and one which fits more clearly the therapeutic understanding of a planned ending. We finish with a brief mention of endings in the context of time-limited groups which, though adding further nuances to the process and meaning of ending, still have much in common with the slow-open group endings already described.

CLINICAL DISCUSSION

Martin Weegmann and Nick Barwick

A premature ending: 'I'm not coming back'

Peter joined an established psychotherapy group, being in fact the first new member since the group began 16 months previously. When his joining was first mentioned in the group, two people seemed to physically recoil at the prospect, one (Sarah) turning the prospect into humour, 'Careful who you invite in, Martin (me), it could be the lion's den in here', and Natalie expressing surprise or puzzlement – 'I thought that the group wouldn't change', she said. Both had seemingly 'forgotten' that, as explained to all in pre-group assessment, the group was a 'slow-open' group.

On joining, Peter looked uncomfortable, eventually expressing the opinion that his needs were different to those of the others. When prompted to say more, by a group member, he said that he was struggling with his role as step-father, to a family in which he felt his step-children neither respected nor listened to him. He came twice, on the second occasion repeating his conviction that the group were 'somewhere else' to him and giving more instances of his family situation, to the apparent annoyance of others. Members seemed to react adversely to his tone of detachment if not disparagement. There was no message from Peter on the next occasion, but Nigel said Peter had told him in the corridor the week before that he would not be coming back. There were no responses to subsequent letters of inquiry.

Discussion

MW: At a general level, Nick, I think it worth us underlining that premature ending is a common experience in all psychotherapy – in fact, about one in five clients will drop out of psychotherapy before completing treatment (Swift & Greenberg, 2012). Therapists usually expect treatment to last significantly longer than do clients, even when this has been 'explained' during assessment. Discerning the reasons why is difficult, or impossible, if the client refuses feedback, as was the case with Peter.

In the group, we can see how Peter appears isolated from the start, and is indifferent and disconnected to the concerns of others. Now in some way it could be argued that he reproduces the problems that he complains of – that he feels like an outsider to his new family, even that in his manner his shows lack of regard to his fellow group members, and so he cuts off a process before it can begin. In their subsequent responses, the members were relieved that he had gone, feeling that he has indeed shown no interest in them. He had delivered a 'monologue' on his situation, but one that did not appear to invite any joining-in or response.

Is this how you would see it, Nick?

NB: Sadly, yes. Peter's experience appears to confirm Eliot's (1940) words from earlier in the *Four Quartets* – 'In my beginning is my end'. For Peter, however, these words provide an insight of dark determinism, rather than the creative, hopeful, time-conflating way forward the poet himself finally discerns. Was Peter, then, doomed to repeat the relational distress that brought him to therapy? Was it inevitable he would end up where he started but with no hope of further exploration and no new knowledge gleaned? Therapeutic hope – that there is a way out of perpetual 'Groundhog Day' – rests to no small degree on a capacity for 'witnessing' (i.e. observing the experience of self and others with compassion but without being consumed) (Barwick, 2004), in all group participants. For witnessing to be possible, particularly at a time when anxieties are running high (which inevitably they do when a new member joins) requires careful preparation – for both newcomer and group.[5]

For Peter, in taking a group history during preparatory sessions, it would have been important to think with him about what it might feel like to join another pre-formed 'family'. Best to be realistic: it's likely to be tough. Is there anything that might help him to hold on and not simply repeat making another beginning into another end? Is there anything, indeed, that might help everyone – himself, the therapist and the group – do this? Such questions aren't designed to provide answers – though they might begin to – but to problematise the process of joining and relating so that it becomes clear these activities require thought and work.

It seems to me, however, that the problem is not just Peter's. It's as if there's a 'psychological fit' between Peter and the group waiting to be realised; one that is evident in the group's reactions to the news of his arrival. Such antagonism – the desire to destroy, *dis*-member, eradicate from mind – needs some unpacking if the level of acting out is to prove containable.[6] Would you agree Martin?

MW: I do agree. It's uncanny and yet very familiar to see the way in which patterns continue and yes, psychotherapy, of any kind, holds out the promise that maybe this time it will not; in narrative terms, that the 'story' can be changed. Peter rejects before he even knows what could happen were he to stay. But even with the most careful, judicious preparation, the person may reject what they are offered, in this case the 'now' of the actual group. When this is so, the conductor's task is still to help make something out of what is a therapeutic failure, to enable useful 'learning from experience'.

NB: Absolutely. Every ending, no matter how unwished for, offers opportunities for learning, for making meaning. Indeed, the very process of making meaning helps build hope in the group's capacity to make meaning; the hope that, even out of therapeutic failure, something creative can be generated and important learning gleaned.

With Peter, I suspect such learning may not, for now, be possible, though I would certainly be inclined to offer individual follow-up in an effort to create, together, a more productive end. As for the group, I suspect the opportunity to work with and through guilt will be important, including the conductor's.

I see Peter's exit as a type of therapeutic suicide; an act of despair born out of a loss of hope in the efficacy of communication; that is, in the capacity of *mature forms of communication* to create shared understanding and to elicit, in and with others, a sense of belonging. Peter's 'suicide' *is* of course a communication but a *primitive* one. It achieves, through projective processes, what its mature counterpart fails to do: a place in the mind of the group. Ironically, Peter will no longer be around to witness the impact he has on others' minds, just as the dead cannot witness the grieving at their grave. Nor do the mourners have an opportunity to make something meaningful from their loss, at least not *with* the departed. And yet, even in such a difficult and sudden ending as this, there remains opportunities for meaning-making. I suspect, for the group, this may entail facing persecutory guilt (guilt that, unfaced, may lead to the dead ends of denial and/or despair), challenging it (the group is not responsible for Peter's 'death' even though they may have contributed to the dynamic out of which it was realised) and transforming it into something more creative, capable of symbolic repair.

In terms of the latter, I have often been moved by the depth of resonance and reflection (the re-working of old experiences of loss) that sudden departure prompts. Memories and thoughts about other relational losses (deaths, divorces, suicides, separations, unexplained relational withdrawals) begin to surface: a whole gamut of 'little deaths' (Kubler-Ross, 1969), including a deeper recognition of enactments within the group, such as retreats from communicative engagement, loss of hope at being understood and the passive aggression inherent, at times, in absences (literal and metaphorical) that an experience of not being thought about can provoke. The opportunity for such exploration is vital for the continued healthy development of the group, especially a group early in its life since, otherwise, as Rosenthal (2005), citing Gustafson (1980) notes, a premature departure can be like 'a hole in the side of the group with cold wind blowing right through' (p. 49).

A premature or appropriate ending? 'But I've got all that I can'

Tracy, having been in the group for 10 months, hinted that she would leave in two. When Mary, who had joined with her, said it would be a shame for the group if she did so, Tracy responded, 'I've got all that I could. It's been good, but I just need to make some key decisions and take action in my life'. Others felt this was a defensive statement, to which Tracy added, 'yeah, but it's my decision, I've got to make it'. Some of the decisions to which she alluded related to an unproductive relationship, one in which she felt stuck by virtue of security needs and a fear of being by herself. Mary could identify with her, herself locked into a joyless marriage. I commented that 'staying in the group' and 'making decisions/taking action' did not have to be mutually exclusive, indeed that by staying in the group those processes might be further strengthened, or clarified, but to no avail. Subsequently, Tracy appeared to avoid reference to the idea of leaving, and indeed, focused on others instead. It was only when Paul reminded her and asked her again how she felt, a month later, that she tersely responded, 'I can't stay on. Sorry'. She left after three more groups. People shared warm farewells, even suggesting that she could still change her mind. She was embarrassed, adding, under her breath, 'I hope I've made the right decision'.

Discussion

MW: Foulkes developed a 'spiral notion' when it comes to matters of endings in a slow-open group. The metaphor here is of a winding staircase on which there are exits at many levels. These are favourable moments where a group member, achieving a certain critical depth of work, must judge whether to leave the group or go on until the next favourable moment or exit presents itself. Their judgement should, suggests Foulkes, be largely in accord with peers – in other words, 'subject to analysis' – though freedom to decide is of course essential.

Now, here the discussion starts because it is unclear if that moment had come and if her peers had really helped her to properly work through her reasons, feelings and the decision itself. And perhaps I too failed to bring it back to the group and to the fore of discussion.

The ending of therapy is of course a loss, where a significant part of the client's life no longer there. As in her real life, there is transition from one place of security, even if that is an unsatisfactory one, to an uncertain place. How will I cope alone? There is a moment at the end when her uncertainty is re-stated, 'have I made the right decision'? One wonders if she lacked a capacity to truly *think* about the ending – the feelings aroused, its meaning, and so forth. Was is an area that could not, in modern terms, be mentalised, so that her action and thought were divorced? On the other hand, we do encourage clients to develop autonomy and maybe her decision to leave mirrors something of the decisions that she wants to take in her outside life – and all that requires courage.

Nick, do you read this in a similar way?

NB: Sometimes groups seem happy to see some members go. Your first scenario is an example of this. In your second, however, it is reluctance not relief the group shows.

Most terminations in groups are experienced, at some level, as a disruption of the 'idealised group illusion' (Schermer & Klein, 1996) – fantasies and basic assumptions of dependency perhaps, of oneness, of permanence – and as an impingement on the enveloping facilitative environment. But this is not, of course, good reason for people not to leave. Although defences against such disruption might be at play here and may well need exploring, the therapist's countertransference, together with the genuine sense of loss – explicitly voiced here by Mary – suggests the group's hesitancy is a response to Tracy not having sufficiently worked something through. At the very least, the group is left, until the final moments of her departure anyway (when she once again becomes aware of her ambivalence – ironically, I think, a sign of health), with an uncertainty that Tracy herself has seemed, for much of these last weeks, less able to bear.

An important aspect of group-analytic therapy is, as you say Martin, to facilitate in individuals a capacity to take up their own authority and, in so doing, to exercise their autonomy. For Tracy, demonstrating a capacity to make decisions is clearly related to this. It is important then, even if the conductor is not convinced of the decision made, to support her capacity to make it. Certainly the group needs to feel free to bring analytic scrutiny to bear upon this communication as with any communication in the group. However, the group, including and especially the conductor, need to be sensitive to enabling Tracy to leave, if and when she wishes to, and to do so with dignity.

All this said, I am, nevertheless, often wary when a group member presents the group with a decision, a *fait accomplit*, especially one that affects the whole group. This is very different than coming with 'thoughts in progress': in this instance, the desire to make a decision and a request for engagement with the process of thinking about it and of making it. It is, on the whole I think, this latter, more open approach that speaks of a more assured sense of internal authority. This is so because implicit in such communicative sharing is both a more realistic understanding of what inter-dependent living entails and a confidence that communication about what is not yet clear in one's own mind leads not to a likely curtailment of agency but to its honing and development. In other words, intimacy and self-agency, rather than being mutually exclusive, are co-creative and the expansion of personal horizons grows out of a 'fusion of horizons', not by defensive efforts to exclude the impact on the self of other ways of seeing.

Rice (1996) suggests that endings which might be deemed premature (as this one might be) can sometimes be prompted during a 'phase change' in a group; for example a change from a period of bonding to a period where difference begins to gain more emphasis and, consequently, conflicts begin to emerge. I'm not sure, from what you describe, whether this might be the case here, but the fact that, following the group's suggestion that Tracy sounded 'defensive', the subject of her departure slips into the background, suggests perhaps a degree of collusion in avoiding difficult ground where individual members might have very different views. Indeed, in the dynamic played out between Tracy and the group, there may be located concerns about how difference can be dealt with and how autonomy can be retained, let alone developed, amidst the growing intimacy of the group.

Ideally all such opportunities for meaning-making would be explored in the group. The nature of the warm farewell and Tracy's greater availability towards the end suggests perhaps, were she to stay, conditions would be ripe for doing so. However, in the light of her departure, this work will be the group's without the benefit of the literal presence of the departed and it is work, I suspect, that will occupy the group, in one way or another, for some time.

A planned ending: 'And I'll try to take the group with me'

Margaret, who was a group member for 4 years, was seen almost as the 'wise woman' of the group. This was on account of several aspects, including, being relatively older (mid-60s when she left), her charm and encouragement, her mature, reflective capacities and the way in which she had tackled considerable adversity in her life. Sarah (mid 20s), for example, said things like, 'We can always rely on you for helping us, and for seeing things' and, 'I can learn a lot from you because you've done so much work on yourself'.

Nursing a disturbed mother and caring for siblings were some of the dominating themes of her early life, together with a stressful job that had involved administration of a care organisation; others in the group both enjoyed her care-giving, 'maternal' sensitivity while simultaneously challenging her gravitation towards the caring role. Increasingly, others wanted Margaret to 'be more selfish' and 'put herself first'. Experiences of job redundancy were another focus, where she was displaced by a much younger, energetic 'entrepreneur', leaving her on the sidelines. Increasing marital tensions and conflicts with her (adult) child reduced the prospects of support outside.

Margaret felt that her time was 'complete' in the group, giving several months' notice before leaving. People were generally supportive of this, but did express concern about her relative isolation. They felt she was sadder also, about life in general.

Discussion

MW: There are several aspects that one could chose to focus on from the vignette – the position of the (significantly) older group member, retirement/redundancy, loss of productivity, and so on. I shall concentrate on her overall 'presence' and patterns in the group and how a process of planned leaving comes about.

Wisdom is hard to define as a quality, which in this context spoke to the way in which Margaret managed life adversity, and gained a certain resilience as a result. Others liked her because she was adept at 'seeing' what they might be going through and was able, with great sensitivity, to help them forward. In their 'golden years', such adults do often acquire a better emotional balance and problem-solving skills but, for Margaret, this also belied a pattern, one developed in the context of premature care-giving. She could be thought of as a 'cork-child' (McDougal, 1986) whose psychic duty was to hold a would-be, should-be container (the mother/the group) together. The fear, were she not to perform, was that the container could explode or not progress. In this way, care-giving provided reassurance, a source of self-esteem, indeed was carried into her occupational life as an adult. Caring was a long-established, crafted ability, but had a heavy price, as pointed out by the others. A 'longer life' brings home the many changing positions, transitions and thresholds that have to be negotiated, and also the way in which patterns become habitual.

As a longer-term treatment, group analysis holds no magical means of knowing when (indeed, when not) a member is ready to leave. But, hopefully, there has been sufficient time in which the person has been able to fully connect with others, to work-through some of their core dilemmas and suffering and to incorporate some of the wider wisdom that group membership provides if seen as no longer located in just one ('wise') person. Others have their opportunities to give feedback over any feeling or decision about leaving, feedback which might not always be comfortable for that person to hear. In this example, there had been a deal of challenging, and an acknowledgement of a dimension of sadness which Margaret carried and/or came to feel. It is a reminder that leaving is seldom a romantic, smooth process for the member who departs, nor for the group who remain.

NB: From your description, one of Margaret's core relational difficulties is her tendency to prioritise others' needs over her own. This behaviour clearly has a long history – 'nursing a disturbed mother and caring for siblings' – and is often enacted in the group. Although group members value her caring capacity and skills, they have also challenged them, experiencing such a stance as 'incomplete'; that is, lacking a counter-balancing capacity for greater selfishness, for 'putting herself first'.

After 4 years in the group, however, Margaret, notifying the group of her intention to leave, refers to her time in the group as being 'complete'. I take this to mean she feels that the core aspect of her main therapeutic task is 'complete'; that she has achieved a more balanced, creative way of relating, of managing competing needs of self and other. Changes in relationships outside the group – emerging conflicts, for example, with her husband and her '(adult) child' – suggest as much, as does, perhaps, her very decision to leave, straining, as it may at some level, against the desire of some group members perhaps who, finding her contributions so valuable, want her to stay.

Although Margaret's enhanced capacity both to acknowledge and express her desire/need brings significant psychic liberation, it also brings sadness. In part, this may be an apt response to the imminent loss of the group. As Garland (2010) suggests:

> even when an individual patient has made for himself the decision to leave, the feeling that predominates is that of *being left*. In the unconscious it makes no difference who made the decision. The outcome is the same – the loss of the object.
>
> (p. 121)

Yet there may be other reasons too. Certainly, for Margaret, with an experience of greater empowerment must come not only a resigned recognition of past unmet, unclaimed needs – a painful loss in itself – but also a poignant awareness of a present and future where, in the pursuit of authenticity, the possibility of losing relationships (and certainly a way of life, of relating) that have served until now to sustain as well as limit her, must be borne. All this, as you say Martin, suggests a far from 'romantic' or 'smooth' ending or road ahead. Nonetheless, it is a realistic one, bringing with it more room for the 'depressive position' (Klein, 1935) out of which creativity can more easily flourish.

As Margaret's departure is explored, the group expresses proper concern about her leaving. There is a recognition of some of the difficulties inherent in her journey ahead. However, unlike with Tracy, the group broadly concurs with her decision. This confirms its likely aptness. In addition, her willingness to give substantial time for discussing her departure itself suggests confidence in her own agency. She will not, she believes, be unhelpfully influenced by the contributions of others, only enriched. Another good sign. Further, her planned departure gives opportunities not only for her, but also for the group, to explore the experience of 'loss'. Does it prompt in the group, for example, a fear of depletion?[7] Or, though recognising her unique contribution, are the remaining members, like Margaret herself, able to think about what they will be able to keep inside even after she has gone. Certainly, the capacity to make life-enhancing meaning out of what is lost, to 'find/Strength in what remains behind' (Wordsworth, 1804/1970), is central to the process of grieving, testing, as it does, whether the learning achieved is 'adhesive' – dependent on concrete repetition with the person or people with whom it was learnt – or 'introjective' – where the lost object is held, as a creative resource, independent of the physical presence of the other, inside (Waddell, 1998). As Margaret says, 'I shall try and take the group with me'.

Yalom (1970/1985) suggests that, for group members who experience a sense of 'completing' their work, termination is, on the whole, less problematic than for individual patients. Having already observed the process of termination of others, they have also experienced, he argues, 'the bittersweet fact that though the therapist is a person with whom they have had a real and meaningful relationship, he or she is also a professional whose attention must shift to others and who will not remain as a permanent and bottomless source of gratification for them' (p. 368). Apart from the fact that this is a rather dyadically oriented (patient-therapist rather than group-oriented) statement, I suspect that the challenge for Margaret is less about whether she feels she can survive without the group (including the therapist) and more about whether she feels the group can survive without her. Perhaps, indeed, her particularly long farewell, useful though it is, speaks something of this concern: a desire to be very sure that all will not fall apart if she goes. This may well be mirrored in the group's own concerns about losing their 'wise woman'. Important for all, then, will be reflecting upon what qualities admired in Margaret may be introjected in the process of her leaving and what adhesively learnt qualities feel more dependent upon her being physically there.

Although there is no indication of regression in Margaret's case, sometimes the original symptoms a member presents at the outset of therapy can forcefully re-present themselves at the end. This can alarm both conductor and group, even prompting a postponement of a planned ending. In group therapy, this might usefully be thought about in terms symptomatic relational enactments. Thus, should the compromised care-giving-receiving system described above – one with Margaret care-giving and others care-receiving – re-emerge in the form, for example, of a series of group member crises matched by a hyper-activated caring response from Margaret and a consequent re-consideration by all of whether it really is a good time for Margaret to leave, it would be worth keeping in mind Wardi's (1989) observation that such regressive symptomatology, though no less intense than its pathological sibling, is transient, offering an opportunity for further 'working through'; hence her reference to it as 'constructive termination regression'.

'Successful termination' in a group can be seen as being a 'gift' to those remaining (Shapiro & Ginzberg, 2002); an opportunity for 'therapeutic harvest' (Schermer & Klein, 1996). This is so, not only because of the rich material evoked and provoked by the experience of separation and individuation that are central to the process of termination, but also because the affectively charged authenticity of communications characteristic of well-managed endings facilitate 'the emergence of the 'true self' experience and the formation of stronger bonds among the ones who are 'left behind' (p. 111).

Reflecting on what I have said about Margaret's ending, I'm aware of offering, perhaps, a fuller response than in the other two cases. I'm aware also of referring more to the literature and of my own need to feel I have said enough. This makes me think of how I, personally, as a conductor, and as a writer, respond to endings. We are, after all, approaching the end of this book.

The anxiety that 'time's winged chariot hurrying near' (Marvell, 1681) provokes is universal, penetrating every aspect of our lives. And I suspect my desire to say more of what there is 'not world enough, and time' to say is, at least in part, a response to just such provocation. It is a desire I often find in myself when approaching the end of time-limited groups, ones in which members have agreed to end both at a predetermined time and together. Unsettled by words not said, not found, of 'something undone', these 'omissions', 'That spread their echoes through a place/And fill the locked-up unbreathed gloom' (Jennings, 1958), can never be fully exorcised, since the work of self-other discovery can never be complete. Yet such *'Ghosts'* – the title of Jennings's hauntingly melancholic poem – can be acknowledged, even if their 'faces' are not yet 'known'. And, in the acknowledgement, we may reach a more depressive (rather than depressed) position; one that, in facing loss, including lost opportunities, finds hope in new ones, aware that 'to make an end is to make a beginning' (Eliot, 1942). This is true because introjective learning, of which the process of therapy is one form, brings with it not only content – *what* we learn (knowledge) – but also a useable understanding of *how* we learn (wisdom), including an awareness of how, sometimes, we do not. Any completeness, then, that we might usefully strive for in group therapy, comes not so much from the actual knowledge that we gain (important though this is, there is always more of that) but from engaging deeply with the work: exploring ourselves in relationship to others *with* others. And it comes also from the realistic hope that we may continue such explorations even after we have left the group because we know what it is like to learn about ourselves through communicating with others – that is, we more readily recognise the life-enhancing import of *community* and of *communion*. This is what Margaret means, I think, when she speaks of taking the group with her and what, perhaps, E. M. Forster means when, through the impassioned plea of *Howard's End*'s (1910) central protagonist Margaret Schlegel, he exhorts the reader to, 'Only connect!'

Notes

1 Exactly how detrimental this influence can be is vividly captured in 'the cold hand situation' (Kahneman *et al.*, 1993), an experiment where participants were twice asked to immerse a hand in painfully cold water. One immersion was for 60 seconds; the other for 90 with the last 30 in water one degree warmer. Clearly, overall, the total pain experienced was least in the shorter immersion. Yet, when given the choice of which to repeat, 80 per cent of participants chose the longer period.
2 I use the term 'slow' advisedly as Kahneman (2011/2012) calls 'slow thinking' an effortful, attentive type of thinking that articulates judgements, makes choices, endorses or rationalises ideas and feelings generated by 'fast thinking'. 'Fast thinking' is, in contrast, automatic, associative, intuitive.
3 A task that can be supported by the group culture of 'mourning', including the rites of mourning which can help articulate the grieving process, 'lightening the burden of responsibility on the bereaved themselves' (Marris, 1986: 32).
4 I am grateful to Murray Cox for this wonderfully telling anecdote.
5 Rosenthal (2005) argues that inadequate preparation, selection and timing of the introduction of new members are the major factors contributing to early drop-out. Further, Rice (1996) cites extensive research suggesting good preparation significantly reduces drop-out.
6 The meaning of the antagonism is likely to be complex but I am reminded of Rosenthal (2005) who, drawing on Lothstein (1978), notes how the 'group

ritualistically sacrifices its deviant to achieve stability' (Rosenthal, 2005: 43). Rosenthal further notes a parallel between a group that rejects new members and 'a society that closes its border to new immigrants' (p. 47).

7 Groups often experience the departure of an engaged member as a loss of an asset. This can often be poignantly so, even when not liked by some – the loss of an opportunity for some members to explore the nature of the relational difficulty experienced.

Epilogue

Martin Weegmann

Among my favourite quotations of Foulkes is this:

> I do not think we should always try to understand. . . . In this connection I tend to leave things unresolved, in mid-air, incomplete ('no closure').
> (Foulkes, 1964, p. 287)

Now it is nigh on impossible to capture complex qualities of group life in writing and, clearly, to isolate particular individuals for purposes of clinical illustration is artificial; artificial in that, even though it is individuals who seek group treatment, 'individual processes' cannot be conceptualised independently of the group matrix in which they occur. That matrix shifts continually and groups are always on the move, open affairs, occupied not only by present content, but also with that which is not-yet said, continually pushing and bumping against the edges of the 'circle of the unexpressed' (Linge, 1966, p. xxxii); each group calls forth another occasion, a further conversation, a next time. Re-translating this back to Foulkes:

> Therapy lies at both ends of the communication process . . . communication becomes plastic, relative and modifiable by group experience, not rigid, absolute and repetitive.
> (Foulkes & Anthony, 1957, pp. 149–150)

Likewise, arguably, is theory. For theory, too, has its locations, historical traditions and particular utility within time and space, so cannot be separated from being part of the ongoing project of group analysis. This having been said, some 'standing back' is always required for critical thinking to take place – do our theories still serve us? what are their limitations, scope and so forth? And how do we endeavour to make them accessible, including for those in different positions within their training and career?

When Nick first asked me to contribute to this project, I was hesitant, thinking, what on earth could I offer that Nick is not already onto? We had trained together and always got on; I recall the pleasure of discussing one of my first psychotherapy publications with him, in which I drew upon literary sources (Eugene O'Neil to be precise) and discovered Nick's love of literature. He struck me then as a creative individual with a wealth of knowledge at his disposal. And I still enjoy his spirit of openness towards theory as well as to how one's group practice can be developed. Overcoming my hesitancy, our dialogue began and I found that I did have something to say. Our communication unfolded and, for a project that at times I felt was over-ambitious, took shape and came into being. I particularly enjoyed our written dialogues for the prompts and clarifications they provided, neither of which was quite there beforehand but which emerged from the act itself. No final answers either, of course, just how we see things at this stage in our mutual careers. No closure.

References

Abelin, E. L. (1971). The role of the father in the separation-individuation process. In J. B. McDevitt & C. F. Settlage (eds), *Separation-Individuation.* New York: International Universities Press.
Abelin, E. L. (1980). Triangulation: The role of the father and origin of core gender identity during the rapprochement sub-phase. In R. F. Lax, S. Bach, & J. A. Burland (eds), *Rapprochement.* New York: Jason Aronson.
Agazarian, Y. (1994). The phases of group development and the systems-centred group. In V. L. Schermer & M. Pines (eds), *Ring of Fire.* London: Routledge.
Agazarian, Y. & Gantt, S. P. (2000). *Autobiography of a Theory.* London: Jessica Kingsley.
Agazarian, Y. & Peters, R. (1981/1995). *The Visible and Invisible Group.* London: Karnac.
Ainsworth, M., Blehar, M., Waters, E., & Wall, S. (1978). *Patterns of Attachment: A Psychological Study of the Strange Situation.* Hillsdale, NJ: Lawrence Erlbaum Associates.
Alexander, F. & French, T. M. (1946). *Psychoanalytic Therapy.* New York: Ronald Press.
Allen, J. G., Fonagy, P., & Bateman, A. (2008). *Mentalizing in Clinical Practice.* Arlington, VA: American Psychiatric Association.
Anthony, E. J. (1971). The history of group psychotherapy. In H. I. Kaplan & B. I. Sadock (eds), *Comprehensive Group Psychotherapy* (1st edn). Baltimore, MD: Williams & Wilkins.
Anthony, E. J. (1983). The group-analytic circle and its ambient network. In M. Pines (ed.), *The Evolution of Group Analysis.* London: Routledge & Kegan Paul.
Anthony, E. J. (1991). The dilemma of therapeutic leadership: The leader who does not lead. In S. Tuttman (ed.), *Psychoanalytic Group Theory and Therapy.* American Group Psychotherapy Association.
Aran, L. W. (2016). The Conductor's Self-disclosure of Negative Countertransference in Group Analytic Psychotherapy. *Group Analysis*, 49, 385–97.
Argelander, H. (1970). Die szeishe Funktion des ich und ihr Anteil an der Symptom und Charakterbildung. *Psyche*, 24, 325–45.
Aron, L. (1996). *A Meeting of Minds: Mutuality in Psychoanalysis.* Hillsdale, NJ: Analytic Press.
Aron, L. (2006). Analytic impasse and the third: Clinical implications of intersubjectivity theory. *International Journal of Psychoanalysis*, 87, 349–68.

As it is in Heaven (2004). Dir. K. Pollack. Distributed by Kino International, USA.
Ashbach, C. & Schermer, V. (1987). *Object Relations, the Self, and the Group.* London: Routledge & Kegan Paul.
Bacal, H. A. (1985a). Object relations in the group from the perspective of self psychology. *International Journal of Group Psychotherapy*, 35, 483–501.
Bacal, H. A. (1985b). Optimal responsiveness and the therapeutic process. In A. Goldberg (ed.), *Progress in Self Psychology.* New York: Guilford Press.
Bacal, H. A. (1991). Reactiveness and responsiveness in the group therapeutic process. In S. Tuttman (ed.), *Psychoanalytic Group Theory and Therapy.* New York: International Universities Press.
Bacal, H. A. (1998). Notes on optimal responsiveness in the group process. In N. H. Harwood & M. Pines (eds), *Self Experiences in Group.* London: Jessica Kingsley.
Bacha, C. (1997). The stranger in the group. *Psychodynamic Counselling*, 3, 7–22.
Bachelard, G. (1969). *The Poetics of Space.* Boston, MA: Beacon Press.
Bakali, J. V., Wilberg, T., Hagtvet, K. A., & Lorentzen, S. (2010). Sources accounting for alliance and cohesion at three stages in group psychotherapy. *Group Dynamics*, 14, 368–83.
Bakali, J. V. I., Wilberg, T., & Lorentzen, S. (2013). Development of group climate in short- and long-term psychodynamic group psychotherapy. *International Journal of Group Psychotherapy*, 63, 366–93.
Barnes, B., Ernst, S., & Hyde, K. (1999) *An Introduction to Groupwork.* London: Macmillan.
Barwick, N. (2000). Core conditions of the psychodynamic environment. In R. J. Hazler & N. Barwick (eds), *The Therapeutic Environment.* Milton Keynes, UK: Open University Press.
Barwick, N. (2001). Underworldly goings on in school: A pedagogue's descent. *Psychodynamic Counselling*, 7, 225–29.
Barwick, N. (2003). Mad desire and feverish melancholy: Reflections on the psychodynamics of writing and presenting. *British Journal of Psychotherapy*, 20, 59–71.
Barwick, N. (2004). Bearing witness: Group analysis as witness training in action. *Group Analysis*, 37, 121–36.
Barwick, N. (2006a). Making room: Developing reflective capacity through group analytic psychotherapy (part one). *Psychodynamic Practice*, 12, 37–52.
Barwick, N. (2006b). Making room: Developing reflective capacity through group analytic psychotherapy (part two). *Psychodynamic Practice*, 12, 53–65.
Barwick, N. (2015). Book Review Essay of *Beyond the Anti-Group* by Nitsun, M. (2015). *Psychodynamic Practice*, 21, 347–53.
Barwick, N. (in press). Writing as developmental process: Staying 'alive' (working title). In M. Weegmann, (ed.), *Psychodynamics of Writing.* London: Karnac.
Bateman, A., & Fonagy, P. (2006). *Mentalization-Based Treatment for Borderline Personality Disorder.* Oxford: Oxford University Press.
Bateson, G. (1972). *An Ecology of Mind.* Chicago, IL: University of Chicago Press.
Bateson, G. (1979). *Mind and Nature.* London: Wildwood House.
Battegay, R. (1994). Cohesive and disintegrative dynamics in group psychotherapy and their moderation by the leader. *Chinese Psychiatry*, 8, 69–82.
Beck, W. (2006). Countertransference in groups. *Group Analysis*, 39, 100–07.

Begovac, B. & Begovac, I. (2013). Cohesion and coherency and a threat of loss in the analytic group. *Group Analysis*, 46, 211–24.
Behr, H. (2004). Commentary on drawing the isolate into the group flow. *Group Analysis*, 37, 76–81.
Behr, H. & Hearst, L. (2005). *Group-Analytic Psychotherapy.* London: Whurr.
Bennis, W. G. & Shephard, H. A. (1956). A theory of group development, *Human Relations*, 9, 415–37.
Bhaktin, M. M. (1986). *Speech Genres and Other Late Essays.* Austin, TX: University of Texas Press.
Bhurruth, M. (2008). Matriculating the matrix. *Group Analysis*, 41, 352–65.
Bick, E. (1968/1988). The experience of the skin in early object-relations. In E. Bott Spillius (ed.), *Melanie Klein Today: Mainly Theory*. London: Routledge.
Bion, W. R. (1952/1989). Group dynamics: A review. In *Experiences in Groups.* London: Tavistock/Routledge.
Bion, W. R. (1959/1984). Attacks on linking. In *Second Thoughts.* London: Karnac.
Bion, W. R. (1961/1989). *Experiences in Groups.* London: Tavistock.
Bion, W. R. (1962a/1984). A theory of thinking. In *Second Thoughts.* London: Karnac.
Bion, W. (1967). Notes on memory and desire. *The Psychoanalytic Forum*, 2, 272–80.
Bion, W. R. (1970). *Attention and Interpretation.* London: Tavistock.
Bion, W. R. (1974/1990). *The Brazilian Lectures.* London: Karnac.
Blackwell, D. (1994). The psyche and the system. In D. Brown & L. Zinkin (eds), *The Psyche and the Social World.* London: Routledge.
Blackwell, D. (2013). Locating 'Nos' in the dialectics of instinct, communication and society. *Group Analysis*, 46, 407–14.
Bollas, C. (1987). *The Shadow of the Object.* London: Free Association Books.
Bollas, C. (1989). *Forces of Destiny.* London: Free Association Books.
Bollas, C. (2008). *The Evocative Object World.* London: Routledge.
Borch, C. (2012). *The Politics of Crowds.* Cambridge, UK: Cambridge University Press.
Boston Change Process Study Group (2010). *Change in Psychotherapy.* New York: Norton.
Bowden, M. (2002). Anti-group attitudes at assessment for psychotherapy. *Psychoanalytic Psychotherapy*, 16, 246–58.
Bowlby, J. (1969). *Attachment and Loss: Attachment.* London: Hogarth Press.
Bowlby, J. (1973). *Attachment and Loss: Separation* London: Hogarth Press.
Bowlby, J. (1980). *Attachment and Loss: Loss.* London: Hogarth Press.
Bowlby, J. (1988). *A Secure Base.* London: Routledge.
Brennan, K. A., Clark, C. L., & Shaver, P. R. (1998). Self-report measurement of adult romantic attachment. In J. A. Simpson & W. S. Rholes (eds), *Attachment Theory and Close Relationships*. New York: Guilford Press.
Bretherton, I. (2000). Emotional availability: An attachment perspective. *Attachment & Human Development*, 2, 233–41.
Britton, R. (1985/1992). The Oedipus situation and the depressive position. In R. Anderson (ed.), *Clinical Lectures on Klein and Bion.* London: Routledge.
Britton, R. (1989). The missing link: Parental sexuality in the Oedipus complex. In J. Steiner (ed.), *The Oedipus Complex Today.* London: Karnac.
Britton, R. (1998). *Belief and Imagination.* London: Routledge.

Britton, R. (2004). Subjectivity, objectivity, and the triangular space. *Psychoanalytic Quarterly*, 73, 47–61.
Brown, D. (1985/2000). Bion and Foulkes: Basic assumptions and beyond. In M. Pines (ed.), *Bion and Group Psychotherapy*. London: Jessica Kingsley.
Brown, D. (1986). Dialogue for change. *Group Analysis*, 19, 25–38.
Brown, D. (1989). A contribution to the understanding of psychosomatic processes in group. *British Journal of Psychotherapy*, 6(6), 5–9.
Brown, D. (1991). Assessment and selection for group. In J. Roberts & M. Pines (eds), *The Practice of Group Analysis*. London: Routledge.
Brown, D. (1994). Self development through subjective interaction. In D. Brown & L. Zinkin (eds), *The Psyche & the Social World*. London: Routledge.
Brown, D. (1998a). Foulkes's basic law of group dynamics 50 years on. *Group Analysis*, 31, 391–419.
Brown, D. (1998b). Fair shares and mutual concern: The role of sibling relationships. *Group Analysis*, 31, 315–26.
Brown, D. (2001). A contribution to the understanding of the social unconscious. *Group Analysis*, 34(1), 29–38.
Brown, D. (2003). Pairing Bion and Foulkes. In R. M. Lipgar & M. Pines (eds), *Building on Bion*. London: Jessica Kingsley.
Brown, D., & Zinkin, L. (1994). The psyche and the social world. In D. Brown & L. Zinkin (eds), *The Psyche and the Social World*. London: Routledge.
Burke, K. (1969). *A Rhetoric of Motives*. Berkeley & Los Angeles, CA: University of California Press.
Burrow, T. (1926a). The laboratory method in psychoanalysis. In E. G. Pertegato & G. O. Pertegato (eds), (2013). *From Psychoanalysis to Group Analysis*. London: Karnac.
Burrow, T. (1926b). On mass neurosis. In E. Pertegato & G. O. Pertegato (eds), (2013). *From Psychoanalysis to Group Analysis*. London: Karnac.
Burrow, T. (1927a). *The Social Basis of Consciousness*. London: Kegan Paul, Trench and Trubner.
Burrow, T. (1927b). The group method of analysis. In E. G. Pertegato & G. O. Pertegato (eds), (2013). *From Psychoanalysis to Group Analysis*. London: Karnac.
Burrow, T. (1927c). The problem of transference. In E. G. Pertegato & G. O. Pertegato (eds), (2013). *From Psychoanalysis to Group Analysis*. London: Karnac.
Burrow, T. (1928a). The autonomy of the 'I' from the standpoint of group analysis. In E. G. Pertegato & G. O. Pertegato (eds), (2013). *From Psychoanalysis to Group Analysis*. London: Karnac.
Burrow, T. (1928b). The basis of group analysis. In E. G. Pertegato & G. O. Pertegato (eds), (2013). *From Psychoanalysis to Group Analysis*. London: Karnac.
Campos, J. (2009). S. H. Foulkes, Pioneer on the Frontiers of the Groups, [Online]. Available at http://arxius.grupdanalisi.org/GDAP/SHFoulkes_JC_ing.pdf (accessed January 2013).
Cano, D. H. (1998). Oneness and Me-ness in the bag. In P. Bion Talamo, F. Borgogno & S.A. Merciai (eds), *Bion's Legacy to Groups*. London: Karnac.
Chused, J. & Raphling, C. (1992). The analyst's mistakes. *Journal of the American Psychoanalytic Association*, 40, 137–49.
Cobban, A. (1965). *A History of Modern France* (Vol. 1). Harmondsworth, UK: Penguin.

Cohen, B. D. & Schermer, V. L. (2001). Therapist self disclosure in group psychotherapy from an intersubjective and self psychological standpoint. *Group*, 25, 41–57.
Coltart, N. (1993). *How to Survive as a Psychotherapist*. New York, Jason Aronson.
Cooper, R. (1999). Foulkes and group analysis. In C. Oakely (ed.), *What is a Group?* London: Rebus Press.
Cortesao, E. L. (1991). Group analysis and aesthetic equilibrium. *Group Analysis*, 24, 271–77.
Cox, J. (2015). Maiden Speech in UK Houses of Parliament, 3rd June [Online]. Available at https://www.parliament.uk/business/news/2016/june/jo-cox-maiden-speech-in-the-house-of-commons/ (accessed 5 December 2016).
Cox, M. & Theilgaard, A. (1987/1997). *Mutative Metaphors*. London: Jessica Kingsley.
Cozolino, L. (2002). *The Neuroscience of Psychotherapy*. New York: Norton.
Cozolino, L. (2006). *The Neuroscience of Human Relationships*. New York: Norton.
Dalal, F. (1998). *Taking the Group Seriously*. London: Jessica Kingsley.
Dalal, F. (2001). The social unconscious: A post-Foulkesian perspective. *Group Analysis*, 34, 539–55.
Dalal, F. (2002a). *Race, Colour and the Process of Racialisation*. Hove, UK: Brunner-Routledge.
Dalal, F. (2002b). The social unconscious: A post-foulkesian perspective. *Group Analysis*, 34, 539–55.
Dalal, F. (2011). The social unconscious. In E. Hopper & H. Weinberg (eds), *The Social Unconscious in Persons, Groups and Societies* (Vol. 1). London: Karnac.
Dalal, F. (2015). Prejudice as ideology: The creation of 'Us' and 'Them' groups in society (and psychoanalysis). *Psychotherapy & Politics International*, 13, 182–93.
Damasio, A. (1999). *The Feeling of What Happens*. New York: Harcourt.
Darwin, C. (1879/2004). *The Descent of Man* (2nd edn). Harmondsworth, UK: Penguin.
Davies, A., Richards, E., & Barwick, N. (2015). *Group Music Therapy*. London: Routledge.
de Maré, P. B. (1972). *Perspectives in Group Psychotherapy*. London: Allen & Unwin.
de Maré, P. B. & Schöllberger, R. (2004). A case for the mind. *Group Analysis*, 37, 339–52.
de Maré, P. B. & Schöllberger, R. (2006). A theory of mind. *Group Analysis*, 39, 65–71.
de Maré, P. B. & Schöllberger, R. (2008). An apologia for the human mind. *Group Analysis*, 41, 5–33.
de Maré, P. B., Piper, R., & Thompson, S. (eds), (1991). *Koinonia: From Hate, Through Dialogue, to Culture in the Large Group*. London: Karnac.
de Waal, F. (2006). *Primates and Philosophers: How Morality Evolved*. Princeton, NJ: Princeton University Press.
Deri, S. (1978). Transitional phenomena. In S. A. Grolnick, L. Barkin & W. Muensterberger (eds), *Between Reality and Fantasy*. New York: Jason Aronson.
Dick, B. M. (1975). A Ten-year study of out-patient analytic group therapy. *British Journal of Psychiatry*, 127, 365–75.
Diel, P. (1980). *Symbolism in Greek Mythology*. Shambhala: Boufler & Hotton.
Doehrman, M. J. G. (1976). Parallel processes in supervision and psychotherapy. *Bulletin of the Menninger Clinic*, 40, 3–104.
Donne, J. (1624). Meditation XVII. In J. Hayward (ed.), *Donne: Complete Verse and Selected Prose*. London: The Nonesuch Press. 1929.

Donne, J. (1633). The good-morrow. In J. Hayward (ed.), *Donne: Complete Verse and Selected Prose*. London: The Nonesuch Press. 1929.

Doron, Y. (2013). Primary maternal preoccupation in a group analytic group. *Group Analysis*, 47, 17–29.

Durkin, H. E. (1983). Some contributions of general systems theory to psychoanalytic group psychotherapy. In M. Pines (ed.), *The Evolution of Group Analysis*. London: Routledge & Kegan Paul.

Ein-Dor, T., Mikulincer, M., Doron, G., & Shaver, P. R. (2010). The attachment paradox: How can so many of us (insecure ones) have no adaptive advantages? *Perspectives on Psychological Science*, 5, 123–41.

The Economist (2016). League of nationalists, *The Economist*, 19 November. [Online]. Available at https://www.economist.com/news/international/21710276-all-around-world-nationalists-are-gaining-ground-why-league-nationalists (accessed 20 November).

Elias, N. (1969). Sociology and psychiatry. In S. H. Foulkes & G. S. Prince (eds), *Psychiatry in a Changing Society*. London: Tavistock.

Elias, N. (1989/1991). *The Symbol Theory*. London: Sage.

Elias, N. (2000). *The Civilizing Process*. E. Jephcott, (rev. edn and trans.). Oxford: Blackwell. First published in German in 1939. 1st English edn: (Vol. 1), *The History of Manners* (1978) Oxford: Blackwell. (Vol. 2), *State Formation and Civilisation* (1982). Oxford: Blackwell.

Elias, N. & Scotson, J. (eds), (1965/1994). *The Established and the Outsiders*. London: Sage.

Eliot, T. S. (1940/1969). East coker. *The Complete Poems and Plays of T. S. Eliot*. London: Faber.

Eliot, T. S. (1942/1969). Little gidding. *The Complete Poems and Plays of T. S. Eliot*. London: Faber.

Emde, R. (1980). Emotional availability: A reciprocal reward system for infants and parents with implications for prevention of psychosocial disorders. In P. M. Taylor (ed.), *Parent-Infant Relationships*. Orlando, FL: Grune & Stratton.

Ettin, M. F. (1993). Links between group process and social, political, and cultural issues. In H. I. Kaplan & B. J. Sadock (eds), *Comprehensive Group Psychotherapy* (3rd edn). Baltimore, MD: Williams & Wilkins.

Ezquerro, A. (2010). Cohesion and coherency in group analysis. *Group Analysis*, 43, 496–504.

Ezriel, H. (1950). A psycho-analytic approach to group treatment. *Psychology and Psychotherapy*, 23, 59–74.

Ezriel, H. (1952). Notes on psychoanalytic group therapy. *Psychiatry*, 15, 119–26.

Ezriel, H. (1973). Psychoanalytic group therapy. In L.R. Wolberg & E.K. Schwartz (eds), *Group Therapy*. New York: Stratton Intercontinental Medical.

Fairbairn, W. F. (1952/2003). *Psychoanalytic Studies of the Personality*. Reprinted Hove, UK: Brunner-Routledge.

Fanthorpe, U. A. (1995). Atlas in *Safe as Houses*. Calstock, UK: Peterloo Poets.

Fanthorpe, U. A. (2010). Atlas in *New and Collected Poems*. London: Enitharmon Press.

Fariss, S. (2011). The social unconscious and the collective unconscious. In E. Hopper, & H. Weinberg (eds), *The Social Unconscious in Persons, Groups, and Societies* (Vol. 1). London: Karnac.

Farrow, T. F. D. & Woodruff, P. W. R. (2007). *Empathy in Mental Illness*. Cambridge, UK: Cambridge University Press.

Ferenczi, S. (1928/1980). The elasticity of the psycho-analytic technique. In M. Blaint (ed.), *Final Contributions to the Problems and Methods of Psycho-Analysis*. London: Maresfield.

Field, T., Vega-Lahr, N., Scafidi, F., & Goldstein, S. (1986). Effects of maternal unavailability on mother-infant interactions. *Infant Behavior and Development*, 9, 473–78.

Flapan, D. & Fenchel, G. H. (1987). Terminations. *Group*, 11, 131–43.

Fleiss, R. (1942). The metapsychology of the analyst. *Psychoanalytic Quarterly*, 11, 211–27.

Fluery, H. J. & Knobel, A. M. (2011). The concept of the Co-Unconscious in moreno's psychodrama. In E. Hopper & H. Weinberg (eds), *The Social Unconscious in Persons, Groups and Societies* (Vol. 1). London: Karnac.

Foguel, B. S. (1994). The group experienced as mother: Early psychic structures in analytic groups. *Group Analysis*, 27, 265–85.

Fonagy, P. (2004). *Attachment Theory and Psychoanalysis*. New York: Other Press.

Fonagy, P. & Target, M. (2008). Attachment, trauma, and psychoanalysis: Where psychoanalysis meets neuroscience. In E. Jurist, A. Slade & S. Bergner (eds), *Mind to Mind*. New York: Other Press.

Fonagy, P., Gergely, G., Jurist, E., & Target, M. (2002). *Affect Regulation, Mentalization, and the Development of the Self*. New York: Other Press.

Fonagy, P., Steele, M., Steele, H., Leigh, T., Kennedy, R., Mattoon, G., & Targe, M. (1995). Attachment, the reflective self and borderline states. In S. Goldberg, R. Muir & J. Kerr (eds), *Attachment Theory: Social Developmental and Clinical Perspectives*. Hillsdale, NJ: The Analytic Press.

Forster, E. M. (1910/1941). *Howards End*. Harmondsworth: Penguin.

Foulkes, E. (1990). S. H Foulkes: A brief memoir. In E. Foulkes (ed.), *Selected Papers*. London: Karnac.

Foulkes, S. H. (1936/1990). Biology in the light of the work of Kurt Goldstein. In E. Foulkes (ed.), *Selected Papers*. London: Karnac.

Foulkes, S. H. (1946/1990). On group analysis. In E. Foulkes (ed.), *Selected Papers*. London: Karnac.

Foulkes, S. H. (1948/1983). *Introduction to group analytic psychotherapy*. London: Karnac.

Foulkes, S. H. (1958/1990). Discussion of L.S. Kubie: Some theoretical concepts underlying the relationship between individual and group psychotherapies. In E. Foulkes (ed.), *Selected Papers*. London: Karnac.

Foulkes, S. H. (1964). *Therapeutic Group Analysis*. London: George Allen & Unwin.

Foulkes, S. H. (1968/1990). Group dynamic processes and group analysis. In E. Foulkes (ed.), *Selected Papers*. London: Karnac.

Foulkes, S. H. (1970/1990). Access to unconscious processes in the group-analytic group. In E. Foulkes (ed.), *Selected Papers*. London: Karnac.

Foulkes, S. H. (1971a/1990). Access to unconscious processes in the group-analytic group. In *Selected Papers*. London: Karnac.

Foulkes, S. H. (1971b/1990). The group as matrix of the individual's mental life. In E. Foulkes (ed.), *Selected Papers*. London: Karnac

Foulkes, S. H. (1972/1990). Oedipus conflict and regression. In E. Foulkes (ed.), *Selected Papers*. London: Karnac.

Foulkes, S. H. (1974/1990). My philosophy in psychotherapy. In E. Foulkes (ed.), *Selected Papers*. London: Karnac.
Foulkes, S. H. (1975a/1986). *Group Analytic Psychotherapy*. London: Karnac.
Foulkes, S. H. (1975b). A short outline of the therapeutic process in group-analytic psychotherapy. *Group Analysis*, 8, 59–63.
Foulkes, S. H. (1977/1990). Notes on the concept of resonance. In E. Foulkes (ed.), *Selected Papers*. London: Karnac.
Foulkes, S. H. & Anthony, E. J. (1957). *Group Psychotherapy: The Psychoanalytic Approach*. London: Karnac.
Foulkes, S. H. & Anthony, E. J. (1965/1984). *Group Psychotherapy: The Psycho-Analytic Approach* (2nd edn), (rev. edn 1973). London: Karnac.
Freud, S. (1900/1976). *The Interpretation of Dreams* (Vol. 4). London: Pelican.
Freud, S. (1913/2002). On initiating treatment. In A. Bance, (trans.), *Wild Analysis*. London: Penguin.
Freud, S. (1914/1950). Remembering, repeating and working-through. *Standard Edition XII*. London: Hogarth.
Freud, S. (1917/1991). Mourning and melancholia. In *On Metapsychology* (Vol. 11). Harmondsworth, UK: Penguin.
Freud, S. (1921/1991). Group psychology and the analysis of the ego. In *Civilization, Society & Religion* (Vol. 12). Harmondsworth, UK: Penguin.
Freud, S. (1926). Letter to Trigant Burrow, 14 November. Cited in J. Campos (1992), 'Burrow, Foulkes and Freud: An Historical Perspective', *Lifwynn Correspondence*, 2, 8.
Freud, S. (1930/1991). Civilization and its discontents. In *Civilization, Society & Religion* (Vol. 12). Harmondsworth, UK: Penguin.
Freud, S. (1932/1991). The Dissection of the Psychical Personality. In *New Introductory Lectures on Psychoanalysis* (Vol. 2). Harmondsworth, UK: Penguin.
Friedman, R. (2002). Dream-telling as a request for containment in group therapy – The royal road through the other. In C. Neri, M. Pines & R. Friedman (eds), *Dreams in Group Psychotherapy*. London: Jessica Kingsley.
Friedman, R. (2004). Dream-telling as a request for containment – Reconsidering the group-analytic approach to work with dreams. *Group Analysis*, 37, 508–24.
Friedman, R. (2012). Dreams and dreamtelling: A group approach. In J. L. Kleinberg (ed.), *The Wiley-Blackwell Handbook of Group Psychotherapy*. Oxford: Wiley Blackwell.
Friedman, R. (2013). Individual or group therapy? Indications for optimal therapy. *Group Analysis*, 46, 164–70.
Friedman, R. (2014). Group analysis today – Developments in intersubjectivity. *Group Analysis*, 47, 194–200.
Friedman, R. (2015a). A soldier's matrix. *Group Analysis*, 48, 239–57.
Friedman, R. (2015b). Using the transpersonal in dreamtelling and conflict. *Group Analysis*, 48, 45–60.
Frogel, S. (2006). The other is a face: On particular moral and humanism. *Metaphor*, 6, 203–19. (In Hebrew). The TAICP, Tel-Aviv.
Frogel, S. (2008). Lecture given to the interdisciplinary forum of Tel-Aviv Institute of Contemporary Psychoanalysis.
Gadamer, H. G. (1975). *Truth and Method*. In J. Weisheimer & D. Marshall (2nd edn). London: Sheed & Ward.

Gans, J. S. (1989). Hostility in group psychotherapy. *International Journal of Group Psychotherapy*, 39, 499–516.

Gantt, S. P. & Hopper, E. (2008a). Two perspectives on a trauma in a training group: The systems-centred approach and the theory of incohesion: Part I. *Group Analysis*, 41, 98–112.

Gantt, S. P. & Hopper, E. (2008b). Two perspectives on a trauma in a training group: The systems-centred approach and the theory of incohesion: Part II. *Group Analysis*, 41(2), 123–39.

Garland, C. (1982). Group-analysis: Taking the non-problem seriously. *Group Analysis*, 15, 4–14.

Garland, C. (ed.), (2010). *The Groups Book*. London: Karnac.

George, C., Kaplan, N., & Main, M. (1985). *The Berkeley Adult Attachment Interview*. University of California. [Online]. Available at http://psychology.sunysb.edu/attachment/measures/content/aai_interview.pdf (accessed 20 February 2013).

Gerson, S. (2004). The relational unconscious. *Psychoanalytic Quarterly*, 73, 63–98.

Gibbard, G. S. & Hartman, J. J. (1973). The significance of utopian fantasies in small groups. *International Journal of Group Psychotherapy*, 23, 125–47.

Gilden, L. (2013). Foreword. In E. G. Pertegato & G. O. Pertegato (eds), *From Psychoanalysis to Group Analysis*. London: Karnac.

Glenn, L. (1987). Attachment theory and group analysis: The group matrix as secure base. *Group Analysis*, 20, 109–22.

Goldstein, K. (1940/1951). *Human Nature in the Light of Psychopathology*. Cambridge, MA: Harvard University Press.

Gordon, J. (1991). Discussion on J. F. Sender's paper: 'Projective identification in group psychotherapy'. *Group Analysis*, 24, 120–2.

Gordon, J. (1994). Bion's post-*Experiences in Groups* thinking on group. In V. L. Schermer & M. Pines (eds), *Ring of Fire*. London: Routledge.

Green, L. (1983). On fusion and individuation processes in small groups. *International Journal of Group Psychotherapy*, 33, 3–19.

Grossmark, R. (2007). The edge of chaos: Enactment, disruption, and emergence in group psychotherapy. *Psychoanalytic Dialogues*. 17, 479–99.

Grotjahn, M. (1977). *The Art and Technique of Analytic Group Therapy*. New York: Jason Aronson.

Grotjahn, M. (1983). Basic Concepts of Group Psychotherapy. In M. Grotjahn, F. Kline & C. Friedman (eds), *Handbook of Group Therapy*. New York: Van Nostrand.

Guntrip, H. (1975). My experience of analysis with Fairbairn and Winnicott. *International Review of Psychoanalysis*, 2, 145–56.

Gustafson, J. (1980). Group therapy supervision. In L. Wolberg & M. Aronson (eds), *Group and Family Therapy*. New York: Brunner/Mazel.

Halton, M. (1999). Bion, Foulkes & the Oedipal Situation. In C. Oakley (ed.), *What is a Group?* London: Rebus.

Hamer, N. (1990). Group-analytic Psychodrama. *Group Analysis*, 23, 245–54.

Hamilton, W. D. (1963). The evolution of altruistic behavior. *American Naturalist*, 97, 56–71.

Harrington, A. (1996). *Reenchanted Science*. New York: W. W. Norton.

Harrison, T. (2000). *Bion, Rickman, Foulkes and the Northfield Experiments*. London: Jessica Kingsley.

Harwood, I. (1983). The application of self-psychology concepts to group psychotherapy. *International Journal of Group Psychotherapy*, 33, 469–87.
Harwood, I. (1986). The need for optimal, available selfobject caretakers. *Group Analysis*, 19, 291–302.
Harwood, I. & Pines, M. (eds), (1998). *Self Experiences in Group*. London: Jessica Kingsley.
Hearst, L. (1993). Our cultural cargo and its vicissitudes in group analysis. *Group Analysis*, 26, 389–405.
Hesse, E. (2008). The adult attachment interview. In J. Cassidy & P. R. Shaver (eds), *Handbook of Attachment* (2nd edn). New York: Guilford Press.
Hinshelwood, R. (1994). Attacks on the reflective space. In V. L. Schermer & M. Pines (eds), *Ring of Fire*. London: Routledge.
Hinshelwood, R. (2004). Two early experimenters with groups. *Group Analysis*, 37, 323–33.
Hinshelwood, R. (2007). Bion and Foulkes: The group-as-a-whole. *Group Analysis*, 40, 344–56.
Hobson, R. P. & Kapur, R. (2005). Working in the transference. *Psychology and Psychotherapy*, 78, 275–93.
Holmes, J. (2010). *Exploring in Security: Towards and Attachment-Informed Psychoanalytic Psychotherapy*. London: Routledge.
Hopper, E. (1997). Traumatic experience in the unconscious life of groups: A fourth basic assumption. *Group Analysis*, 30, 439–70.
Hopper, E. (2001). The social unconscious. *Group Analysis*, 34, 9–27.
Hopper, E. (2002). Letter to the editor commenting on: 'The social unconscious: A post-Foulkesian perspective' (by Farhad Dalal). *Group Analysis*, 35, 333–35.
Hopper, E. (2003a) The problem of context in group-analytic psychotherapy. In *The Social Unconscious*. London: Jessica Kingsley.
Hopper, E. (2003b). The social unconscious in clinical work. In *The Social Unconscious*. London: Jessica Kingsley.
Hopper, E. (2003c). *Traumatic Experience in the Unconscious Life of Groups*. London: Jessica Kingsley.
Hopper, E. (2003d). *The Social Unconscious*. London: Jessica Kingsley.
Hopper, E. (2006). theoretical and conceptual notes concerning transference and countertransference processes in groups and by groups, and the social unconscious, part I. *Group Analysis*, 39, 549–59.
Hopper, E. (2007). Theoretical and conceptual notes concerning transference and countertransference processes in groups and by groups, and the social unconscious, part II. *Group Analysis*, 40, 21–34.
Hopper, E. (2009). The theory of the basic assumption of incohesion: Aggregation/massification or (Ba) I:A/M. *British Journal of Psychotherapy*, 25, 214–29.
Hopper, E. (2016). *The Social Unconscious in Persons, Groups and Societies* (Vol. 2). London: Karnac.
Hopper, E. & Weinberg, H. (2011). *The Social Unconscious in Persons, Groups and Societies* (Vol. 1). London: Karnac.
Horwitz, L. (1977). A group-centered approach to group psychotherapy. *International Journal of Group Psychotherapy*, 27, 423–39.
Hume, F. (2010). Bion and group psychotherapy: Bion and Foulkes at the Tavistock. In C. Garland (ed.), *The Groups Book*. London: Karnac.

Hutchinson, S. (2009). Foulkesian Authority. *Group Analysis*, 42, 354–60.
Inglehart, R. F. & Norris, P. (2016). Trump, Brexit and the Rise of Populism. [Online]. Available at https://research.hks.harvard.edu/publications/workingpapers/citation.aspx?PubId=11325&type=FN&PersonId=83 (Accessed 5 December 2016).
Jacobson, L. (1989). The group as an object in the cultural field. *International Journal of Group Psychotherapy*, 39, 475–98.
James, C. D. (1982). Transitional phenomena and the matrix in group psychotherapy. In M. Pines & L. Rafalson (eds), *The Individual and the Group*. London: Plenum Press.
James, C. D. (1984). Bion's 'containing' and Winnicott's 'holding' in the context of the group matrix. *International Journal of Group Psychotherapy*, 34, 1–13.
James, C. D. (1994). 'Holding' and 'Containing' in the group and society. In D. Brown & L. Zinkin (eds), *The Psyche and the Social World*. London: Routledge.
Jennings, E. (1958/1986). Ghosts. *Collected Poems*. Manchester, UK: Carcanet.
Johnson, J. E., Burlingame, G, M., Olsen, J. A., Davies, D. R., & Gleave, R. L. (2005). Group climate, cohesion, alliance and empathy in group psychotherapy. *Journal of Counseling Psychology*, 52, 310–21.
Joseph, B. (1985). Transference – the total situation. *International Journal of Psycho-Analysis*, 66, 447–54.
Joyce, R. (2006). *The Evolution of Morality*. Cambridge, MA: MIT.
Jung, C. (1968/1991). *Archetypes and the Collective Unconscious* (2nd edn and trans.), R.F.C. Hull. London: Routledge.
Kahneman, D. (2011/2012). Two Selves. In *Thinking, Fast and Slow*. London: Penguin.
Kahneman, D., Frederickson, B. L, Schreiber, C. A., & Redelmeier, A. (1993). When more pain is preferred to less: Adding a better end. *Psychological Science*, 4, 401–05.
Karterud, S. (2011). Constructing and mentalizing the matrix. *Group Analysis*, 44, 357–73.
Karterud, S. (2015a). *Mentalization-Based Group Therapy*. Oxford: Oxford University Press.
Karterud, S. (2015b). On structure & leadership in mentalization-based group therapy & group analysis. *Group Analysis*, 48, 137–49.
Katerud, S. & Stone, W. (2004). The group self: A neglected aspect of group psychotherapy. *Group Analysis*, 36, 7–22.
Kauff, P. (1977). The termination process and its relation to the separation-individuation phase of development. *International Journal of Group Psychotherapy*, 27, 3–18.
Kennard, D., Roberts, J., & Winter, D. (1993). *A Workbook of Group Analytic Interventions*. London: Routledge.
Kernberg, O. (1965). Notes on countertransference. *Journal of the American Psychoanalytic Association*, 13, 38–56.
Khantzian, E., Halliday, K., & McAuliffe, W. (1990). *Addiction and the Vulnerable Self: Modified Dynamic Group Therapy for Substance Abusers*. New York: Guilford Press.
King, Jnr M. L. (1963/1964). Letter from birmingham city jail. In *Why Can't We Wait?* New York: New American Library.
Klein, M. (1929/1988). Infantile anxiety-situations reflected in a work of art and in the creative impulse. In *Love, Guilt and Reparation*. London: Virago Press.

Klein, M. (1935/1988). A contribution to the psychogenesis of manic-depressive states. In *Love, Guilt and Reparation.* London: Virago Press.
Klein, M. (1940/1988). Mourning and its relation to manic-depressive states. In *Love, Guilt and Reparation.* London: Virago Press.
Klein, M. (1946/1988). Notes on some schizoid mechanisms. In *Envy and Gratitude.* London: Virago Press.
Klein, M. (1952/1988). Some theoretical conclusions regarding the emotional life of the infant. In *Envy and Gratitude.* London: Virago Press.
Kohut, H. (1959). Introspection, empathy, and psychoanalysis: An examination of the relation between mode of observation and theory. In P. H. Ornstein (ed.), *The Search for the Self* (Vol. 1). New York: International Universities Press.
Kohut, H. (1971). *The Analysis of the Self.* New York: International Universities Press.
Kohut, H. (1976). Creativeness, charisma, group psychology. In J. E. Gedo & G. H. Pollock (eds), *Freud: The Fusion of Science and Humanism.* New York: International Universities Press.
Kohut, H. (1977). *The Restoration of the Self.* New York: International Universities Press.
Kohut, H. (1984). *How Does Analysis Cure?* Chicago, IL: University of Chicago Press.
Kohut, H. & Wolf, E. (1978). The 'disorders of the self' and their treatment. *International Journal of Psychoanalysis*, 59, 413–25.
Kosseff, J. W. (1975). The leader using object-relations theory. In Z. A. Liff & J. Aronson (eds), *The Leader in the Group.* New York: Jason Aronson.
Koukis, A. (2016). *On Group Analysis and Beyond.* London: Karnac.
Kubler-Ross, E. (1969). *On Death and Dying.* New York: Scribner.
Lacan, J. (1973/1998). *The Four Fundamental Concepts of Psychoanalysis.* A. Miller, (ed.), A. Sheridan, (Trans.). New York: W.W. Norton.
Lavie, J. (2005). The lost roots of the theory of group analysis: 'Taking interrelational individuals seriously'!. *Group Analysis*, 38, 519–35.
Lavie, J. (2007). 'Open People', 'Homo Clausus' and the '5th Basic Assumption': Bridging concepts between Foulkes's and Bion's traditions, *Funzione Gamma.* [Online] Available at http://funzionegamma.it/wp-content/uploads/open-people-19e.pdf (accessed 3 December 2012).
Lawrence, W. G. (1998). *Social Dreaming @ Work.* London: Karnac.
Lawrence, W. G. (2003). Narcissism v social-ism governing thinking in social systems. In R. M. Lipgar & M. Pines (eds), *Building on Bion – Branches.* London: Jessica Kingsley.
Lawrence, W. G. & Biran, H. (2002). The complementarity of social dreaming and therapeutic dreaming. In C. Neri, M. Pines & R. Friedman (eds), *Dreams in Group Psychotherapy.* London: Jessica Kingsley.
Lawrence, W. G., Bain, A., & Gould, L. (1996/2000). The fifth basic assumption. In W. G. Lawrence (ed.), *Tongued with Fire.* London: Karnac.
Le Bon, G. (1895). *The Crowd: A Study of the Popular Mind.* London: Benn.
Leitner, L. M. (1995). Optimal therapeutic distance. In R. A. Neimeyer & M. J. Mahoney (eds), *Constructivism in Psychotherapy.* Washington, DC: American Psychological Association.
Leowald, H. (1986) Transference-countertransference. *Journal of the American Psychoanalytic Association*, 34, 275–89.

Levinas, E. (1982). *Totality and Infinity*. London: Klewer Academic.
Lewin, K. (1951). *Field Theory in Social Science*. New York: Harper & Row.
Lewis, T., Amini, F., & Lannon, R. (2001). *A General Theory of Love*. London: Vintage.
Lichtenberg, J. D. (1983). The influence of values and value judgements on the psychoanalytic encounter. *Psychoanalytic Inquiry*, 3, 647–64.
Linehan, M. (1993). *Skills Training Manual for Treating Borderline Personality Disorder*. New York: Guilford Press.
Linge, D. (ed. and trans.) (1966). Introduction. In H. Gadamer (ed.), *Philosophical Hermeneutics*. Berkeley, CA: University of California Press.
Lipgar, R. M. & Pines, M. (eds), (2003). *Building on Bion- Branches*. London: Jessica Kingsley.
Lorentzen, S. (2014). *Group Analytic Psychotherapy*. London: Routledge.
Lorentzen, S., Sexton, H. C., & Høglend, P. (2004). Therapeutic alliance, cohesion and outcome in a long-term analytic group. *Nordic Journal of Psychiatry*, 58, 33–40.
Lothstein, L. (1978). The group dropout revisited. *American Journal of Psychiatry*, 135, 1492–95.
Lovas, G. S. (2005). Gender and patterns of emotional availability in mother-toddler and father-toddler dyads. *Infant Mental Health Journal*, 26, 327–53.
Maar, V. (1989). Attempts at grasping the self during the termination phase of group-analytic psychotherapy. *Group Analysis*, 22, 99–104.
MacDonald, P. (2004). Life and death in an analytic group. *Group Analysis*, 37, 23–42.
MacKenzie, K. R. (1997). *Time-Managed Group Psychotherapy*. Washington, DC: American Psychiatric Association.
Mahoney, P. (2001). *Psychoanalysis and Discourse*. London: Taylor & Francis.
Main, M. & Goldwyn, S. (1995). Interview based adult attachment classification: Related to infant-mother and infant-father attachment. *Developmental Psychology*, 19, 227–39.
Main, M. & Solomon, J. (1990). Procedures for identifying infants as disorganized/disoriented during the ainsworth strange situation. In M. Greenberg, D. Cicchetti, E. M. Cummings (eds), *Attachment in the Preschool Years*. Chicago, IL: University of Chicago Press.
Malan, D. H. (1979). *Individual Psychotherapy and the Science of Psychodynamics*. London: Butterworth.
Malan, D. H., Balfour, F. G. H., Hood, V. G., & Shooter, A. M N. (1976). Group psychotherapy: A long-term follow-up study. *Archives of General Psychiatry*, 33, 1303–15.
Mallinckrodt, B., Porter, M., & Kivlighan, D. (2005). Client attachment to therapist, depth of in-session exploration, and object relations in brief psychotherapy. *Psychotherapy*, 42, 85–100.
Malloch, S. & Trevarthen C. (eds), (2009). *Communicative Musicality: Exploring the Basis of Human Companionship*. Oxford: Oxford University Press.
Maratos, J. (1996). The emergence of self through group. *Group Analysis*, 29, 161–68.
Markova, G. & Legerstee, G. (2006). Contingency, imitation and affect sharing: Foundations of infants' social awareness. *Developmental Psychology*, 42, 132–41.
Marmarosh, C. L., Martin, R. D., & Speigel, E. B. (2013). *Attachment in Group Psychotherapy*. Washington, DC: American Psychological Association.

Maroda, K. (1991). *The Power of the Countertransference*. Northvale, NJ: Jason Aronson.
Marris, P. (1986). *Loss and Change*. Revised edition. London: Routledge.
Marris, P. (1992). Grief, loss of meaning and society. *Bereavement Care*, 11, 18–22.
Marrone, M. (1994). Attachment theory and group analysis. In D. Brown & L. Zinkin (eds), *The Psyche and the Social World*. London: Routledge.
Marrone, M. (1998). *Attachment and Interaction*. London: Jessica Kingsley.
Marrone, M. (2014). *Attachment and Interaction* (2nd edn). London: Jessica Kingsley.
Marsh, L. C. (1933). An experiment in group treatment of patients at Worcester State Hospital. *Mental Hygiene*, 17, 396–416.
Marvell, A. (1681/1972). To his coy mistress. In *Andrew Marvell: The Complete Poems*. Harmondsworth, UK: Penguin.
Marziali, E., Munroe-Blum, H., & McCleary, L. (1997). The contribution of group cohesion and group alliance to the outcome of group psychotherapy. *International Journal of Group Psychotherapy*, 47, 475–97.
McDougal, J. (1986). *Theatres of the Mind*. London: Free Association Books.
Mead, G. H. (1934). *Mind, Self and Society*. Chicago, IL: Chicago University Press.
Meins, E. (1997). *Security of Attachment and the Social Development of Cognition*. Hove, UK: Psychology Press.
Meltzer, D. (1968). *The Psycho-Analytic Process*. Perthshire, UK: Clunie Press.
Mendez, C. L., Coddou, F., & Maturana, H. (1988). The bringing forth of pathology. *Irish Journal of Psychology*, 9, 144–72.
Merleau-Ponty, M. (1964). *The Primacy of Perception*. Evanston, IL: Northwestern University Press.
Mermelstein, J. (2000). The role of the concordance and complementarity in psychoanalytic treatment. *Psychoanalytic Psychology*, 17, 706–29.
Mikulincer, M. & Shaver, P. R. (2007). *Attachment in Adulthood*. New York: Guilford Press.
Miller, J. G. (1969). Living systems: Basic concepts. In W. Gray, L. Duhl, & N. Rizzo (eds), *General Systems Theory and Psychiatry*. Boston, MA: Little Brown.
Mills, R. (2005). *Suspended Animation: Pain, Pleasure and Punishment in Medieval Culture*. London: Reaktion.
Mitchell, S. (1988). *Relational Concepts in Psychoanalysis*. Cambridge, MA: Harvard University Press.
Morgan, G. (1986). *Images of Organization*. London: Sage.
Nava, A. S. (2007). Empathy and group analysis. *Group Analysis*, 40, 13–28.
Neeman-Kantor, A.-K. (2013). *Secure Presence*. Unpublished PsyD. Dissertation. School of Psychology, Sacramento.
Neri, C., Pines, M., & Friedman, R. (eds), (2002). *Dream in Group Psychotherapy*. London: Jessica Kingsley.
Neumann, E. (1963). *The Great Mother*. London: Routledge & Kegan Paul.
Nicolis, G. & Prigogine, I. (1989). *Exploring Complexity*. New York: W.H. Freeman.
Nietzsche, F. (1882–84/1977). *Nachgelassene fragmente*. Berlin: De Gruyter.
Nietzsche, F. (1886/1973). *Beyond Good and Evil*. R. J. Hollingdale, (trans.) Harmondsworth, UK: Penguin.
Nitsun, M. (1989). Early development: Linking the individual and the group. *Group Analysis*, 22, 249–60.

Nitsun, M. (1991). The anti-group: Destructive forces in the group and their therapeutic potential. *Group Analysis*, 24, 7–20.

Nitsun, M. (1994). The primal scene in group analysis. In D. Brown & L. Zinkin (eds), *The Psyche and the Social World*. London: Routledge.

Nitsun, M. (1996). *The Anti-Group*. London: Routledge.

Nitsun, M. (2006). *The Group as an Object of Desire*. London: Routledge.

Nitsun, M. (2009). Authority and revolt: The challenges of group leadership. *Group Analysis*, 42, 325–48.

Nitsun, M. (2015). *Beyond the Anti-Group*. London: Routledge.

Nitzgen, D. (2001). Training in democracy, democracy in training: Notes on group analysis and democracy. *Group Analysis*, 34, 331–47.

Nitzgen, D. (2008). The group analytic movement sixty years on: Revisiting Introduction to group analytic psychotherapy by S. H. Foulkes. *Group Analysis*. 41, 325–46.

Nitzgen, D. (2011). The concept of the social unconscious in the work of S. H. Foulkes. In E. Hopper & H. Weinberg (eds), *The Social Unconscious in Persons, Groups and Societies* (Vol. 1). London: Karnac.

Nitzgen, D. (2013a). Free association, group association and group dialogue. *Group Analysis*, 46, 144–63.

Nitzgen, D. (2013b). On the location of nos. *Group Analysis*, 46, 395–406.

Nitzgen, D. (2013c). Group analysis and complexity theory. *Group Analysis*, 46, 314–27.

Nitzgen, D. (2015). Group psychotherapy: The psychoanalytic approach, by S. H. Foulkes & E. J. Anthony. From the first to the second edition. *Group Analysis*, 48, 126–36.

Nitzgen, D. (2016). Reflections on group analysis and philosophy. *Group Analysis*, 49, 19–36.

Noack, A. (2011). Introduction. In E. Hopper, & H. Weinberg (eds), *The Social Unconscious in Persons, Groups, and Societies* (Vol. 1). London: Karnac.

Ofer, G. (2013). Group processes in the movie, 'as it is in heaven': Leadership that enhances; leadership that stifles. *Group Analysis*, *46*, 299–313.

Ogden, T. H. (1979). On projective identification. *International Journal of Psychoanalysis*, 60, 357–73.

Ogden, T. H. (1992a). The dialectically constituted/decentred subject of psychoanalysis, I. *International Journal of Psychoanalysis*, 73, 517–26.

Ogden, T. H. (1992b). The dialectically constituted/decentred subject of psychoanalysis, II. *International Journal of Psychoanalysis*, 73, 613–26.

Ogden, T. H. (2004). The analytic third. *Psychoanalytical Quarterly*, 73, 167–95.

Orange, D. M. (1995). *Emotional Understanding*. New York: Guilford Press.

Orange, D. M. (2009). The face of the other: Beyond individuality in psychotherapy and psychoanalysis. Presented at the *International Association of Psychoanalytic Self Psychology Annual Conference*, Chicago.

Orange, D. M., Atwood, G., & Stolorow, R. (1997). *Working Intersubjectively*. Hillsdale, NJ: Analytic Press.

Ormay, T. (2012). *The Social Nature of Persons*. London: Karnac.

Ormay, T. (2013). One person is no person. *Group Analysis*, 46, 344–68.

Ormont, L. R. (1999). Progressive emotional communication: Criteria for a well-functioning group. *Group Analysis*, 32, 139–50.

Ormont, L. R. (2004). Drawing the isolate into the group flow. *Group Analysis*, 37, 65–76.
Ornstein, A. (2012). Mass murder and the individual: Psychoanalytic reflections on perpetrators and their victims. *International Journal of Group Psychotherapy*, 62, 1–20.
Ornstein, P. (1981). The bipolar self in the psychoanalytic treatment process. *Journal of the American Psychoanalytic Association*, 2, 353–75.
Padel, J. (1985). Ego in current thinking. *International Review of Psychoanalysis*, 12, 273–83.
Parkes, C. M. & Weiss, R. S. (1983). *Recovery from Bereavement*. New York: Basic Books.
Pertegato, E. G. (1994). Trigant Burrow tra Freud e Foulkes: la fondazione della gruppoanalisi e transformazioni epistemologiche della psicoanalisi (Trigant Burrow between Freud and Foulkes: The Foundation of Group-Analysis and Epistemological Transformations of Psychoanalysis). *Rivista Italiana di Gruppoanalisi*, 9, 7–44.
Pertegato, E. G. (1999). Trigant Burrow and unearthing the origin of group analysis. *Group Analysis*, 32, 269–84.
Pertegato, E. G. (2014). Foulkes' roots in Trigant Burrow's writings. *Group Analysis*, 47, 312–28.
Pertegato, E. G. & Pertegato, G. O. (2013). *Psychoanalysis to Group Analysis: The Pioneering Work of Trigant Burrow*. London: Karnac.
Pines, M. (1978). Group analytic psychotherapy of the borderline patient'. *Group Analysis*, 11, 115–26.
Pines, M. (1979). How a group develops over time. *Group Analysis*, 12, 109–13.
Pines, M. (1980). What to expect in the psychotherapy of the borderline patient. *Group Analysis*, 15, 3.
Pines, M. (1982/1998). Reflections on mirroring. In *Circular Reflections*. London: Jessica Kingsley.
Pines, M. (1983). On mirroring in group psychotherapy. *Group*, 7, 3–17.
Pines, M. (1984/1998). Group analytic psychotherapy and the borderline patient. In *Circular Reflections*. London: Jessica Kingsley.
Pines, M. (1985a/1998). Psychic development and the group analytic situation. In *Circular Reflections*. London: Jessica Kingsley.
Pines, M. (1985b/1998). Mirroring and child development. In *Circular Reflections*. London: Jessica Kingsley.
Pines, M. (1990). Group analysis and the Corrective Emotional Experience: Is it relevant? *Psychoanalytic Inquiry*, 10, 389–408.
Pines, M. (1993). Interpretation: Why, for whom and when. In D. Kennard, J. Roberts & D. A. Winter (eds), *A Work Book of Group-Analytic Interventions*. London: Routledge.
Pines, M. (1994a). The group as-a-whole. In D. Brown & L. Zinkin (eds), *The Psyche and the Social World*. London: Jessica Kingsley.
Pines, M. (1994b). Borderline phenomena in analytic groups. In V. L. Schermer & M. Pines (eds), *Ring of Fire*. London: Routledge.
Pines, M. (1996). Interpretation, dialogue, response: Changing perspectives in psychoanalytic theory and technique. Unpublished talk.
Pines, M. (2003a). Social brain and social group: how mirroring connects people. *Group Analysis*, 36, 507–13.

Pines, M. (2003b). Bion and Foulkes on empathy. In R.M. Lipgar & M. Pines (eds), *Building on Bion: Roots*. London: Jessica Kingsley.
Pines, M. (2013). Foreword. In E. G. Pertegato & G. O. Pertegato (eds), *From Psychoanalysis to Group Analysis*. London: Karnac.
Pines, M. & Schermer, V. L. (1994). An editorial introduction: Silence = death. In V. L. Schermer & M. Pines (eds), *Ring of Fire*. London: Routledge.
Pines, M., Hearst, L., & Behr, H. (1982). Group analysis. In G. M. Garza (ed.), *Basic Approaches to Group Psychotherapy and Counseling* (3rd edn). Springfield, IL: Charles Thomas.
Pisani, R. A. (2014). A comparison between the art of conducting in group analysis and the art of conducting an orchestra. *Group-Analytic Contexts*, 64, 33–45.
Potthoff, P. (2014). Foulkes and intersubjectivity. *Group Analysis*, 47, 268–82.
Potthoff, P. & Moini-Afchari, U. (2014). Mentalization-based treatment in groups – a paradigm shift or old wine in new skin. *Group Analysis*, 47, 3–16.
Powell, A. (1983). The music of the group. *Group Analysis*, 16, 3–19.
Powell, A. (1991). Matrix, mind and matter. *Group Analysis*, 24, 299–322.
Powell, A. (1994). Towards a unifying concept of the group matrix. In D. Brown & L. Zinkin (eds), *The Psyche and the Social World*. London: Routledge.
Power, K. (2012). Book review. In T. Ormay (ed.), *The Social Nature of Persons*. *Group Analysis*, 45, 391–93.
Power, K. (2013). Book review. In E. G. Pertegato & G. O. Pertegato (eds), *Psychoanalysis to Group Analysis: The Pioneering Work of Trigant Burrow*. *Group Analysis*, 46, 33–6.
Preston, S. D. & de Waal, F. B. M. (2002). Empathy: Its ultimate and proximate bases. *Behavioural and Brain Sciences*, 25, 1–72.
Prinz, W. (1997). Perception and action planning. In *European Journal of Cognitive Psychology*, 9, 129–54.
Prodgers, A. (1990). The dual nature of the group as mother: The uroboric container. *Group Analysis*, 23, 17–23.
Prodgers, A. (1991). Countertransference: The conductor's emotional response within the group setting. *Group Analysis*, 24, 389–407.
Quintaneiro, T. (2004). The concept of figuration or configuration in Norbert Elias's sociological theory. M. Mitre, (trans.) (2006). *Teoria & Sociedade*, Belo Horizonte, 12, 54–69. [Online] Available at: http://socialsciences.scielo.org/scielo.php?pid=s1518-44712006000200002&script=sci_arttext (accessed 5 November 2012).
Raphael-Leff, J. (1984). Myths and modes of motherhood. *British Journal of Psychotherapy*, 1, 14–18.
Redl, F. (1942). Group emotion and leadership. *Psychiatry: Journal for the Study of Interpersonal Processes*, 5, 573–96.
Renik O. (1993). Analytic interaction: Conceptualizing technique in light of the analyst's irreducible subjectivity. *Psychoanalytic Quarterly*, 62, 553–71.
Rice, C. (1996). Premature termination of group therapy. *International Journal of Group Psychotherapy*, 46, 5–23.
Rilke, R. M. (2003). Arrival. In M. Hamburger, (trans.), *Dance of the Orange: Selected Poems*. Maidstone: Crescent Moon.
Rippa, B. (1994). Groups in Israel during the Gulf War. *Group Analysis*, 27, 87–94.

Rizzolatti, G., Fogassi, L., & Gallese, V. (2001). Neurophysiological mechanisms underlying the understanding and imitation of action. *Nature Review Neuroscience*, 2, 661–70.

Roberts, J. (1983). Foulkes's concept of the matrix. *Group Analysis*, 15, 111–26.

Roberts, J. (1991a). Intervening to establish and maintain a therapeutic environment. In D. Kennard, J. Roberts & D. A. Winter (eds), *A Work Book of Group-analytic Interventions*. London: Routledge.

Roberts, J. (1991b). Destructive phases in groups. In J. Roberts & M. Pines (eds), *The Practice of Group Analysis*. London: Routledge.

Roberts, J. (1993). Interventions. In D. Kennard, J, Roberts & D. A. Winter, *A Work Book of Group-Analytic Interventions*. London: Routledge.

Roberts, J. & Pines, M. (1992). Group-analytic psychotherapy. *International Journal of Group Psychotherapy*, 42, 469–94.

Rogers, C. (1987). On putting it into words: The balance between projective identification and dialogue in the group. *Group Analysis*, 20, 99–107.

Rogers, C. R. (1957). The necessary and sufficient conditions of therapeutic personality change. *Journal of Consultant Psychology*, 21, 95–103.

Rosenthal, L. (1987). *Resolving Resistances in Group Psychotherapy*, Northvale, NJ: Jason Aronson.

Rosenthal, L. (2005). Castouts and dropouts: Premature termination in group analysis. *Modern Psychoanalysis*, 30, 40–53.

Rouchy, J. C. (1995). Identification and groups of belonging. *Group Analysis*, 28, 129–41.

Rutan, J. S., Stone, W., & Shay, J. (2014). *Psychodynamic Group Therapy* (5th edn). New York: Guilford Press.

Rutter, M. (1995). Clinical implications of attachment concepts: Retrospect and prospect. *Journal of Child Psychology & Psychiatry*, 36, 549–571.

Rycroft, C. (1985). *Psycho-Analysis and Beyond*. London: Hogarth Press.

Sargeant, R. (2011). Imperfection and disillusionment as therapeutic agents. *Group Analysis*, 44, 40–51.

Sartre, J.-P. (1943). *Le regard*. Paris: Chalimard.

Scanlon, C. (2015). On the perversity of an imagined psychological solution to very real social problems of unemployment (work-lessness) and social exclusion (worth-lessness): A group analytic critique. *Group Analysis*, 48, 31–44.

Scheidlinger, S. (1964). Identification, the sense of belonging and of identity, in small groups. *International Journal of Group Psychotherapy*, 14, 291–306.

Scheidlinger, S. (1992). Why did freud drop the theme of group psychology? *Journal of the American Psychoanalytical Association*, 40, 1230–32.

Schermer, V. L. (1985/2000). Beyond bion: The basic assumption states revisited. In M. Pines (ed.), *Bion and Group Psychotherapy*. London: Jessica Kingsley Publishers.

Schermer, V. L. (2010a). Reflections on 'reflections on mirroring'. *Group Analysis*, 43, 214–27.

Schermer, V. L. (2010b). Mirror neurons: Their relevance for group psychotherapy. *International Journal of Group Psychotherapy*, 60, 485–511.

Schermer, V. L. (2012a). Group-as-a-whole and complexity theories: Part I. *Group Analysis*, 45, 275–88.

Schermer, V. L. (2012b). Group-as-a-whole and complexity theories: Part II. *Group Analysis*, 45, 481–97.

Schermer, V. L. & Klein R. H. (1996). Termination in group Psychotherapy from the perspective of contemporary Object relations theory and self psychology. *International Journal of Group Psychotherapy*, 46, 99–115.
Schermer, V. L. & Pines. M. (eds), (1994). *Ring of Fire: Primitive Affects and Object Relations in Group Psychotherapy.* London: Routledge.
Schlachet, P. (1986). The concept of group space. *International Journal of Group Psychotherapy*, 36, 33–53.
Schlapobersky, J. (1994). The language of the group: Monologue, dialogue and discourse in group analysis. In D. Brown & L. Zinkin (eds), *The Psyche and the Social World.* London: Routledge.
Schlapobersky, J. (2016). *From the Couch to the Circle: Group-Analytic Psychotherapy in Practice.* London: Routledge.
Schlapobersky, J. & Pines, M. (2009). Group methods in adult psychiatry. In M. Gelder, N. Andreasen, J. Lopez-Ibor & J. Geddes (eds), *The New Oxford Textbook of Psychiatry.* Oxford: Oxford University Press.
Scholz, R. (2003). The foundation matrix. *Group Analysis*, 36, 48–54.
Schore, J. R. & Schore, A. (2008). The central role of affect regulation in development treatment. *Clinical Social Work Journal*, 36, 9–20.
Schore, A. N. (1994). *Affect Regulation and the Origin of the Self: The Neurobiology of Emotional Development.* Mahwah, NJ: Lawrence Erlbaum Associates.
Schore, A. N. (2002) Advances in neuropsychoanalysis, attachment theory and trauma research. *Psychoanalytic Inquiry*, 22, 433–84.
Schulte, P. (2000). Holding in mind: Intersubjectivity, subject relations and the group. *Group Analysis*, 33, 531–44.
Segal, H. (1977). Countertransference. *International Journal of Psychoanalytic Psychotherapy*, 6, 31–7.
Segalla, R. (2012). The therapeutic work of the group: Finding the self through finding the other. In I. Harwood, W. Stone, & M. Pines (eds), *Self Experiences in Group, Revisited.* London: Routledge.
Shapiro, E. & Ginzberg, R. (2002). Parting gifts: Termination rituals in group therapy. *International Journal of Group Psychotherapy*, 52, 319–36.
Singer, T. & Kimbles, S. (eds), (2004). *The Cultural Complex.* London: Brunner-Routledge.
Skynner, A. C. R. (1982). Reflections. *The Bethlem and Maudsley Gazette*, 30, 14–16.
Skynner, A. C. R. (1983/1987). Group analysis and family therapy. In J. Schlapobersky (ed.), *Explorations with Families: Group Analysis & Family Therapy.* London: Routledge.
Slavendy, J. T. (1993). Selection and preparation of patients and organisation of the group. In H. J. Kaplan & B. J. Sadock (eds), *Comprehensive Group Psychotherapy* (3rd edn). Baltimore, MD: Williams & Wilkins.
Smith, E. R., Murphy, J., & Coates, S. (1999). Attachment to groups: Theory and measurement. *Journal of Personality and Social Psychology*, 77, 94–110.
Smith, K. K. & Berg, D. N. (1988). *Paradoxes of Group Life.* London: Jossey-Bass.
Sordano, A. (2013). The roots of human dialogue. *Group Analysis*, 46, 375–85.
Source, J. & Emde, R. N. (1981). Mother's presence is not enough: Effect of emotional availability on infant exploration. *Developmental Psychology*, 17, 737–45.
Spiegelman, J. M. & Mansfield, V. (1996). On the physics and psychology of the transference as an interactive field. *Journal of Analytical Psychology*, 41, 179–202.

Sroufe, L. A. (1996). *Emotional Development*. Cambridge: Cambridge University Press.
Sroufe, L. A., Egeland, B., Carlson, E., & Collins, W. A. (2005). *The Development of the Person*. New York: Guilford Press.
Stacey, R. (2000). Reflexivity, self-organization and emergence in the group matrix. *Group Analysis*, 33, 501–14.
Stacey, R. (2001). Complexity theory and the group matrix. *Group Analysis*, 34, 221–40.
Stacey, R. (2003). *Complexity and Group Processes*. London: Brunner-Routledge.
Stacey, R. (2005). Affects and cognition in a social theory of unconscious processes. *Group Analysis*, 38, 159–76.
Stein, M. (ed.), (1995). *The Interactive Field in Analysis*. Wilmette, IL: Chiron.
Steiner, J. (2011). *Seeing and Being Seen: Emerging from a Psychic Retreat*. Hove, UK: Routledge.
Stern, D. (1977). *The First Relationship: Infant and Mother*. Cambridge, MA: Harvard University Press.
Stern, D. (1985). *The Interpersonal World of the Infant*. New York: Basic Books.
Stern, D. (1999). Vitality contours: The temporal contour of feelings as a basic unit for constructing the infant's social experience. In P. Rochat (ed.), *Early Social Cognition*. New York: Lawrence Erlbaum Associates
Stern, D. (2004). *The Present Moment in Psychotherapy and Everyday Life*. New York: Norton.
Stern, D., Sandler, L. W., Nahum, J. P., Harrison, A. M., Lyons-Ruth, K., Morgan, A. C., Bruschweiler-Stern, N., & Tronick, E. Z. (1998). Non-interpretative mechanisms in psychoanalytic therapy. *International Journal of Psychoanalysis*, 79, 903–21.
Stolorow, R. D. & Atwood, G. E. (1992). *Context of Being; The Intersubjective Foundations of Psychological Life*. Hillsdale, NJ: Analytic Press.
Stolorow, R. D., Brandchaft, B., & Atwood, G. E. (1987). *Psychoanalytic Treatment: An Intersubjective Approach*. Hillsdale, NJ: Analytic Press.
Stolorow, R., Atwood, G., & Orange, D. (2002). *Worlds of Experience*. New York: Basic Books.
Stone, E. (2001). Culture, politics and group therapy. *Group Analysis*, 34, 501–14.
Stone, W. N. (1995). Frustration, anger and the significance of alter-ego transferences in group psychotherapy. *International Journal of Group Psychotherapy*, 45, 287–302.
Stone, W. N. (2009). *Contributions of Self Psychology to Group Psychotherapy*. London: Karnac.
Stone, W. N. & Whitman, R. M. (1977). Contributions of the psychology of the self to group process and group therapy. *International Journal of Group Psychotherapy*, 27, 343–59.
Strich, S. (1983). Music and the patterns of human interactions. *Group Analysis*, 16, 20–29.
Sullivan, H. S. (1954). *The Psychiatric Interview*. New York: W. W. Norton.
Swift, J. K. & Greenberg, R. P. (2012). Premature discontinuation in adult psychotherapy. *Consulting and Clinical Psychology*, 80, 547–559.
Symington, N. (1986). *The Analytic Experience*. London: Free Association Books.
Symington, J. & Symington, N. (1996). *The Clinical Thinking of Wilfred Bion*. London: Routledge.

Syz, H. (1927). On a social approach to neurotic conditions. *Journal of Nervous and Mental Disease*, 66, 601–15.
Thornton, C. (2004). Borrowing my self: An exploration of exchange as a group-specific therapeutic factor. *Group Analysis*, 37, 305–20.
Thygesen, B. (1992). 'Diversity' as a group-specific therapeutic factor in group-analytic psychotherapy. *Group Analysis*, 25, 75–86.
Thygesen, B. (2008). Resonance: No music without resonance – without resonance no group. *Group Analysis*, 41, 63–83.
Tolpin, M. (1971). On the beginnings of a cohesive self. *The Psychoanalytic Study of the Child*, 25, 273–30.
Trevarthen, C. (1977). Descriptive analyses of infant communicative behaviour. In H. R. Schaffer (ed.), *Studies in Mother-Infant Interaction*. New York: Academic Press.
Trevarthen, C. (1979). Communication and cooperation in early infancy: A description of primary intersubjectivity. In M. Bullowa (ed.), *Before Speech*. Cambridge, UK: Cambridge University Press.
Trevarthen, C. (2005). Stepping away from the mirror: Pride and shame in adventures of companionship. In S. Carter, L. Amherl, K. Grossman, S. Hardy, M. Lamb, & W. Porgess (eds), *Attachment and Bonding*. Cambridge, MA: MIT Press.
Tubert-Oklander, J. (2010). The matrix of despair: From despair to desire through dialogue. *Group Analysis*, 43, 127–40.
Tubert-Oklander, J. (2014). *The One and the Many*. London: Karnac.
Tuckman, B. (1965). Developmental sequences in small groups. *Psychological Bulletin*, 63, 384–99.
Tuckman, B. W. & Jensen, M. A. C. (1977). Stages of small group development revisited. *Group and Organizational Studies*, 2, 419–27.
Turquet, P. (1974). Leadership: The individual and the group. In G. S. Gibbard, J. J. Hartman & R. D. Mann (eds), *Analysis of the Group*. San Francisco, CA: Jossey-Bass.
Tuttman, S. (1994). Therapeutic responses to the expression of aggression by members in groups. In V. L. Schermer & M. Pines (eds), *Ring of Fire*. London: Routledge.
Urlic, I. (2010). The phenomenon of silence. *Group Analysis*, 43, 337–53.
van Ijzendoorn, M. H., & Sagi A. (1999). Cross-cultural patterns of attachment. In J. Cassidy & P. R. Shaver (eds), *Handbook of Attachment*. New York: Guilford Press.
Vella, N. (1999). Freud on groups. In C. Oakley (ed.), *What is a Group?* London: Rebus Press.
Vlastelica, M., Pavlovic, S., & Urlic, I. (2003) Patient's ranking of therapeutic factors in group analysis. *Collegium Antropologicum*, 27, 779–88.
Volkan, V. D. (2001). Transgenerational transmissions and chosen traumas: An aspect of large group identity. *Group Analysis*, 34, 79–97.
von Bertalanffy, L. (1968). *General Systems Theory* (rev. edn) New York: George Braziller.
von Fraunhofer, N. (2008) What's in it for me? The development from immature to mature dependence in groups. *Group Analysis*, 41, 278–90.
Vygotsky, L. S. (1962). *Thought and Language*. Cambridge, MA: MIT Press.
Waddell, M. (1998). *Inside Lives: Psychoanlaysis and the Growth of Personality*. London: Duckworth.

Wardi, D. (1989). The termination process in the group process. *Group Analysis*, 22, 87–99.
Watzlawick, P., Beavin, J., & Jackson, D. (1967). *Pragmatics of Human Communication*. New York: W. W. Norton.
Weber, R. (2016). Research review: Attachment theory and group therapy. *International Journal of Group Psychotherapy*, 66, 456–460.
Weegmann, M. (2001). Working intersubjectively: What does it mean for theory and therapy? *Group Analysis*, 34, 515–30.
Weegmann, M. (2011). Working intersubjectively: What does it mean for theory and therapy? In E. Hopper, & H. Weinberg (eds), *The Social Unconscious in Persons, Groups, and Societies* (Vol. 1). London: Karnac.
Weegmann, M. (2014). *The World Within the Group: Developing Theory for Group Analysis*. London: Karnac.
Weegmann, M. (2016). *Permission to Narrate: Explorations in Group Analysis, Psychoanalysis, Culture*. London: Karnac.
Weinberg, H. (2007). So what is the social unconscious anyway? *Group Analysis*, 40, 307–22.
Weinberg, H. (2016). 'Impossible groups that flourish in leaking containers' – Challenging group analytic theory? *Group Analysis*, 49, 330–49.
Weinberg, H. & Toder, M. (2004). The hall of mirrors in small, large and virtual groups. *Group Analysis*, 37, 492–507.
Weldon, E. (1997). Let the treatment fit the crime: Forensic group psychotherapy. *Group Analysis*, 30, 9–26.
Whitaker, D. S. & Lieberman, M. A. (1964). *Psychotherapy through the Group Process*. New York: Prentice-Hall.
Winnicott, D. W. (1942/1991). Why children play. In *The Child, The Family and the Outside World*. London: Penguin.
Winnicott, D. W. (1947/1992). Hate in the countertransference. In *Through Paediatrics to Psycho-Analysis*. London: Karnac.
Winnicott, D. W. (1951/1992). Transitional objects and transitional phenomena. In *Through Paediatrics to Psycho-Analysis*. London: Karnac.
Winnicott, D. W. (1953/1974). Transitional objects and transitional phenomena. In *Playing and Reality*. Harmondsworth, UK: Pelican.
Winnicott, D. W. (1954/1992). Metapsychological and clinical aspects of regression within the psycho-analytical set-up. In *Through Paediatrics to Psycho-Analysis*. London: Karnac.
Winnicott, D. W. (1956/1992). Primary maternal preoccupation. In *Through Paediatrics to Psycho-Analysis*, London: Karnac.
Winnicott, D. W. (1960a/1990). The theory of the parent-infant relationship. In *The Maturational Processes and the Facilitating Environment*. London: Karnac.
Winnicott, D. W. (1960b/1990). Ego distortion in terms of true and false self. In *The Maturational Processes and the Facilitating Environment*. London: Karnac.
Winnicott, D. W. (1962/1990). Ego integration in child development. In *The Maturational Processes and the Facilitating Environment*. London: Karnac.
Winnicott, D. W. (1963/1990). Development of the capacity for concern. In C. Winnicott, R. Shepherd & M. Davis (eds), *Deprivation and Delinquency*. London: Routledge.

Winnicott, D. W. (1964/1991). Roots of aggression. In *The Child, The Family, and the Outside World*. Harmondsworth, UK: Penguin.
Winnicott, D. W. (1965/1989). The relationship of a mother to her baby at the beginning. In *The Family and Individual Development*. London: Routledge.
Winnicott, D. W. (1968/1989). The squiggle game. In C. Winnicott, R. Shepherd & M. Davis (eds), *Psycho-Analytic Explorations*. London: Karnac.
Winnicott, D. W. (1970/1986). Living creatively. In C. Winnicott, R. Shepherd & M. Davis (eds), *Home is Where We Start From*. Harmondsworth, UK: Penguin.
Winnicott, D. W. (1971a/1974). Playing: A theoretical statement. In *Playing and Reality*. Harmondsworth, UK: Pelican.
Winnicott, D. W. (1971b/1974). The use of an object and relating through identification. In *Playing and Reality*. Harmondsworth, UK: Pelican.
Wolf, E. S. (1980). On the developmental line of selfobject relations. In A. Goldberg (ed.), *Advances in Self Psychology*. New York: International Universities Press.
Wolf, E. S. (1988). *Treating the Self*. New York: Guilford Press.
Wood, D. (2016). On working with opaque silence in group psychotherapy. *Group Analysis*, 49, 233–48.
Wooster, G. (1983). Resistance in groups as developmental difficulty in triangulation. *Group Analysis*, 16, 30–40.
Wordsworth, W. (1804/1970). Intimations of Immortality. In G. H. Hartman (ed.), *The Selected Poetry and Prose of Wordsworth*. New York: Signet Classics.
Wotton, L. (2012). Between the notes: A musical understanding of change in group analysis. *Group Analysis*, 46, 48–60.
Wotton, L. (2013). Concerto for group analysis. *Group Analysis*, 46, 386–94.
Wotton, L. (2015). Improvising a home amongst strangers. *Group Analysis*, 48, 447–54.
Yalom, I. D. (1970/1985). *The Theory and Practice of Group Psychotherapy* (3rd edn). New York: Basic Books.
Yalom, I. D. & Leszcz, M. (2005). *The Theory and Practice of Group Psychotherapy* (5th edn). New York: Basic Books.
Yeats, W. B. (1931/1950). Remorse for intemperate speech. In *Collected Poems of W. B. Yeats*. London: Macmillan.
Yogev, H. (2008). Holding in relational theory and group analysis. *Group Analysis*, 41, 373–90.
Yogev, H. (2013). The development of empathy and group analysis. *Group Analysis*, 46, 61–80.
Zinkin, L. (1979). The collective and the personal. *Journal of Analytic Psychology*, 24, 227–50.
Zinkin, L. (1983). Malignant mirroring. *Group Analysis*, 16, 113–26.
Zinkin, L. (1989). The group as container and contained. *Group Analysis*, 22, 227–34.
Zinkin, L. (1994). Exchange as a therapeutic factor in group analysis. In D. Brown & L. Zinkin (eds), *The Psyche and the Social World*. London: Routledge.
Zinkin, L. (1998). *Dialogue in the Analytic Setting*. London: Jessica Kingsley.

Author index

Entries in italics refer to notes.

Abelin, E. L. 44
Adorno, T. 11, *16*, 51
Agazarian, Y. 55, 68, 113
Ainsworth, M. 87, 88
Alexander, F. 22, 97
Allen, J. G. 92
Anthony, E. J. 14, *68*, 111
Aran, L. W. 66
Argelander, H. 67
Aron, L. 49, 66
Ashbach, C. *101*
Atwood, G. *49*

Bacal, H. A. 97
Bacha, C. *29*
Bachelard, G. 62
Bakali, J. V. 20
Balint, M.
Barnes, B. 78, 80
Barwick, N. 3, *16*, 43, 59, 74, 110, *115,* 140, 141, 146, 151, 161, 171
Bateman, A. 92
Bateson, G. 45, 113
Battegay, R. 83
Beck, W. 67
Begovac, B. *29*
Begovac, I. *29*
Behr, H. 6, 11, 46, 54, *68,* 72, 75, *80,* 114
Bennis, W. G. 21, 28
Berg, D. N. 116
Bertalanffy, L. 113
Bhaktin, M. M. 114

Bhurruth, M. 32, 71
Bick, E. 141, *150,* 151
Bion, W. R. 3, 28, 39, *68,* 81, 82, 83, 85, 91, 98, 101, *101, 102*, 103, 104, 105, 106, 107, 108, 109, 110, 111, 113, *115,* 136
Biran, H. 62
Blackwell, D. *50,* 77, 113
Bollas, C. 27, 42, 61, 82, 137
Borch, C. *16*
Boston Change Process Study Group, 97
Bowden, M. 134
Bowlby, J. 87, 90, 91, *102*
Brennan, K. A. 88
Bretherton, I. 96
British Psycho-Analytic Society, 16
Britton, R. *16,* 43, 106, 107
Brown, D. 25, 36, 46, 47, 54, *69,* 72, 74, 90, 91, 97, 106, 113, 114, 120, 153
Burke, K. 37
Burrow, T. 6, 7, 8, 12, 13, 14

Campos, J. 7, 8, 9, *16*
Cano, D. H. *115*
Cassel Hospital, The 3
Chused, J. 95
Clark, C. L. 88
Cobban, A. *16*
Cohen, B. D. 66
Coltart, N. 132
Cooper, R. 11, *16*
Cortesao, E. L. 113
Cox, J. xix, xx

Cox, M. 62, *179*
Cozolino, L. 42, 92

Dalal, F. 25, 26, *30*, 45, 113
Damasio, A. 42
Darwin, C. 47, 48
Davies, A. xix
de Mare, P. B. 27, 29, 47, *49*, 53, *68*
de Waal, F. 48, 99
Deri, S. 84
Dick, B. M. 21, *29*
Diel, P. 43
Doehrman, M. J. G. *150*
Donne, J. xx, xxiii, 161
Doron, Y. 85, *101*
Durkin, H. E. 113

Economist, The xx
Ein-Dor, T. 91
Elias, N. 8, 11, 12, 14, *16*, 17, 25, 45, 113, 114
Eliot, T. S. 168, 171, 179
Emde, R. 96
Erasmus, D. xiv, 120
Ernst, S. 78, 80
Ettin, M. F. 32
Evans, B. *163*
Ezquerro, A. 21
Ezriel, H. 105

Fairbairn, W. F. 21, 99
Fanthorpe, U. A. xv
Fariss, S. *30*
Farrow, T. F. D 39
Fenchel, G. H. 168
Ferenczi, S. xxi
Field, T. 96
Flapan, D. 168
Fleiss, R. 94
Fluery, H. J. 30
Foguel, B. S. 85
Fonagy, P. 91, 92, 142, 146
Forster, E. M. 179
Foulkes, E. 12
Foulkes, S. H. xii, xiii, xxi, 3, 4, 5, 8, 9, 10, 11, 12, 13, 14, 15, *16*, 18, 19, 20, 22, 23, 24, 25, 26, 27, 28, *29*, 30, 31, 32, 33, 34, 35, 36, 37, 38, 39, 40, 41, 42, 43, 45, 46, 47, 48, *49*, *50*, 51, 52, 53, 54, 55, 56, 61, 62, 64, 65, 66, *68*, *69*, 70, 71,72, 75, 76, 81, 82, 83, 100, 101, 103, 104, 105, 107, 110, 113, 114, *115*, *116*, 120, 123, 127, 136, 137, 139, 140, 141, 142, 146, 155, 162, 167, 168, 173, 181
Frankfurt School, 10, 11
French, T. M. 22, 97
Freud, S. 4, 5, 6, 7, 8, 10, *16*, 22, 23, 25, 26, 28, 47, 48, 59, 62, 63, *68*, 101, *116*, 164, 166
Friedman, R. 45, *49*, 54, 55, 62, 63, 140
Frogel, S. 98

Gadamer, H. G. xii, xiv, xxi, 37, 100, 124, 127
Gans, J. S. 112
Gantt, S. P. 113
Garland, C. 36, 105, *115*, 129, 177
Gelb, A. 9, *16*
George, C. 88
Gerson, S. 39
Gibbard, G. S. 100
Gilden, L. 7
Ginsberg, R. 164, 178
Glenn, L. 89, *102*
Goldstein, K. 8, 9, 10, 14, *16, 26, 113,* 114
Goldwyn, S. 95
Gordon, J. 111, 152
Green, L. 101
Grossmark, R. *68, 101*
Greenberg, R. P. 171
Grotjahn, M. 28, 62
Guntrip, H. *101*
Gustafson, J. 172

Halton, M. 107, *115*
Hamer, N. *30*
Hamilton, W. D. 47
Harrington, A. *16*
Harrison, T. 3, *16*
Hartman, J. J. 100
Harwood, I. 95, 96, 136
Hearst, L. xi, 6, 11, 46, 54, *68*, 72, 114, 137
Hesse, E. 89

Author index

Hinshelwood, R. 7, *30*, *68*, 104, 105, 111
Hobson, R. P. 64
Holmes, J. 88, 89, 124, 132
Hopper, E. xix, 24, 26, 29, 33, *49*, 54, 65, 71, 77, *80*, 108, 109, 113, 114, 143
Horwitz, L. 105
Hume, F. 105
Hutchinson, S. 51
Hyde, K. 78, 80

Inglehart, R. F. xx
Institute of Group Analysis, 102
Institute of Human Relations, Lucerne, 3
Institute of Psychoanalysis, Frankfurt, 1o
Institute of Social Studies, Frankfurt, 11, 16

Jacobson, L. 86
James, C. D. 85, *101*
Jennings, E. 179
Jensen, M. A. C. *29*
Johnson, J. E. 20
Joseph, B. 64
Joyce, R. 48
Jung, C. 35, 39

Kahneman, D. 164, 165, 168, *179*
Kaplan, N. 88
Kapur, R. 64
Karterud, S. 92, 93, 96
Kauff, P. 168
Keats, J. *101*
Kennard, D. 60, *69*
Kernberg, O. 65
Khantzian, E. 162
Kimbles, S. *30*
King, Martin-Luther, Jnr. vii
Klein, M. xii, 81, 107, 112, 166, 177
Klein, R. H. 174
Knobel, A. M. *30*
Kohut, H. xii, 41, 95, 96, 133, 143
Kosseff, J. W. *68*
Koukis, A. *68*
Kubler-Ross, E. 158, 166, 172

Lacan, J. 41, 142
Lavie, J. 15, 108
Lawrence, W. G. 62, 108
Le Bon, G. 5, 6, *16*, 105
Leitner, L. M. 143
Leowald, H. 65
Leszcz M. 66
Levinas, E. 98, 100
Lewin, K. *16*, 80
Lewis, T. 39
Lichtenberg, J. D. *69*
Lieberman, 73, 122, 153
Linehan, M. 163
Linge, D. 181
Lorentzen, S. 20, 21, *29*, *30*, 56, 58
Lothstein, L. *179*
Lovas, G. S. 96

Maar, V. 79, 168
MacDonald, P. *29*
MacKenzie, K. R. 21, *29*
Mahoney, P. 161
Main, M. 88, 89, 91
Malan, D. H. 64, 105
Mallinckrodt, B. 91
Malloch, S. 39
Mansfield, V. 39
Marmarosh, C. L. *102*
Maroda, K. 66
Marris, P. 165, 166, 167, *179*
Marrone, M. 89, 90, 92, *102*, 133
Marsh, L. C. 15
Marvell, A. 178
Marziali, E. 20
Maudesley Hospital, 3
McDougal, J. 176
Mead, G. H. 114
Meins, E. 92
Meltzer, D. 64
Mendez, C. L. 111
Merleau-Ponty, M. 46
Mermelstein, J. *69*
Mikulincer, M. *102*
Miller, J. G. 113
Mills, R. *50*
Mitchell, S. *49*, 66
Moini-Afchari, U. 93
Morgan, G. 113

Nava, A. S. 98
Neeman-Kantor, A. K. 58
Neri, C. 62
Neumann, E. 100
Nicolis, G. 114
Nietzsche, F. vii
Nitsun, M. xii, xiii, 26, *29*, 42, 46, 47, *50*, 51, 60, 85, 107, 109, 110, 111, 112, 113, *116*, 131, *163*
Nitzgen, D. 10, 26, 29, *30*, 32, 34, 46, 47, *50*, 51, 52, *68*, *116*
Noack, A. *30*
Norris, P. xx

Ofer, G. 52, 98, *102*
Ogden, T. H. 39, 82, 113
Orange, D. M. *49*, 65, 100
Ormay, T. 47, 48
Ormont, L. R. 75, 138
Ornstein, A. 96, *102*

Padel, J. 45
Parkes, C. M. 167
Pertegato, E. G. 8, 12, 13, 14
Pertegato, G. O. 8, 12, 13, 14
Peters, R. 113
Pines, M. 4, 8, 13, 20, 22, 29, 31, 36, 38, 41, 43, 44, 46, 47, 53, 54, 55, 61, *68*, 72, 76, 80, 81, 90, 95, 97, 133, 136, 140, 141, 142
Pisani, R. A. *68*
Potthoff, P. *50*, 66, 93
Powell, A. 32, *68*
Power, K. 14, 48
Preston, S. D. 99
Prigogine, I. 114
Prinz, W. 99
Prodgers, A. 65, *69*, 100, 101

Quintaneiro, T. 12

Raphael-Leff, J. 100
Raphling, C. 95
Rattle, S. 162
Redl, F. 34
Renik, O. 66
Rice, C. 174, *179*
Richards, E. xix

Rilke, R. M. 142
Rippa, B. 77
Rizzolatti, G. 99
Roberts, J. 33, 59, *69*, 72, 76, 95
Rogers, C. 67, 83
Rogers, C. R. 10, 94
Rosenthal, L. 112, 172, *179*, *180*
Rouchy, J. C. 20
Rutan, J. S. *115*, 168
Rutter, M. 90
Rycroft, C. 101

Sagi, A. *102*
Sargeant, R. 85
Sartre, J.-P. 98
Scanlon, C. 26
Scheidlinger, S. 8, 75
Schermer, V. L. 42, 66, *101*, 104, 113, *115*, 140, 174, 178
Schlachet, P. 87
Schlapobersky, J. xi, xxii, 21, 22, 36, 39, 40, 41, 47, *50*
Schollberger, R. *49*
Scholz, R. 33
Schore, A. N. 88, 91, 92, *102*
Schore, J. *102*
Schulte, P. 66, 99, 140, 142
Scotson, J. 113
Segal, H. 82
Segalla, R. 100
Seglow, I. *16*
Shakespeare, W. xiv, 124
Shapiro, E. 164, 178
Shaver, P. R. 88, *102*
Shephard, H. A. 21, 28
Singer, T. *30*
Skynner, A. C. R. *29*, 60
Slavendy, J. T. 56
Smith, E. R. 91
Smith, K. K. *116*
Solomon, J. 89
Sordano, A. *50*
Source, J. 96
Spiegelman, J. M. 39
Sroufe, L. A. 91
St Bartholomew's Hospital, 3
Stacey, R. 113, 114, *116*
Stein, M. 39

Steiner, J. 136
Stern, D. 39, 41, 46, *49*, 63, 97, 129, 146, 148
Stolorow, R. D. 37, *49*
Stone, E. 32
Stone, W. N. 95, 96, *115*
Strich, S. *68*
Sullivan, H. S. 155
Swift, J. K. 171
Symington, J. *102*
Symington, N. *101, 102*
Syz, H. 13

Target, M. 92
Tatum, A. 155
Tavistock, The 3, 105, 106, 108, *115*
Theilgaard, A. 62
Thornton, C. 45
Thygesen, B. 20, *29*, 38, 39
Toder, M. 42
Tolpin, M. 133
Trevarthen, C. 39, 61, 136, 148
Tubert-Oklander, J *16*, 36, 49
Tuckman, B. W. 21, 22, *29*
Turquet, P. 108
Tuttman, S. 112

Urlic, I. *80,* 119

van Ijzendoorn, M. H. *102*
Vella, N. 4, *116*
Vlastelica, M. 119
Volkan, V. D. 29
von Bertalanffy, L. 113

von Fraunhofer, N. 21, 22
Vygotsky, L. S. 114

Waddell, M. 177
Wardi, D. 79, *163*, 165, 178
Watzlawick, P. 77
Weber, R. 91
Weegmann, M. 4, 34, 37, *49, 50, 69,* 130, 138
Weinberg, H. 24, 26, 33, 42, *49,* 58, *68,* 69
Weiss, R. S. 167
Weldon, E. 47
Wertheimer, M. *16*
Whitaker, D. S. 73, 122, 153
Whitman, R. M. 95
Winnicott, D. W. 23, 41, 84, 85, 86, 87, 91, 94, *101*, 112, 140, 142, 156, 158, 162, 166
Winter, D. *69*
Wolf, E. S. 95, 97, 133, 136, 143
Wood, D. 77, 78, *115*
Woodruff, P. W. R. 39
Wooster, G. 41, 44
Wordsworth, W. 161, 177
Wotton, L. 38, 39, *50, 68*

Yalom, I. D 21, 22, 66, 162, 168, 177
Yeats, W. B. 139, 143
Yogev, H. 86, 99

Zinkin, L. xxii, *30*, 32, 35, 41, 42, 43, 45, 83, 90, 91, 94, 152

Subject index

Entries in italics refer to notes.

abandonment 77, 85, 88, 101, 109, 126, 147, 148, 157, 166, 168
absence xxi, 19, 36, 38, 56, 57–58, 60, 79, 85–86, 95, *101*, 109, 121–22, 153, 155–57, 158, 160, 168, 172
abuse 20, 36, 76, 83, 98, 128, 152–53
acting out 56, 104, 123, 152, 171
affective life 88, 91, 126–27, 129, 142
aggression 27–28, 55, 65, 73, 76, 84, 86, *101*, 104, 106, 109, 129, 139, 146, 149, 156, 158, 161, 172; and anti-group 110–12; and basic assumptions 104–10
alienation xiii, 7, *116*
alliance 20, 57, 91, 95, 111, 120, 126, 143–44
amplification 40
analysis vs interpretation 27, 61–62; *see also* interpretation
analytical psychology and group analysis *30*, 32, 35, 39–40, 100
anger *29*, 35, 60–61, 66, 81, 128–29, 132, 147, 156, 159
anti-group xiii, *29*, 60, 64, 74–76, 109–13, *116*, 122, 147, 156; developmental 110, 112–13; pathological 110–12
anxiety in groups: and aggression 112; annihilatory 19, 101, 107, 110; attachment 77, 144; at the beginning 22, 51, 131; conductor's 143, 148, 151–53, 162; and containment 82; defences against 71–73; and impingement 84; and interpretation 61; and loss/ending 157, 166, 178; paranoid 107; and the primal scene 107; primitive/archaic 74, 85–86, 140; relational 106; separation 74, 103, 163; stranger 112, 171; survival *101*
assessment 54–56, 91, 107, 110, 125, 131–34, 143–45, 170, 171
assumptions 24, 25, 26, 94, 114
attachment: and alienation *116*; anxiety 77, 144; behaviour 88, 90, 96; and exploring 87–91, 96, 123, 133; figure 89, 166; and friction and 'relational moments' 22; interview 91, 110; and intimacy 22; and loss/separation 91, 166–67, 169; patient-therapist 57; pattern 54, 79, 88–92, *102*; process 123; relationship 166–69; repertoire 89; style 91, 144; theory 87–90, 94–95, *102*, 131, 133, 138, 142; *see also* secure base
attunement 39, 79, 85, 89, 96–97, 142, 148
authenticity 90, 119, 143, 177–78
authority xiii, 11, 21–22, 27–28, *30*, 47, 51–52, 62–64, *68*, 75, 79, 93, 106, 108, 111, 127, 132–33, 139, 146, 149, 151, 156, 174; *see also* conductor
auxiliary ego 84, 85, 140

barometric event 28
basic assumption theory: 3, 39, 103–09; and the anti-group 109–10;

dependency (baD) 103, 106, 174; flight (baF) 103, 106; Group (baG) *115*; incohesion: aggregation/massification (baI:a/m) 77, 108–09; me-ness (baM) 108, *115*; oneness (baO) 108; pairing (baP) 104, 106
basic law of group dynamics 46
bearing witness *see* witnessing
belonging 21, 36, 39, 42, 47, 48, *80*, 89, 95, 106–07, 110, *116*, 121, 126–27, 147, 157, *163*, 169, 172
borderline personality disorder xii, xiii, 54, 89, 92–93, 110, *115*, 124, 141, 162
boundary: and the analytic setting 60, 85; and attachment style 91; and authority 46–47; and dynamic administration 53–54, 56–58, 60, 79–80, 125; and exclusion *50*; and group development 21–22, 56; incidents 19, 56–57, 60; issues 22, 85; national xx–xxi; permeability and impermeability of xxi, 20, 32; and resonance 39; and safety 57–58, 77, 80; and self 94, 108, 133; and skin 141, 148

CBT *see* cognitive behavioural therapy
cognitive behavioural therapy 19, 125
coherence in groups 20–21, *29*, 33, 70, 79, 85–86, 90, 94, 115, 121, 124, 127, 138, 143
cohesion in groups 6, 20–21, *29*, 47, 54, 57, 70, 83, 85, 90, 95–96, 100, 109, 113, 115, *116*, 120, 123, 125, 129, 143
collective unconscious *see* unconscious
combined group psychotherapy 18, *29*
communication: articulate xxi, 35, 62, 65, 70, 77, 83; and assessment 132; and attachment 88, 91; and the 'autistic' 35, 71, 112; behavioural 36; and the boundary 57–58; and countertransference 66–68; blockage/blocks/breakdowns in 61, 70, 71, *116*; and complexity theory 114; and ending 178; and exchange 45; facilitating 70–71; and figure-ground relations 10; fluid/free 14, 28, 33, 36, 64, 70, 71, 86, 106; and free association/free-floating discussion 50, 86; and 'group space' 134; of holding 85; and inter-dependence 174, 179; and interpretation 61–62, 111; levels of 35–36, 41, 79, 106, 112; and location 33, 112; mature 172; and mentalising 9; and mirroring 42, 99; and monologuing 72; and music xiv, 39; network/web of 9, 23–24, 28, 31, 57, 80; open and closed 35, 37; pattern(s) 144, 154; and play 86–87; primitive 67, 81, 112, 172; process of xxii, 41, 60, 64, 73, 112, 127, 180, 18; progressive emotional 138; and projective identification 67, 81–83; quality of 21–22; and reception 82; resistance to 61, 65, 71–79; and resonance 38–39, 65, 120; restricted 122; and rhetoric 37–38; and selection 54; and social facts 32; theory of 34–35; and the therapeutic process xiii, 35–36, 53, 123, 181; in time-and-place 14, 71; and translation 34–38; unfolding 120, 123, 182; *see also* dialogue in groups; discourse; matrix; monologue; free-floating discussion; silence
communion 38, 77; phatic 72
community 4, 12–13, 15, 25, 30–31, 46, 77, 90, 127, 179
complexity theory 114
composition of groups 18, 20, 35, 53–54, 134; *see also* selection of group members
condensation 40
conduct, principles of 56–57
conductor: and the anti-group xiii, 110–12; attachment-oriented 89–91; and authority 51–52; and basic assumptions 106; and boundaries 57–58; use of countertransference 65–68, 82, 145–46; definition of 19; as dynamic administrator 51, 53–58, 60; and empathy 59, 69, 96–99, 119–20,146 ; and ending 158–61,

168, 172, 174, 178; as facilitator of communication 70–78, 106; as father 28, 35, 52, *68*, 100, 107, 159; female vs male *29*; feminine vs masculine 59–60; as group member 52–53; and interpretation 27, 61–65; interventions, active vs passive 19, 41, 51, 58–59, 60, 71, 74–75, 79–80, 90, 93–94, 107–08, 120, 123, 125, 162; interventions, types of 60–68; as leader 24; linking psychic and social-historical facts 32; and mentalisation 93–94; as mother 28, 68, 82–83, 85, 96, 98, *101*, 106, 140; and the orchestral analogy 11, 51–52, *68*, 108, 122, 155, 162; as parent/caregiver 57, 61, 66, 74, 79, 80, 89, 93, 106, 107; and play 64, 86, 155–56, 162; preparation of group members 56–57, 74; qualities 119–20; use of rhetoric 37; response to scapegoating 34, 76, 83; and selection 54–56; and theory 138; as therapist 11, 19, 58–80; in time-and-place 14, 28, 66–67, 70–71, 168; and Transference *28, 35; see also* authority; countertransference; empathy; interpretations; leader; interventions; leadership; transference interpretations

configuration xiii, 33–34, 49, 59, 70, 72, 91, 107, 109; see *also* figuration; figure-ground

conjoint group psychotherapy 18, *29*, 93

contact-shunning 109, 143, 177; *see also* merger-hungry

container 41, 42, 58, 66, 67, *69, 82–83*, 112, 129, 176; -contained 109

containing and containment 19, 21, 33, 41, 54–55, 58, 66, 72–73, 80, 81–83, 91–92, 100–01, 108, 109–10, 112, 114, 121, 139, 145–46, 148, 151–52, 157, 159–60, 166; *see also* projective identification

context xi–xii, xix–xxiii; and meaning xix, 10, *16*, 26, 37, 59; see also *social context*

conversation *see* communication

core phenomena in groups *see* communication; group mind; location; matrix; translation

corrective developmental dialogues 133

corrective emotional experience 22, 90, 97–98

corrective family group experience 64

corrective interaction 29

corrective recapitulation 71

corrective re-encounter 41

countertransference 53, 65–68, *69*, 77, 80, 82, 94, 112, 114, 139, 145, 147, 149, 155, 159, 160, 169; disclosure 65–66, 159; *see also* containment; projective identification; resonance

cultural cargos 137–38

culture of inquiry 59, 119, 127

death *see* loss

death instinct 24, *116*; *see also* Thanatos

defence xi, 6, 23, 25, *30*, 33, 39, 56, 74–75, 81, 99,1 03, 106, 111, 139, 143, 147, 151, 157, 174; *see also* social defences

dependence 21, 63, 73, 93, 108, 157, 163

dependency 74, 86, 88, 104, 106, 148, 174; *see also* basic assumption dependency (baD)

depressive position 177, 179

development of groups 20–22, 25, 28, 34, 51, 58, 61

developmental anti-group *see* anti-groups

developmental psychology and group analysis 49, 94–96, 136

dialogue in groups 22, 36–37, 44–45, 70, 72, 92, 120–21, 127, 130, 133, 136, 182; *see also* communication

difference, in groups xxi, 19, 20, 22, 42, 45–46, 48, 51, 70, 73, 76–77, *80*, 86, 104, 107, 109, 114, 121–23, 129, 162, 174–75

dimensions of psychotherapy 22, 129, 140

disavowals 25

disclosure: by the conductor 64, 66, *69*, 94; by group members 22, 56, 129, 146
discourse in groups 22, 34, 36, 37, 64, 70, 72, 77, 120; see also communication
diversity xix, 20, 72, 95, 96, 115, *116*, 119
dreams 34, 35, 38, 40, 62–63, 142, 145–46, 159
drive 4, 10, 48, 81, 104, 106, 114; drive theory 5, 34, 47
drop-out 56, 60, 78, *80*, 85, 125, 14–145, 147, 171, *179*
dynamic administration 58, *68*, 85, 133; see also conductor as dynamic administrator
dynamic matrix see matrix

ego 4, 16, 23, 29, 30, 39, 46, 48, 67–68, 94; alter- 95; auxiliary 84–85, 140; -consciousness 39; -identity *115*; training in action 29, 93; see also superego
emotional availability 56, 92, 96, 97
emotional contagion 39, 99
empathic attunement see attunement
empathic failure 95–97, 99
empathic resonance see resonance
empathy 36, 47, 92, 94–100, 120; training in action 99; and the conductor 59, 69, 98, 119–20, 146, 153
enabling solution 73, 122, 153; see also focal conflict; restrictive solution
enactment 43, 45, 49, 58, 67, *68*, 72, 87, 97, 121, 148, 172, 176, 176
ending 18, 135, 160, 164–80; and meaning 165–67; planned 169–70, 175–78; premature 169–75; and the remembering self 164–65; scratched 168–69; as termination 167–68; see also termination
engagement xxiii, 19, 22, 30, 99–100, 102, 108, 122, 136, 172, 174; lack of 160
engulfment 77, 101, 109, *115*; mimetic 42

envy 6, 106–08, 110
exchange, as group specific factor 21, 36, 45–46, 73, 79, 108, 121, 127, 140–41, 143, 145, 146, 148, 153, 160; see also reciprocity
exclusion 28, 34, 43–44, 55, 106–07
exclusion criteria 56
exclusionary matrix 34; see also scapegoating
experiencing self 164–65
exploring see attachment

facilitating environment 102, 138; see also holding
facilitation: guided and open 60, 69; of communication xxii, 35, 62, 70–80
false self 84–85, 90, 142
family and the group 4, 7, 10–11, 15, 18, 28, 31, 35, 64, 71, *80*, 87, 92, 96, *102*, 107, 126, 131–32, 137, 171
father, in the group 4, 27–28, 35, 44, 52, *68*, 87, 100, 107, 137, 152, 159, 170; see also conductor
field theory *16*
fight-flight see basic assumption theory
figuration 11–12, 14, 33; see also configuration, figure-ground
figure-ground xiii, 10, *16*, 33, 59, 71, 130, 147, 155
focal conflict 73; see also enabling solution; restrictive solution
foundation matrix see matrix
free association 4, 26–27, 31, *50*, 59, 93
free floating discussion 16, 27, 36, 61, 66, 73, 86; see also group association
fusion of horizons xxi, 37, 127, 174

gaze 28, 41, 43, 95, 98, 109, 136
gestalt configuration 33, 59, 71
gestalt psychology and group analysis 4, 9–10, *16*
group association 26–27, 93–94; see also free floating discussion
group as forum 46
group as mother 28, 31, 41, 45, 81–102, 107, 176

group-analytic culture 21, 46, 51, 56, 61, 63, 73, 76
group-as-a-whole 13, 22, 28, 42, 61, 66–67, 73, 77, 85–86, 91, 94, 96, 100, 110, 122–23, 125, 147; interpretations 104, 111; interventions 110; observations 79; projections 82, 112
group mentality 5, 103, 105, 108, 110
group mind 31, 33–34, *49,* 58, 145, 172
group self 96; *see also* self-psychology
group specific (therapeutic) factors 14, 22, 31, 38–50; *see also* amplification; condensation; exchange; mirroring; resonance; socialising process
guilt xii, 4, 25, 28, 78, 95, 132, 148, 153, 160, 169, 172

here-and-now *see* communication in time-and-place
heterogeneous group psychotherapy group 20, 163
holding 53, *69,* 74, 83–87, 109, 123, 148, 166
holism 9, 10, *16*
Homo Clausus vs Homines Apertis 11, *40*
homogenous group psychotherapy group 18, 20, 29, 163
humanistic psychology and group analysis 34

id 4, 23, 25, *30*, 48
idealisation *16*, 28, 66, 68, 83, 95–96, 100–01, 106, 174
identification 6, 44–45, 54–55, 63, 135–37, 160, 162–63; narcissistic *16*, 112; oedipal 137; over-identification 20, 112, 138; transient 75; trial 94
identity xxi, 19, 20, 23–24, 39, 41–42, 48, 51, 74, 77, 84, 86, 108–09, 115, 143, 145–46
impingement 53–54, 57, 84–85, 141, 145, 148, 170, 174
independence 21, 51, 73–74, 96, 126, 177
individualism 7, 8, 11, 13, 29, 32, 106, 108, 141

individuation 22, *29*, 42, 44, 100, 141, 168–69, 178
insight and outsight 47, 79
instinct 5–6, 24–26, 38, 114, *116*; social 47–48
integration, psychological 41, 44, 73, 76, 92,
interconnectedness xx, xxi, xxii, 3–16, 18, 26, 31, 49–50, 71, 115
inter-dependence 11–12, 15, 21, *50*, 54, 74, 86, 108, *115*, 120, 174
intermediate area of experiencing 84, 87, 156, 162; *see also* play; transitional space
internal working models 87–91, 133; *see also* attachment theory
interpretation 27, 70, 58, 85, 61–66, 69, 73, 75, 77–79, 90, 93, 95, 104–06, 109, 111, 156; *see also* transference interpretation
intersubjectivity and group analysis 33, 36–37, 45, *49–50*, 63, 65–66, *69*, 83, 92, 95–97, 99–100, *102*, 140, 142
intervention, by the conductor xi, 34, 52, 55, 57, 58–67, *69*, 70–80, 83, 94, 110, 121, 123–25, 127, 129, 155; *see also* conductor interventions, active vs passive; conductor interventions, types of; counter-transference disclosure; facilitation (guided and open); interpretation; maintenance; modelling; self-disclosure; transference interpretation
intimacy 19, 21–22, 36, 46, 54, 56, 74, 112, 140, 143, 148, 153, 156–57, 174–75
intolerable imbalance 123, 125, 127
introjection 44, 82, 151, 178; re-introjection 52, 67
introjective learning 177, 179
invisible group 68
isolation, in groups xiii, xxi, 10, 20, *29*, 35–36, 38, 42, 46–47, 49, 61, *69*, 71, 74–78, *80*, 101, 121, 126, 135, 141, 162, 171

jealousy 6, 44, 106, 141, 143

language 24–25, 30, 35, 37–38, 45, 61, 72, *80*, 86, 111, 114, 134, 153, 160; see also communication
leader xx, 6–7, *16*, 21, 24, 28, 51–52, *68*, 98, 103–06, 110, 124; activity *115*
leadership *68*, 125; growth-enhancing 52; transformational 98; see also authority; conductor
limbic resonance see resonance
linear relations 110, 140, 143
listening 45, 55, 63, 70, 72, 96, 98, 126, 144, 147–48
location xix, 11, 33–34, *49*, 53, 63, 65, 71–73, 75–76, 78, 91, 93, 101, 112, 123, 147, 159, 175, 176
loss xxi, 28–29, *30,* 36, 42, 54, 74, 77, 84, 91, 104, 106–07, 112, *115*, 145, 148, 157–61, 165–79, *180*; see also ending

maintenance *15*, 57, 60, *69*
malignant mirroring see mirroring
matrix 31–33, 48, 52, 57, 64–65, 71–73, 89, 93, 114, 128–29, 131, 134, 147, 159, 161, 181; communicational 71; dynamic 31, 33, 35, 46, 62–63, 71, 76, 80, 89, 122, 127, 145, 148, 151–52; exclusionary 34; foundation 32, 33, 62–63, 80; intersubjective 96; mentalising 93; over-cohesive 20; personal/of self 31, 41, 62–63, 76; populated 120, 125, 134; relational *49*; resistance to joining 74–76; and resonance 39; social 32, 71; social dreaming 62
mature group 10, 21–22, 54, 57, 64, 66, 86, 98, 122, 125, 128–29, 130; see also development of groups
mentalisation 91- 94, 142, 173
merger *16*, 77, 95, 99, 106, 143, 145–46; merger-hungry 109, 143, 148
metaphor, in groups xxii, 35, 72, 86, 111, 121, 134, 156, 172–73
mimetic engulfment 42
mirror neurons 65, 99
mirroring 14, 20, 38, 40–42, 45–46, 79, 82, 91, 93–96, 99, 129, 133, 135–36, 142, 145, 148, 155; communicational 42; malignant xxii, 42–44, 73, 83, 94, *101, 122,* 132, 143, 152, 155; negative 34, 42–43; triadic 43–44
model of three see triadic mirroring, witnessing
modelling 52, 59, *69*, 86, 90, 94, 97, 112
moments 22, 63, 97, 129, 130
monologue 22, 36, 70, 72, 120–21, 146–47, 149, *150*, 153, 155, 171
mother, as the group see group as mother
mother, in the group 20, 27–28, 68, 81–102, 106–07, 127–28, 147, 153–54, 175–76; see also conductor as mother
mother-infant relations 20, 24, 36, 39, 41, 44, 45, 47, 81–102, 106–07, 141–42; see also the group as mother

narcissism xiii, 6, 42, 44, 54, 56, *68*, 83, 95, 112, 141, 146
narcissistic identification *16*, *68*, 83, 112
narcissistic needs 95, 105, 143
negative capability 101
negative mirroring see mirroring
network xxi, 9, 10–12, 33, 35, 54, 57, 70–71, 113; see also communication; figurations; matrix
neuroscience xxii, 9–10, 95, 98–99, *102,* 113–14, *115*
Noah's Ark principle 20, 54
Northfield Experiments 3, *68*, 103–04
nos 48

object: bad 34; combined *115*; external 151; focal *68*; good/good enough/helpful/sustaining 77, 89, 96, *115*, 148; group *50*, 111; hated 6; idealised 106; internal 97; lost 74, 177; loved 106, 107; merger with subject 99; mother 84, 85; part 133; part object transference 27, 35; primal 115; primary 74, *80*; social 24; subject- 49; survival of 84; third 20; transitional *68*, 84, *101*; the truth of *102*; usage 112; whole object transference 27, 35; see also selfobject

object relations 43, 66, 90, *102*, 107, 109, 111
oedipal: complex 106; dynamics *16*; identification 137; myth 106; negotiations 74, situation 43, 74, 106–07; transference 28
optimal responsiveness 65, 97
organising principles 37, *49*
orthodox vs radical Foulkes 4, 25, 113
outsight *see* insight

pairing *see* basic assumption theory
parallel process *150*
pathological anti-group *see* anti-group
personification 28, 32, 109, 143
phyloanalysis and group analysis 7
play 37, 64, 70, 83–87, *101*, 112, 136, 137–38, 140, 155–56, 162
preparation: of the group 57, 133, 134, 160, 171; pre-group 56–57, 74, 79, 91, *102*, 162, 171–72, *179*
primal scene 74, 106, 107
process dynamics *see* group specific factors
projection: 24–25, 27, 34–35, 41, 43–44, 52, 62–64, 66–67, 73, 82, 85, 106, 110, 112
projective identification: 43, 66–67, 75–76, 81–83, 94, 110, 114, 140, 146, 152
projective level of communication 35, 7; *see also* communication, levels of
projective mechanisms/processes xxii, 25, 67, 172
proximity and attachment 88–89, 111; *see also* attachment
psychoanalysis and group analysis 3, 4–9, 13, *16*, *17*, 18, 21, 23, 26, 31, 35, 81, 90, 106, 113
psychological analysis and group analysis 8–10

reciprocity 12, 21, 41, 45, 55, 96–97, 120, 140, 146, 148; *see also* exchange
re-enactment *see* enactment
reflective ability/capacity 4, *69*, 70, 92, 175

reflective activity 44, 58, 140
reflective dimension *see* dimensions of psychotherapy
reflective function 91–94; *see also* mentalisation
reflective process 59, 122, 165
reflective space 58, *68*, 122–23, 125
regression xxi, 5, 67, 78, 106–07, 110, *116*, 157, 163, 178
remembering self 164–65, 168
reparation 22, 78, 87, 89, 97, 112, 121–22, 136, 140, 172; *see also* dimensions of therapy
resilience 84, 88–89, *101*, *102*, 121–22, 133, 175
resistance 25–26, 39; to communication 61, 65, 71–79, 146
resonance 18, 20, 35, 38–42, 45, *50*, 63, 65–67, 71, 78–79, 90–91, 93, 99, 111–12, 120, 143, 146, 155, 172; and countertransference 65–67, 112, 143; empathic 39, 95–97, 99; limbic 39
restrictive solution 73; *see also* enabling solution; focal conflict
reverie 58, 82, 91
rivalry 6, *29*, 44, 105–06, *115*, 133–34, 156
role suction 34, *49*; *see also* valency
roles, played by group members *29*, 34, 36, 70, 75–76, 87, 109, 126, 129, 160, 175

safety, in and of groups 20, 22, 28, 53, 57–58, *68–69*, 70, 72, 76–77, 85–86, 89, 95, 103, 120–22, 124, 137, 153, 156, 158, 161–62
scapegoating 20, 26, 34, 60, 76, 83, 141
scenic understanding 67
secure base xxi, 87–89, 90, 93, *102*, 162; *see also* attachment
selection of group members 20, 54–57, 74, 79, 107, 110, *115*, *179*; *see also* assessment
selfobject 95–97, 136, 138
self-psychology and group analysis *49*, 95, *102*, 133; *see also* selfobject

setting 124, 153; analytic 53–54, 85, 120, 123; boundaries of 56; forensic 47; group 23; NHS 139; one-to-one *80*; organisational 53–54; physical 53, 57; social 43
sharing, in groups 20, 45, 54, 63, 71, 74, 79, *80*, 87, 95–96, 99, 107, 120, 129, 154, 174; *see also* disclosure; reciprocity
sibling relationships 6, 7, 27, *29*, 35, 66, 74–75, 86–87, 152, 157, 163, 175, 176
silence, in groups 42, 58, 76, 77–78, *80*, 109, 121, 125, 144, 147, 149, 155, 158–59
skin: developing 151–54; group analytic 139, 148, *150*; psychic 141, 145, 148, 151–52; second 151; *see also* boundary
slow open psychotherapy groups 18, 21, 58, 78, 134, 163, 170, 173
social bonds 7, 20, 38, 72
social context xii, xx–xxi, 4, 10, 11, 14, 24, 26, 29, 32, 42, 46, 47, 53, 71, 114
social defences 25
social instinct *see* instinct social
unconscious *see* unconscious
social matrix *see* matrix
social mind 13, 24, 26, 41–42
socialising process 46–48, 49
sociology and group analysis 3, 4, 8, 11–12, *16*, 24–26, 34, 37, 47, 132, *163*, 166
spatial relations 110, 140
splitting xxii, 19, 23, 27, 35, 55, 66–67, 100, 113, 115
squiggle game 86, 138
stranger group 19, 32, *116*
structural oppression 25
subgroups 19, 34, 42, 73, 77, 82, 112
superego 12, *30*, 46–48, 51–52; *see also* authority
surviving xiii, xxi, 23, 47, 73, 83–87, 88, 94, *101*, 106, 110, 112, 128, 140, 149, 151, *163*, 166, 178
syncretic paradigm *49*
systems 6, 9–10, 24, 31, 36, 42, 44, 81, 88–92, 110, 113, *116*, 129, 178

Tavistock model 3, 105, 106, *115*; and the inductive approach 105
termination 22, 30, 58, 163, 167–68, *170*, 174, 177–78
Thanatos 104–06, 108, 113; *see also* death instinct
therapeutic alliance *see* alliance
therapeutic community 3, 124
therapist *see* conductor
third position 43, 44; *see also* model of three; triadic mirroring; witnessing
time-limited psychotherapy group 18, 20, 21, 58, 79, 169–70, 178
tolerable imbalance 123, 125, 155
training in action: countertransference 68; ego 29, 93; empathy 99; witness 43–44, 67
transference 4, 22, 24, 27–29, 31, 35, 52, 54, 57, 61, 63–65, 67, *68*, 71, 79–80, *80*, 87, 94, 96, 100, 107–08, 114, 145, 152
transference interpretation 27, 61, 63–65, 66, 105, 107–08
transference level 35, 71; *see also* communication, levels of
transformational leadership *see* leadership
transitional object 68, 84, 101
transitional space 84, 86–87, 112
translation 34–38, 60–62, 65, 71, 79, *116*, 123
trauma xiii, 3, 23, 29, 39, 54, 67, *68*, 74, *80*, 95, 97, 105–07, 109, 111, 115, 142–43, 146, 148, 162, 166–68
triadic mirroring 43–44; *see also* oedipal; mirroring; witnessing
triadic relations 28, 57, 74; *see also* oedipal; triadic mirroring; witnessing
true self 84, 142, 178
trust: and baM 108; basic 73–74; and boundary incidents 19; in the conductor 119, 132; and containment 82; and ending 168; in the group 22, 59, 60, *68*, 93, 120–23, 125, 129, 140, 152; lack of 19, 56, 73–74, 83, 92–93, 100, 106, 108, 115, 122–23, 128, 145,

149, 153; and the oedipal situation 106; and secure base 88; 93; and 'transference love' 52
turn-taking 72–73, 93, 148

unconscious, the 4, 13, 22–26, 27, 29, *30*, 31, 35–39, 42, 54, 62, 72, *102*, 114; collective *30*, 35, 39–40; co-unconscious *30*; interpersonal 23–24, 62; social 13, 23–27, 29, 32, 47–48, 62, 76–77, 113–14; transpersonal 23–24

valency *17*, 28, 39–40, 104
vitality contours 148

witnessing 43–44, 67, 106, 128, 140, 171–72; *see also* model of three; oedipal; triadic mirroring
working through 22, 47, 127

Taylor & Francis eBooks

Helping you to choose the right eBooks for your Library

Add Routledge titles to your library's digital collection today. Taylor and Francis ebooks contains over 50,000 titles in the Humanities, Social Sciences, Behavioural Sciences, Built Environment and Law.

Choose from a range of subject packages or create your own!

Benefits for you
- Free MARC records
- COUNTER-compliant usage statistics
- Flexible purchase and pricing options
- All titles DRM-free.

REQUEST YOUR FREE INSTITUTIONAL TRIAL TODAY

Free Trials Available
We offer free trials to qualifying academic, corporate and government customers.

Benefits for your user
- Off-site, anytime access via Athens or referring URL
- Print or copy pages or chapters
- Full content search
- Bookmark, highlight and annotate text
- Access to thousands of pages of quality research at the click of a button.

eCollections – Choose from over 30 subject eCollections, including:

Archaeology	Language Learning
Architecture	Law
Asian Studies	Literature
Business & Management	Media & Communication
Classical Studies	Middle East Studies
Construction	Music
Creative & Media Arts	Philosophy
Criminology & Criminal Justice	Planning
Economics	Politics
Education	Psychology & Mental Health
Energy	Religion
Engineering	Security
English Language & Linguistics	Social Work
Environment & Sustainability	Sociology
Geography	Sport
Health Studies	Theatre & Performance
History	Tourism, Hospitality & Events

For more information, pricing enquiries or to order a free trial, please contact your local sales team:
www.tandfebooks.com/page/sales

The home of Routledge books

www.tandfebooks.com